METAL

METAL

Design and Construction

by

A. FRANK SHIRLEY, F.C.C.Ed.

Formerly Head of Technical Studies
City of Leeds and Carnegie College
University Examiner and Moderator for G.C.E. Examinations at
Ordinary and Advanced Levels

Illustrated by

G. GANNON

HULTON EDUCATIONAL PUBLICATIONS

ISBN 0 7175 0653 3

This edition first published 1973 by Hulton Educational Publications Ltd.,
Raans Road, Amersham, Bucks.

Text set in 11 pt. Monotype Times Roman, printed by photolithography,
and bound in Great Britain at The Pitman Press, Bath

Foreword

Metal is a comparatively new educational material and much research and experience is necessary in order that its possibilities can be well understood and exploited. The average pupil now accepts the workshop as a natural classroom which should be a stimulating and progressive educational centre. The aim of this book is to help pupils and teachers a little further on the way towards this objective.

This new volume supersedes METALWORK—TECHNIQUES FOR SCHOOL WORKSHOPS, which was written ten years ago, has served its purpose and is now out of print. Craft education has developed so much in recent years that a new book was essential with a new approach and to include several sections on design and history. The old book was a metalwork textbook for CSE and GCE examinations but the new one has been prepared against a rapidly changing educational background for a wider range of young people of both sexes who are living in a new technological world. The school examinations have been further considered as it is realised that, although the traditional practical test will soon become an anachronism, skills, techniques and technology will always be essential and that the emphasis now must be on considering the problems, sometimes obvious but always inevitable in craft, problems of design, of selection of materials, tools and processes. This problem-solving involves greater intellectual study, wider reading and the ability to discriminate and communicate. This book caters for these changes but it also makes learning easier by its systematic arrangement, analogical development and its many illustrations.

The many new plates in this volume have been selected for their own sake and are independent of the text. They show new work, fine craftsmanship and introduce famous designers who are working in our time and amidst our surroundings. I am grateful to friends who have assisted me by giving advice and reading through notes, suggestions and proofs especially G. H. Bantock, Professor of Education at the University of Leicester, C. H. Wilson, Managing Director of Boxford Machine Tools and A. H. Moore and R. A. A. Rignall, Senior Lecturers at the City of Leeds and Carnegie College. I am indebted to the painstaking care which has been exercised by Mr. H. Gannon in the drawing of sketches and diagrams and to the various firms, organisations and individual designers who have contributed details and up-to-date photographs of their work and their equipment.

Contents

List of Plates

1

Problem Solving: An Introduction to Assignments

Tools assist men and women to solve their practical problems—to make, to repair, to improve, to change, to display, and to vary the size and shape of all kinds of materials so as to further ideas and provide for certain needs. The working out of these assignments involves the solving of various problems. If the problem has already been solved and there are detailed instructions to follow, step by step—as in some simple do-it-yourself examples—then the assignment becomes a matter of copying. In some schools, students are told what to do, a little at a time, so that they all proceed at the same speed, copying their teacher as he demonstrates, step by step. In both cases, copying and problem-solving, tools are used and skill and techniques are essential, but original thinking is not involved in copying. It is the thinking that is the basis of designing. The assignments suggested in this volume involve solving problems and as such can be design-exercises—design briefs.

The design of a small, simple article—such as a label, a pendant or a brooch—does not present many problems, but there are difficulties if the practical problem involves repairing something or an assignment like making a cupboard, an improvement for a car, or putting up a clothes-line, or fixing a shelf. In all these cases there are basic problems to be solved, questions to be asked and answered, and the *approach* is the same. Firstly, one thinks about the assignment generally and then lists in precise language the problems which arise—the questions and some likely answers, and these will suggest ideas which should be put down on paper, together with sketches and notes, and sometimes with dimensions and detailed drawings. Some of the ideas can be discarded almost at once, others are tested, and some accepted. Eventually, the best ideas are selected and worked out carefully, possibly with a working-drawing; finally, a complete *practical* answer is obtained. This is design realisation, which in schools includes the ultimate production.

Consider *putting up a shelf* as an assignment. The general problem concerns the uses of the shelf: what is it for? Where is it going? There are at least seven questions:

Questions

(1) What is going on the shelf?
(2) Where is it to be fitted?
(3) Is it to be of wood or metal (Dexion)?
(4) What size will it be? (How strong must it be? If wood, what length, width and thickness?)
(5) How is it to be supported at the ends?
(6) Will it need extra support?
(7) Finish?

Answers

(1) The shelf is for saucepans and is to be fitted in the kitchen.
(2) It is to be fixed within an alcove.
(3) Wood is suitable for a kitchen shelf and it can be cut accurately and easily to fit the alcove.
(4) The alcove is 2 metres wide and 300 millimetres deep. The largest saucepan is 250 mm in diameter—so the shelf can be the length and width of the alcove. Saucepans are not very heavy, so wood planed to 16–19 mm thick will be strong enough.

DESIGNING A SHELF

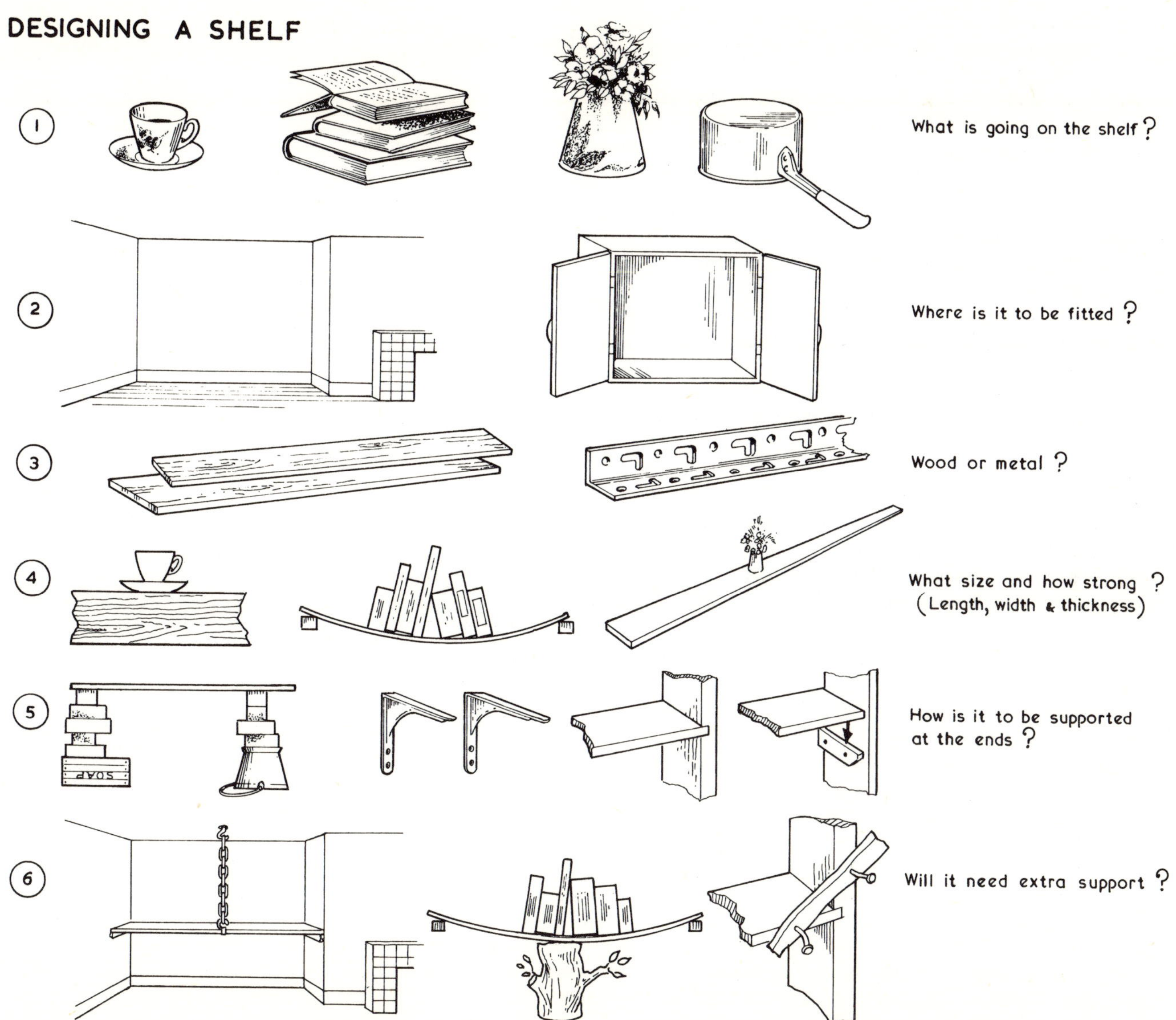

(5) The shelf will be supported on bearers screwed against the side walls which will have to be plugged.
(6) The shelf is not long and the saucepans should not cause it to sag. The bearers should provide sufficient support.
(7) It can be painted to match the kitchen, and washable plastic material can cover the top.

Further considerations. Method and order of procedure? The size of the bearers, number and size of screws? Should there be some means of supporting saucepan-lids under the shelf? A well-designed kitchen is important in a modern home and the putting up of a shelf in the kitchen is an important design exercise. Finally look again at Question (6) and consider how, if it were a long shelf extra support would be provided.

Three assignments suitable for beginners in metalwork will be considered, to be followed by an advanced design brief—the drawing examination set in 1971 by London University in their GCE Ordinary Level Metalwork Examination.

Assignment (1) A Key label

(*a*) *Approach.* General thinking about the problem. Consider a bunch of keys without a label affixed. What happens if they are lost? Think of all the keys for all the cupboards in a workshop. What happens if any are lost? How could you tell which key fits which cupboard? Can they be labelled? What kind of label is suitable and desirable? How do we design and make a label? What is the order of working?

(*b*) *Definite questions*—(i) *Size?* Is the label to go in my pocket, or hang on the wall? If hanging, what is the size of the key? If it were the key of a shed or store or a hotel key, it might be left lying around and a large, wooden label might prevent it being lost. When small cupboard keys are to hang together, small thin labels are preferable and if they

ASSIGNMENT I **KEY LABEL**

10
J.S. B.G. 231
LIBRARY SHED WORKSHOP
CYCLES MR. JONES B.A.C
SMITH HUT 140

Select a shape. If the selection is difficult it may be easier to eliminate
(a) shapes that are difficult to make, (b) shapes with sharp corners,
(c) shapes unsuitable e.g. too small for the necessary inscription.
What is to go on the label is bound to affect the shape e.g. a long name needs a long label.

are to be kept in a pocket or handbag labels cannot be heavy or bulky; they should be small and smooth. (ii) *Material?* If large, the key-label might be of wood, if small it could be of metal or plastic. If it is to be made of metal, the label could be of aluminium which is light in weight and colour and can be marked easily; copper, brass and gilding-metal are attractive metals, can be polished bright, and can be easily punched or engraved; mild steel is cheap, but might rust if left about; stainless steel looks well, but is hard and difficult to mark and is expensive. Odd pieces of copper, brass and gilding-metal might be suitable for this assignment. (iii) *Shape?* Does the lettering which is to go on the key-label need a special shape—a long name needs a long label? Maybe one of the small, odd pieces of metal may suggest a suitable shape. Otherwise draw on a sheet of paper a number of possible shapes and select the one you like best. (iv) *How is the label to be fixed to the key?* If fixed by means of a key-ring the label will be small and will have a small hole for the ring drilled in the corner or the side. If the label were of plastic sheet, the hole might wear, become enlarged and break out at the edge—a good reason for using metal. (v) *Thickness?* If too thin the label will bend too easily and buckle and it may not be possible to punch or cut the name but if too thick the label will be heavy and clumsy. (vi) *Marking on the label—How will it be done?* Filing, punching, piercing, engraving, or etching? Once these questions have been answered satisfactorily a good label can be drawn, cut out with hacksaw or tinman's snips and filed to shape. Beginners will find it easy to punch the name or number, but it should be drawn out first. The illustration offers ideas for shape, but not for size. Many other shapes can be suggested.

Assignment (2) A Pendant

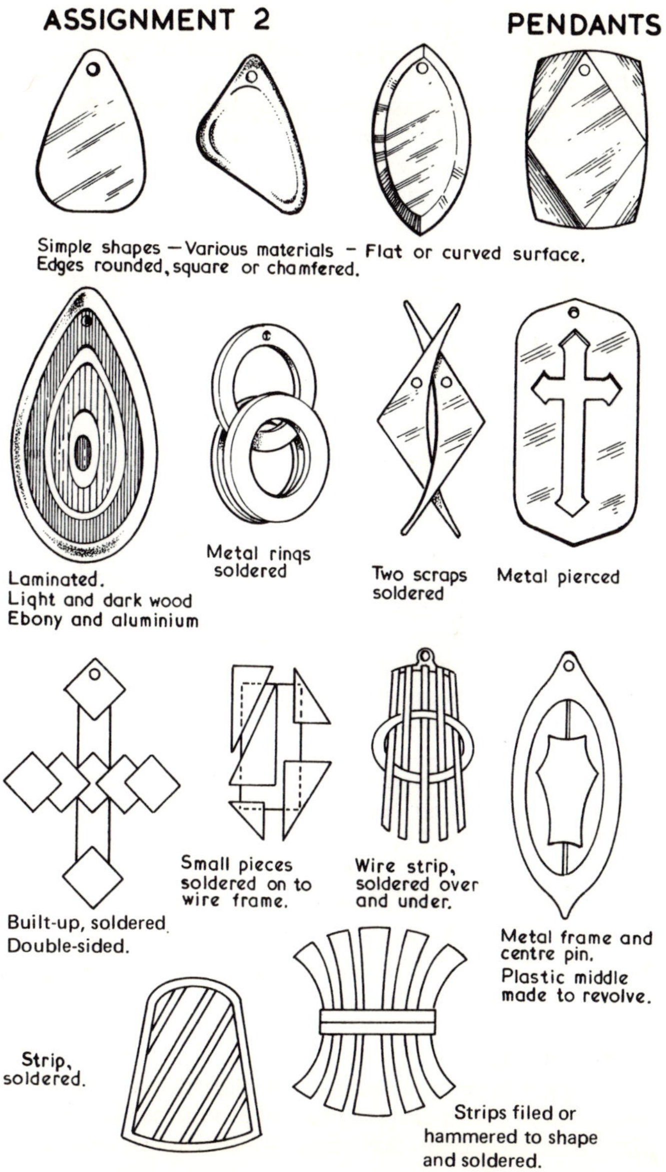

This book deals with metalwork and the assignments are suitable for metal, but metal need not be used exclusively. If another material, such as wood, stone, glass, or plastic is thought to be more suitable, or is preferred for personal taste, then it may be wrong to use metal. Designing a pendant presents such a case. It is wise to collect all odd pieces of attractive material and the pendant might be made from this collection. An oddment might be chosen and the shape worked out from the material.

General thoughts. It must look good—a pleasant material, an attractive shape—and smooth and clean so that it does not tear or mark a dress.

Questions

(1) *Is the pendant to be made from an odd piece of material?* Or is it to be made with complete freedom of choice?

(2) *How is it to hang?* On a leather thong, metal chain, nylon cord, or plaited embroidery thread? How will it be fixed—one or two holes in the pendant, or rings or loops soldered on the top or the back?

(3) *Size and kind of pendant?* A one-piece shape, plain or decorated, or a built-up unit?

(4) *Is it to show only one side?* Can it be double-sided?

(5) *Finish?* How will it be polished? Will it need cleaning? If of metal, should it be given a protective finish (e.g., lacquer)?

Assignment (3) A Leaf Brooch

General thoughts. How can an attractive brooch be made that looks something like a leaf and which a girl will wish to wear?

Questions

(1) *Use?* Is it to be pinned or clipped on to a dress. What pin or clip is to be fixed to the brooch? Advanced students can make such fittings, but

ASSIGNMENT 3

beginners would be wise to buy them. Two suitable pins are illustrated, the first of high quality with a locking catch, and the second a cheap, simple pin. They can both be purchased in several sizes.

(2) *Material?* Wood, metal or plastic? The latter offers a variety of colours, but the pin is metal—and it is easy to soft-solder metal to metal. We have in the workshops choices of metal as well as the necessary tools and equipment so metal will be convenient. The brooch is to be polished bright and the metal must soft-solder easily, so brass, copper and gilding-metal are all suitable and again we can look for odd pieces, provided they are of suitable thicknesses.

(3) *Shape and size?* This can be decided by collecting leaves and making sketches of them. The size may have to be modified a little to suit the size of the metal used. The best leaf shape is selected, cut out and either stuck on the metal or held there while a soft pencil is used to draw around it.

(4) *Manufacture?* Cut the metal accurately and carefully with tinman's snips and if necessary file to shape. Then solder the pin in position.

Further design problems. Shall the leaf be left flat or can the ends be slightly curved by hammering over a stake, bearing in mind that the pin must be soldered on to a flat surface? Shall the edges be decorated with file or punch marks? Shall veins be marked by filing, engraving or etching? Can we build up a leaf brooch, or make one from wire bent to the outside shape as shown in the illustration? With such brooches the concealing of the pin might present difficulties.

The leaf is a useful motif in jewelry and might be used for pendants, earrings and cuff-links. Pins, clips and other fittings (called 'findings' in the jewelry trade) can be glued on with Araldite. Experiments should be carried out using other materials, e.g., grained or inlaid wood—marquetry—and wood in conjunction with metal, or coloured plastics.

This introduction to metalwork has included two jewelry assignments, but most of the assignments suggested on p. 26 would serve equally well. Jewelry, however, has unlimited possibilities for girls as well as boys as design briefs and as exercises in fine craftwork. These can lead to all kinds of decorative arrangements of metal, wood and stones, and can provide an introduction to *lapidary*—the selection, cutting, polishing, and mounting of a great variety of stones. The stones can be comparatively inexpensive (e.g., quartz and agate) or could be metallic ores (such as haematite or pyrites). Ordinary stones may be selected and prepared and this work can make the selection and collection of pebbles from the beach during a school outing a worth-while exercise. This kind of interest is important today when it is realised that studies of materials are as important as techniques, and lapidary may create an interest in semi-precious stones and gems.

The drawing shows a preliminary idea from a design sheet for a jig to clamp pieces of irregularly shaped thin metal between the studs and the jaw whilst drawfiling. The jig is held in a vice when in use.

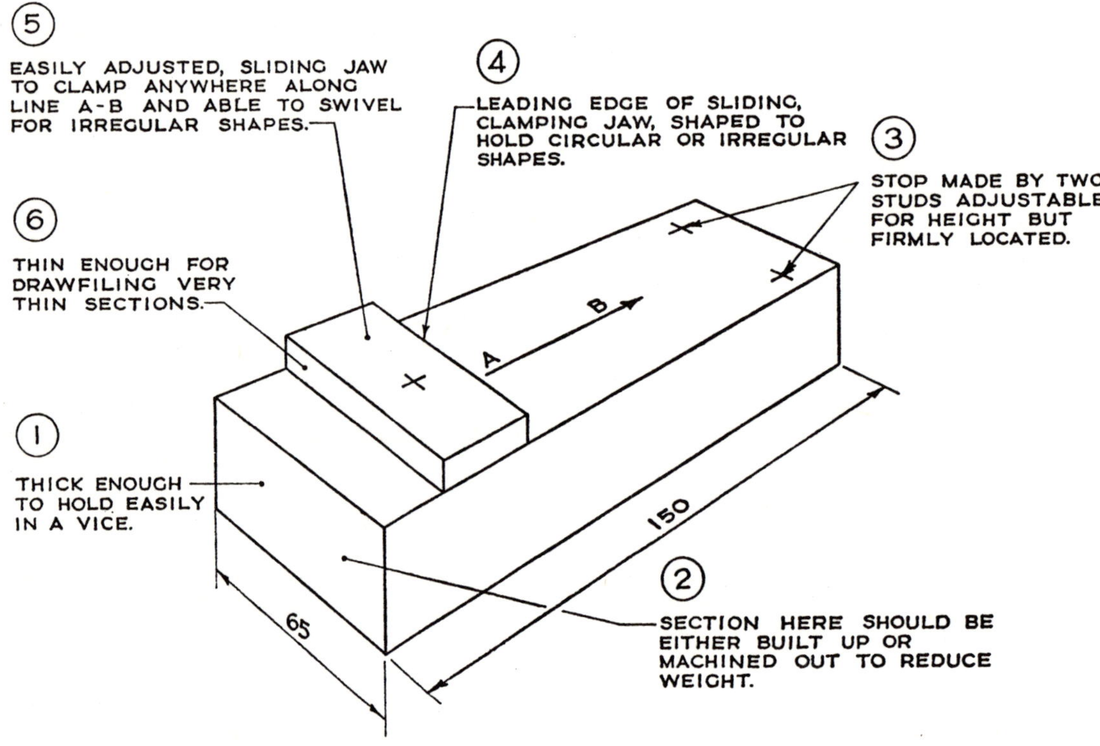

Dimensions in millimetres.

You will see from the notes that several problems are still to be overcome. These have been numbered for your convenience.

On the small piece of paper make preliminary sketches to solve each of the *six* problems posed. You may sketch several ideas for each before you finally decide upon a preferred solution.

Suggested Answer for the Drawing and Design Question set by London University GCE Ordinary Level Handicraft Examination (Summer, 1971)

1. The thickness will depend on whether the base is a plain rectangular piece of metal, whether it is to be built up, or whether part is to be cut away. Measure thicknesses (e.g., of a piece of wood or a book and study sizes on your rule). A piece of metal, 5 mm thick, would be rather thin to fit in the vice unless it were built up, but 10 mm might do, and 15 mm must be considered. A 20 mm block would be thick, but not too thick—especially if part were machined out for lightness; but 25 mm would be too thick unless much were cut away, and this would be a waste of time and metal; 30 mm would be much too thick, ugly and clumsy. The answer should be between 5 mm and 20 mm thick, 5 mm if it is to be built up, 10–15 mm if left as it is, and 20 mm if part is to be machined out.

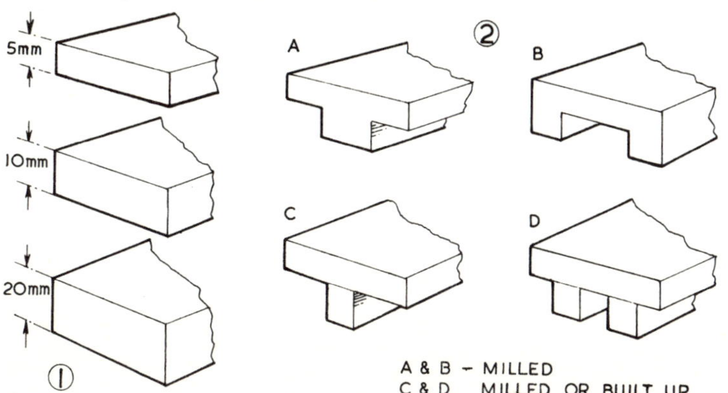

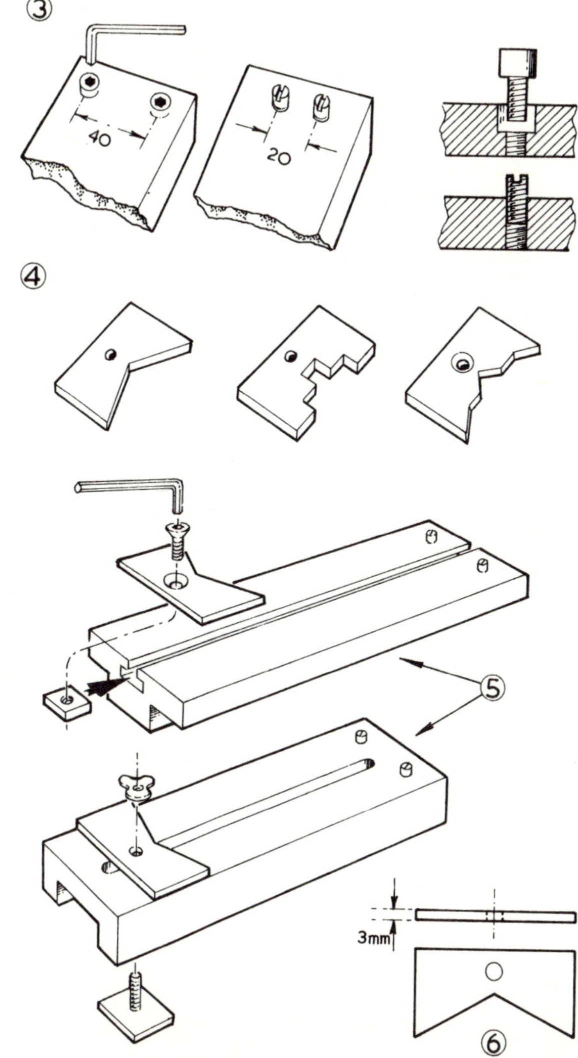

2. The usual practice is to remove metal in a *milling machine*—a heavy, rigid machine designed to remove metal quickly by shaving off metal with a revolving cutter, either along or across the main piece, so forming rectangular slots. Alternatively, the body could be built up by brazing or welding one or two strips underneath, but the clamp must be flat on top. A brazed or welded box-construction using thin metal, 2–3 mm thick, would probably distort while heating and would not be so rigid, while the complicated drilling of holes or the cutting out of rectangular pieces of metal is not practicable. Several possible answers are suggested.

3. The studs must be adjustable so that thin metal, down to 2 mm, can be drawfiled. They cannot have heads therefore, unless holes are counterbored to receive them. The studs must be threaded and the holes tapped so that there is an up-and-down adjustment of 0–5 mm. As they will have to be screwed from the top, the appropriate recesses for screwdriver or Allen key should be shown. Strip metal of varying width will have to be held against the studs for drawfiling—so the position of the studs is important, not too far apart nor too close together—probably between 20 and 40 mm apart. Material less than 20 mm wide could be held against one stud while it is being filed.

4. A plain 'Vee' is probably the best answer, certainly better than a semi-circle, but more complicated alternatives like those suggested might be acceptable.

5. The jaw must slide along the clamp and be free to revolve. A longitudinal slot with a clamping device must be considered. This can be a plain slot part-way along, or a 'Tee'-slot milled out for the whole length, with a coach-bolt with a square-neck fitting into the plain-slot or a 'Tee'-bolt fitting into the 'Tee'-slot with a nut at the top. If on top it will be easier to tighten, and if it were a wing nut or a knurled nut or a drilled nut with a tommy-bar, it could be tightened by hand. Other ideas include a square or hexagonal nut which could be tightened by a spanner or a specially made flat nut which would not interfere with drawfiling. Screws requiring tightening from above can be managed by the methods already suggested for the nut or they should have countersunk heads to be used with a screwdriver or Allen key. Other possibilities might employ a cam device or a vice-action, screwing-up from the end.

6. The actual clamping plate must not be thick, but it has to be kept flat. The best thickness is probably 2–4 mm.

Plate 1. **Kitchenware by David Mellor**

Heavy gauge aluminium saucepans with teak knob and handles

Plate 2. **Stainless Steel Jewelry**

A stainless steel choker with three interchangeable centre pieces designed and made by Ann Marie Shillite of Walsall, Staffs. Exhibited at the Steel Appeal Exhibition at the London and Glasgow Design Centres 1972

2

Basic Design in Jewelry

In jewelry the principles of basic design hold good in exactly the same way as they do for the design of any other article. Just as a coffee table or a knife has to be considered in terms of use, situation (where it will be used), material, construction, decoration, finish and many other factors, so with jewelry a number of questions have to be asked. But in jewelry the problems are less complicated because appearance is fundamental and the first and overriding question is, "How will it look?" This may not be an easy question to answer but it does control other questions such as use, construction and material. The use or purpose is concerned with how and where it will be worn and by whom, man or woman, young or old and whether it is to decorate a person, e.g. a ring, or an article of clothing, e.g. a brooch or tiepin. The strength depends on the construction which must be reliable but it must be subservient so that the piece looks right, e.g. making the metal of a claw-setting for a cut stone so thin that light can get behind and all round the stone. Then the polished facets will reflect the light and the stone will shine brightly. The material, whether it be the metal or the stone, is always selected for appearance but the cost is often a deciding factor.

Jewelry is like a picture, usually viewed from the front and seldom from the back; basically it consists of shapes forming a pattern and it offers many opportunities for experimenting. Some pieces can consist of one shape with or without a pattern, perhaps a pendant, brooch or cuff-link, but other articles such as bracelets or necklaces may consist of several pieces of the same shape joined together. A study of simple shapes, their arrangement and repetition can be a basic design exercise specially applicable to jewelry. Such exercises are particularly suitable for beginners studying design in metalwork. They can be developed as pattern work in which any motif can be repeated—straight lines, bent lines (suggested by setting out a number of short pieces of wire all bent in one or two ways), simple shapes and even letters or numbers. Many examples are suggested here and it is hoped that they will prompt pupils to apply and arrange their own units. There are countless ways of arranging units and all kinds of units can be used. Two or more different units can be fitted together to form an individual motif, e.g. squares and circles overlapping or intertwining, and more complex shapes, regular and irregular, joined together and decorated with lines.

Lines can be the basis of the simplest designs and they offer the widest variations. Three examples are illustrated—a ring with line decoration

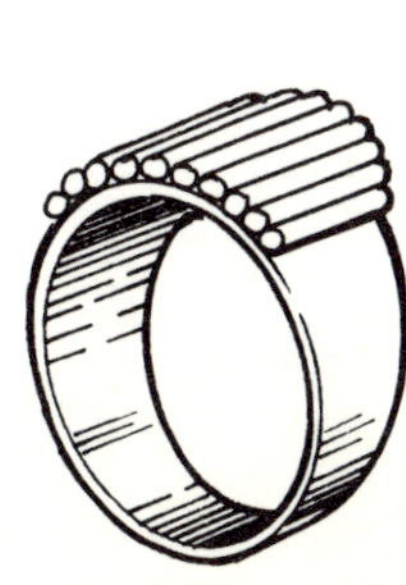

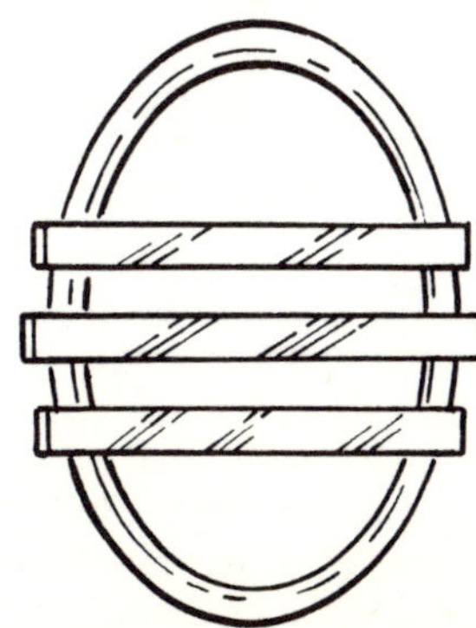

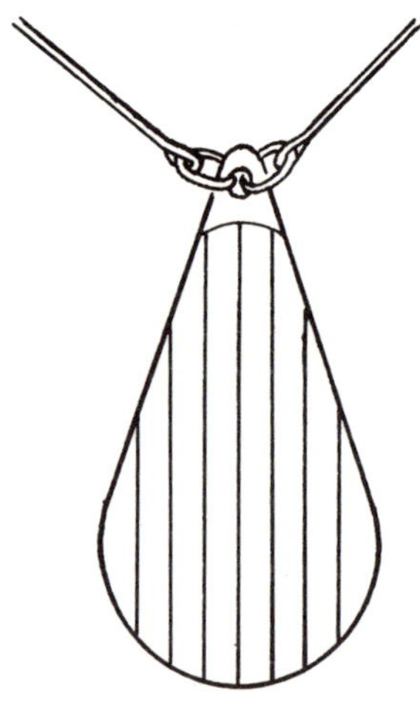

effected by soldering together pieces of round wire, a brooch on which the lines are strips of rectangular metal and a pendant showing lines scored or filed or possibly sawn in which case the line appearance can be produced by grooves and if they are wide enough the lower levels of the grooves will give a space effect. These basic line exercises can be the beginnings of excellent design briefs but the brooch suggests the greatest variety. Strips of so many sizes can be fitted together in so many ways, soldered closely together or separated as illustrated. On p. 17 the strips are all of the same section soldered on to a circle but more strips could be used and they could be fixed to different shapes or on to other strips set out at right angles or obliquely. The strips could vary in width and thickness as well as length and they do not have to have an underneath piece. Strips might be arranged together all in one plane by soldering two or more very short strips between the longer strips and by this method the spaces so formed could be as interesting as the lines: or the strips can be soldered in different planes, e.g. one up, one down, alternatively—but an essential and final operation for every brooch is fixing on the pin (*see* p. 12) so that it (the pin) cannot be seen from the front when the brooch is in place.

Shapes can be thin pieces of metal or outlines of wire. They can be joined together by soldering or by wire links or the shapes can be interlocking and the whole series of units can be fixed rigidly or loosely for a bracelet or necklace. Decoration can be applied to shapes as shown by the lines added to the pendant shape shown here. This can be extended to patterns possibly cut with a burin or etched with acid. Similarly basic design in shapes can be extended to using two metals and soldering them to a third or to piercing, i.e. cutting out the shapes with a piercing saw and leaving the holes (possibly the cut out shapes could be used elsewhere).

When experimenting for basic designs it is better to begin with felt pens on large sheets of paper. The easy flowing thick dark lines lead to more ideas whereas thin sharp lines appear hard and can be stultifying, especially if they are set out on small pieces of paper. Some students achieve better results by cutting out and experimenting with a series of shapes rather than by drawing and, finally, having settled for a good arrangement, pasting them down—white on black card or vice versa. The use of three colours, say black and white on a green background suggests two or three metals and this can lead on to three dimensional basic designs by cutting out forms in polystyrene and fixing the polystyrene units to card or making plastic models of finished pieces. Students can suggest many designs for brooches; school badges, foliage—leaf and flower forms can be built up from wire and flat units. Initials and monograms, two or more letters intertwined, are excellent especially if

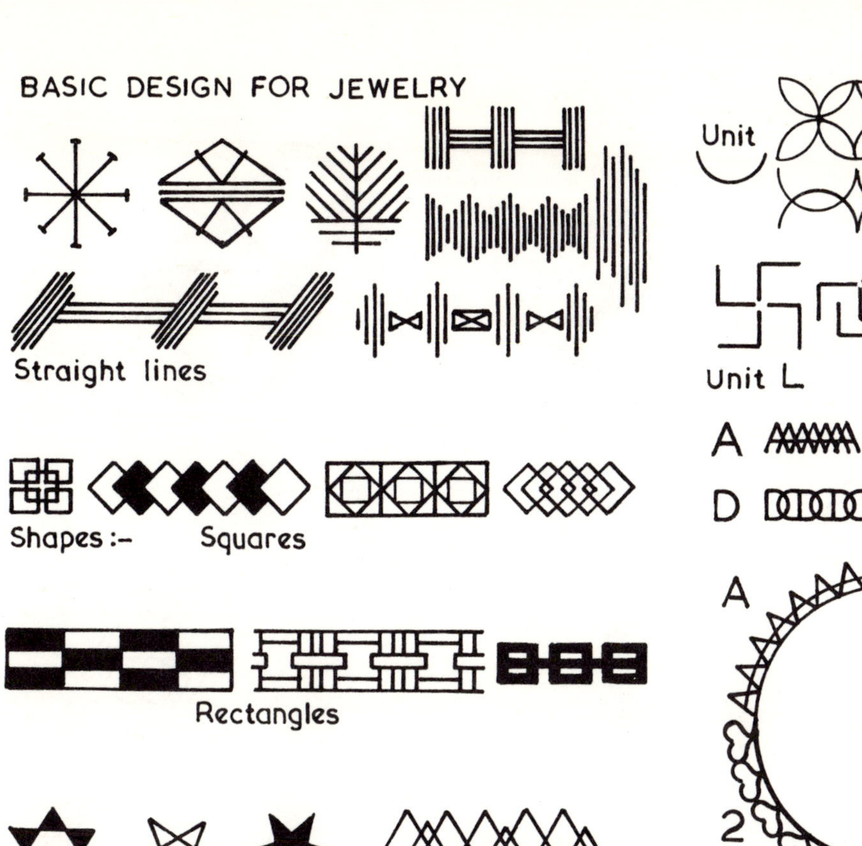
BASIC DESIGN FOR JEWELRY
Straight lines
Shapes :-
Squares
Rectangles
Triangles
Circles

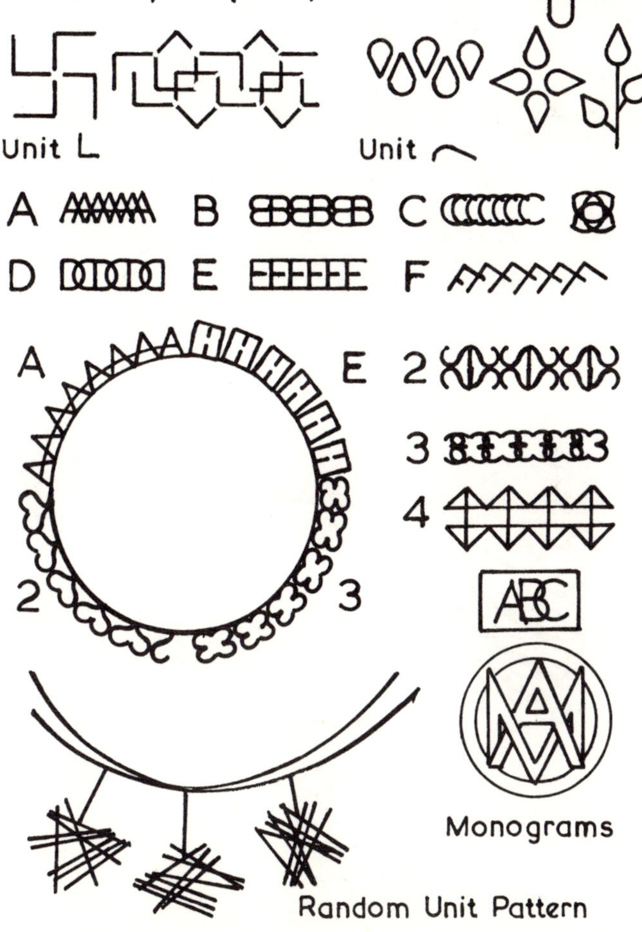
Unit
Unit
Unit L
Unit
A
B
C
D
E
F
A
E
2
3
4
2
3
ABC
Monograms
Random Unit Pattern

MODERN JEWELRY

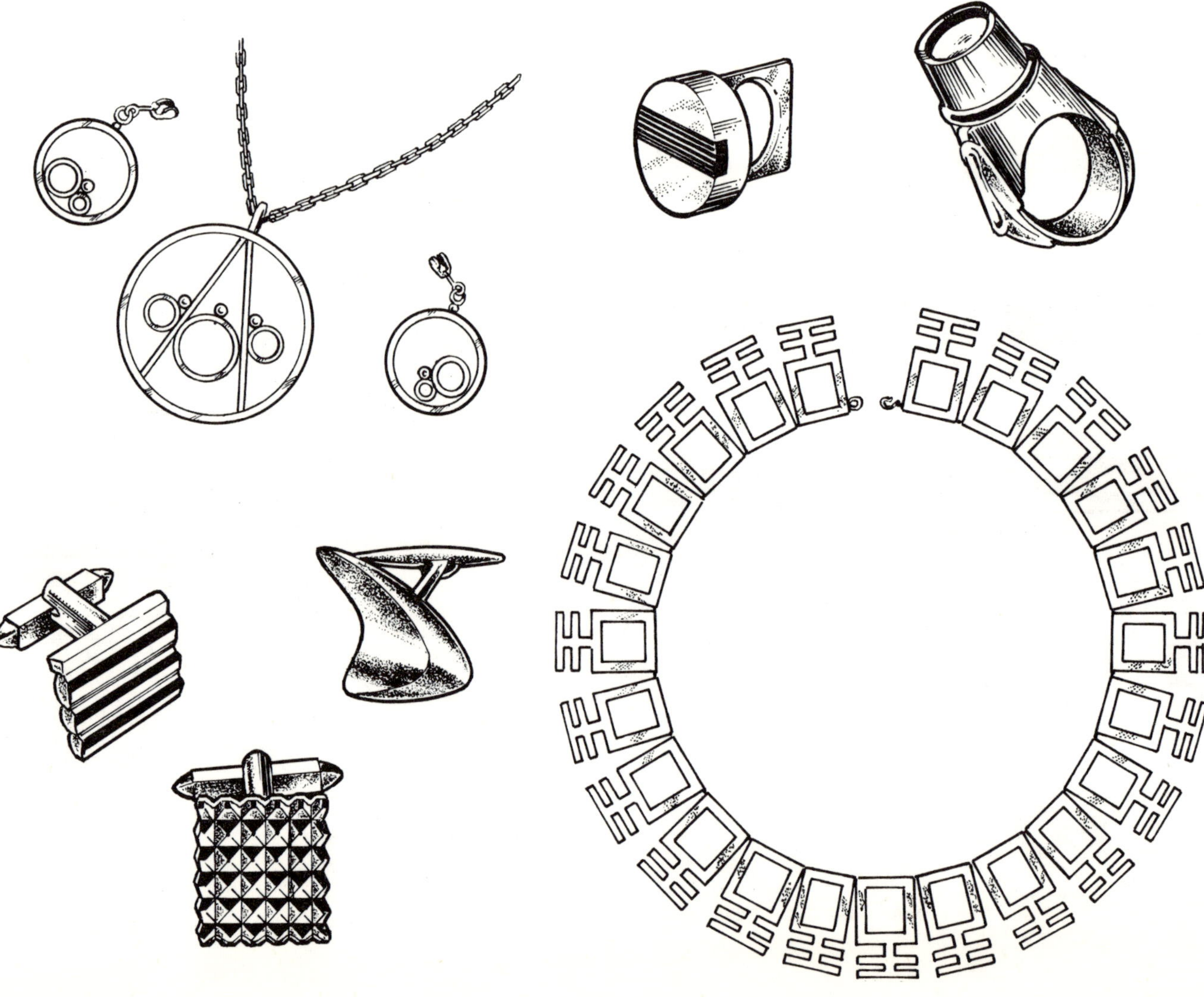

an under-and-over strip design is adapted. Another plan which can be used to form a unit which might be suitable for a brooch is to hold about a dozen small strips—say 50 mm panel pins—and carefully drop them together on to white paper and copy this arrangement. If it is not suitable for a brooch it will certainly serve as a repeat pattern for a necklace as suggested on p. 19.

Many ideas for school jewelry can be obtained from shop windows or supermarkets and pp. 20 and 22 show examples of good jewelry in silver and gold in which the simple arrangement of lines and shapes is obvious.

Page 20 shows a pendant and earrings based on circles designed by William and Lilian Hall and gold cuff-links based on lines and squares designed and made by K. Weiss Limited. The third cuff-link is of silver, moulded to a three-dimensional shape by Henning Koppel of Georg Jensen Ltd of Copenhagen. Henning Koppel is a famous designer who began as a sculptor and many of his works have been purchased by important museums all over the world. He designed the large brooch on p. 22 and the silver pitcher on p. 190. The necklace on this page, designed by M. L. Letki, illustrates an attractive and successful repetition of a simple unit consisting of a square and three lines. The two rings are of very different styles, one with a circular motif of silver and onyx designed by Joel Degan and the other is of conical form with a stone of rock crystal mounted with a "rub over" setting and designed by the Swedish silversmith, Torun Bulow-Hube, who worked in France for twelve years and like Henning Koppel is internationally renowned. Torun says her jewellery should be beautiful and as perfect as a delicate piece of mechanism "evoking a world in which form and function reflect each other". On p. 22 are illustrated a bracelet and earrings based on line scrolls and pair of "drop" shaped earrings of gold wire with small stones set between the wires all designed and manufactured by Corocraft Limited. The chokers, both made of wire shaped and flattened are by Dasdales Limited. The circular brooch is of gold set with pearls and was designed for Georg Jensen Ltd by Nanna Ditzel. The other two brooches are sophisticated shapes, the lower one designed by Ernest Blyth for Ivan Tarratt and Associates and the one above it by Henning Koppel for Georg Jensen Ltd.

MODERN JEWELRY

3

Fitting—Vices

The vice is the first tool seen when entering the school metalwork room. As a vice is used to hold the metal which is filed and cut, it should be at the correct height, i.e. the vice jaws should be at the same height as the student's elbow when it is close to his side.

The Parallel Vice is the best vice for fitting, i.e. filing, sawing, chiselling and screwing. The size of the vice depends on the width of its jaws which vary between 60 mm and 200 mm; 80 mm and 100 mm are most suitable for schools. The body is made of cast iron, the screw and handle of mild steel and the jaws, which are screwed to the body, of hardened cast steel. The outside surfaces of these jaws are cut, criss-crossed, so that they are rough and will grip the metal firmly, but this means that they can damage the work. Fitters turn them round, file them smooth, change the jaws or face them with brass, but the usual practice is to protect the work by covering the jaws with vice clamps. These can be of soft metal, 18-gauge copper or aluminium, which can be made in school, or the Record vice clamps of fibre, fastened to metal as shown opposite, or of lead which might be cast in the school foundry (*see* p. 121). The parallel vice shown is an instantaneous grip vice. It can be opened and closed easily without turning the screw. The screw is a buttress thread (*see* p. 45) and it turns in a half-nut which can be disengaged by moving the small lever near the handle.

The Leg Vice is an older and stronger kind of vice which is used for heavier work, especially when the work is hammered. It is fixed to the bench and into the floor and is most useful when fixed near the forge. Leg vices are made of mild steel with cast steel jaws welded in position. The jaw sizes vary between 80 mm and 180 mm and the screw is a square thread.

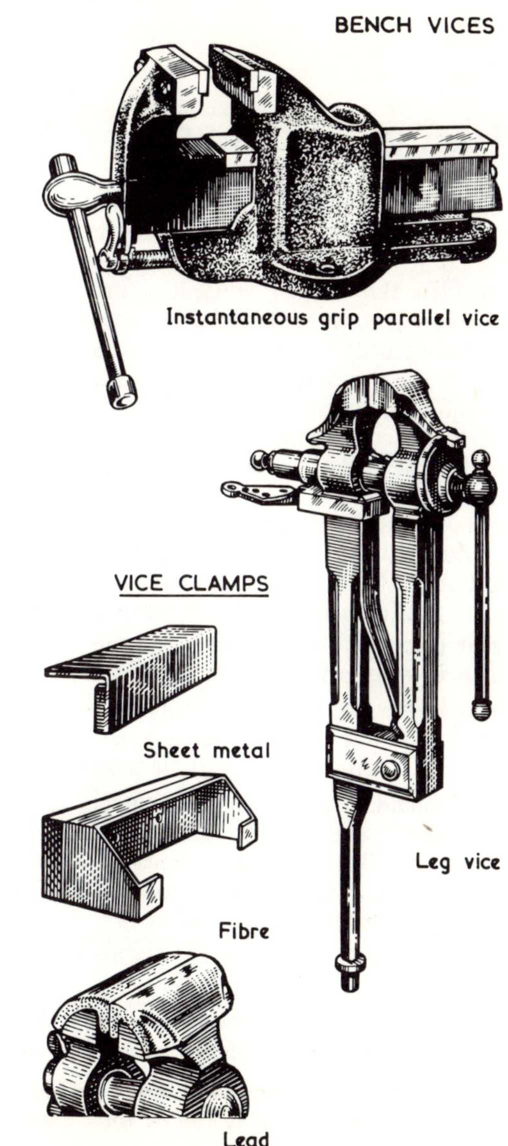

4

Fitting—Files and Filing

The file is the most important hand tool in the school metalwork room. There are very many different kinds of files that vary in cut, length and shape, but those commonly used in the school workshop are illustrated. Files are measured by their length, excluding the tang, and when ordering a file it is necessary to state the length, shape and cut, e.g. 200 mm half-round bastard. The cut is the degree of roughness or smoothness and is described as coarse, bastard, second cut, smooth and dead smooth—but coarse and dead smooth files are seldom used in schools. Most files are double cut, i.e. the teeth are formed by two series of parallel cuts made with a reciprocating chisel. The two series of cuts do not slope equally, as diagonal teeth with two different slopes are more effective. On single-cut files the teeth are formed by a single series of chisel cuts.

Flat Files have double cut teeth on all four sides, taper a little in width and thickness, and are rectangular in section.

Hand Files are also rectangular in section with double cut teeth but have one edge smooth, a safe edge, for working in corners when only one surface is to be filed.

Half-round Files are double cut on the flat side, but on second cut and smooth files the curved side has a series of short parallel cuts going right down the file, while the bastard files are double cut on both sides. All half-round files taper in width and thickness.

Square Files are double cut on all four sides and usually taper slightly.

Round Files have single cuts, each row intersecting slightly, and tapering round files are called "rat tails".

Triangular or **Three-square Files** are double cut on each face, parallel for two thirds of their length and taper to a point.

Knife-edge Files have two sloping side faces, double cut, meeting at a sharp edge which cuts like a saw, and have a single cut narrow edge at the back.

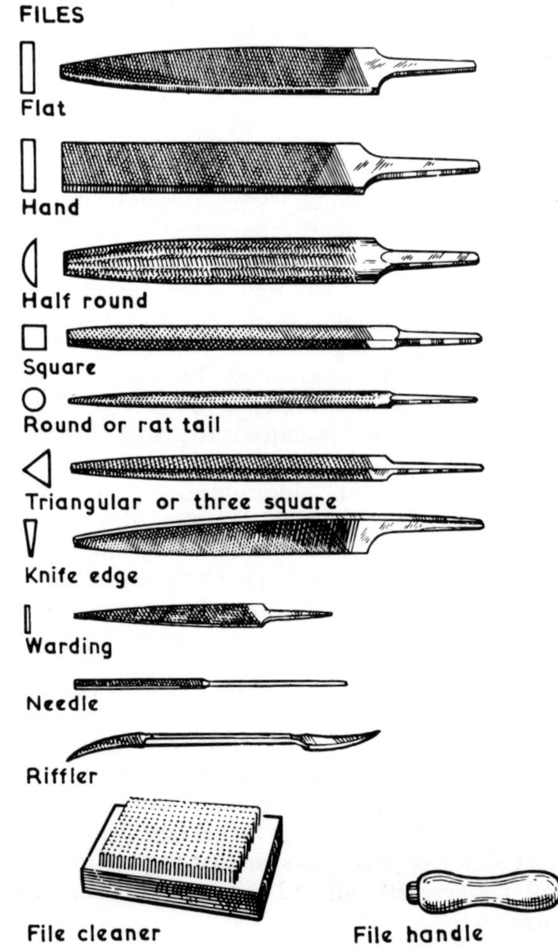

Warding Files are small, generally between 75 and 200 mm long and thin and were used largely by locksmiths, hence the name.

Needle Files, sometimes called Swiss pattern files, are small, 120–180 mm long. They are made in many shapes from small section rod, and, instead of a tang, part of this rod is left as a handle. They are used by jewellers, silversmiths, die makers and watchmakers, as are **Rifflers,** which are 145 and 175 mm long and have small curved files at each end.

Filing. When filing, the student should stand upright with the left foot forward, holding the file handle in the right hand and grasping the other end of the file with the thumb and the first two fingers. The work, usually held in a vice, should be about elbow height and the file is pushed lengthways slightly diagonally, across the work so that it cuts on the forward stroke.

When the surfaces of thin flat work have to be filed the metal can be fastened to wood with small nails or screws, or held in a filing clamp. The wood or clamp (*see* pp. 14 and 35) is held in a vice.

Drawfiling consists of holding the file at each end and pushing and pulling the file sideways along the work. This produces a finer finish than normal filing, all the file marks being parallel with the length of the metal.

Use of Files. A file with a tang should never be used without a handle, which must fit securely and be of convenient size. Files must be kept clean, free of filings, that is, "pinnings", which scratch the work. The filings can be removed by tapping the file on the bench and by rubbing with a wire brush, a file card or cleaner. New files must be used carefully on iron and steel to prevent chipping and tooth breakage, but if used first on brass or other non-ferrous metals the file will give better service.

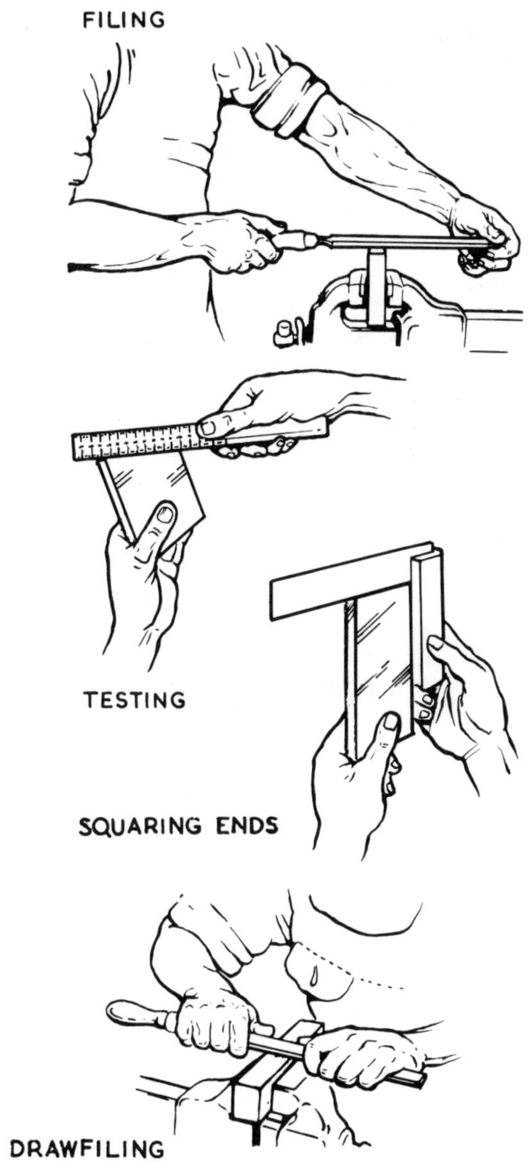

Assignments

All assignments involve questions—material?—shape?—size?—use?—and how is it to be made? These you must answer so that you are able to prepare a dimensional sketch indicating materials, construction and order of working and then, if necessary, an accurate working drawing.

Filing can be very tedious, and unnecessary filing must be avoided especially in the beginning so whenever possible have metal cut accurately to size. When this is not possible use metal with a good surface, polished bright if convenient, and the correct width so that you have to file only the ends. Look around your house, school, garage and garden to find metal articles which can be made from strip, metal which is smooth along its edges as well as its sides, and think whether you can make them by just cutting to length and filing the ends and bending to shape. This is a problem and all assignments have problems. All those opposite have a definite purpose and this must be considered before deciding upon the kind and size of metal to use but they can all be made from strip.

(1) Nameplate. What is it for? Where is it going? What is to be on it? What metal should be used? Is this metal available? How is it to be fixed in position? Does it need screw holes? How many? Where? This exercise like many others involves filing the ends square (*see* p. 25).

(2) What metal is strong enough for a tyre lever? It should not be thick and heavy. Its shape has been designed over the years for a specific purpose and a boy cannot improve on it, but a tyre lever is a functional tool and should be made only if it is to be used, preferably on your own cycle.

(3) Pipe clip. The size of the pipe determines the size of the clip and the material from which it should be made.

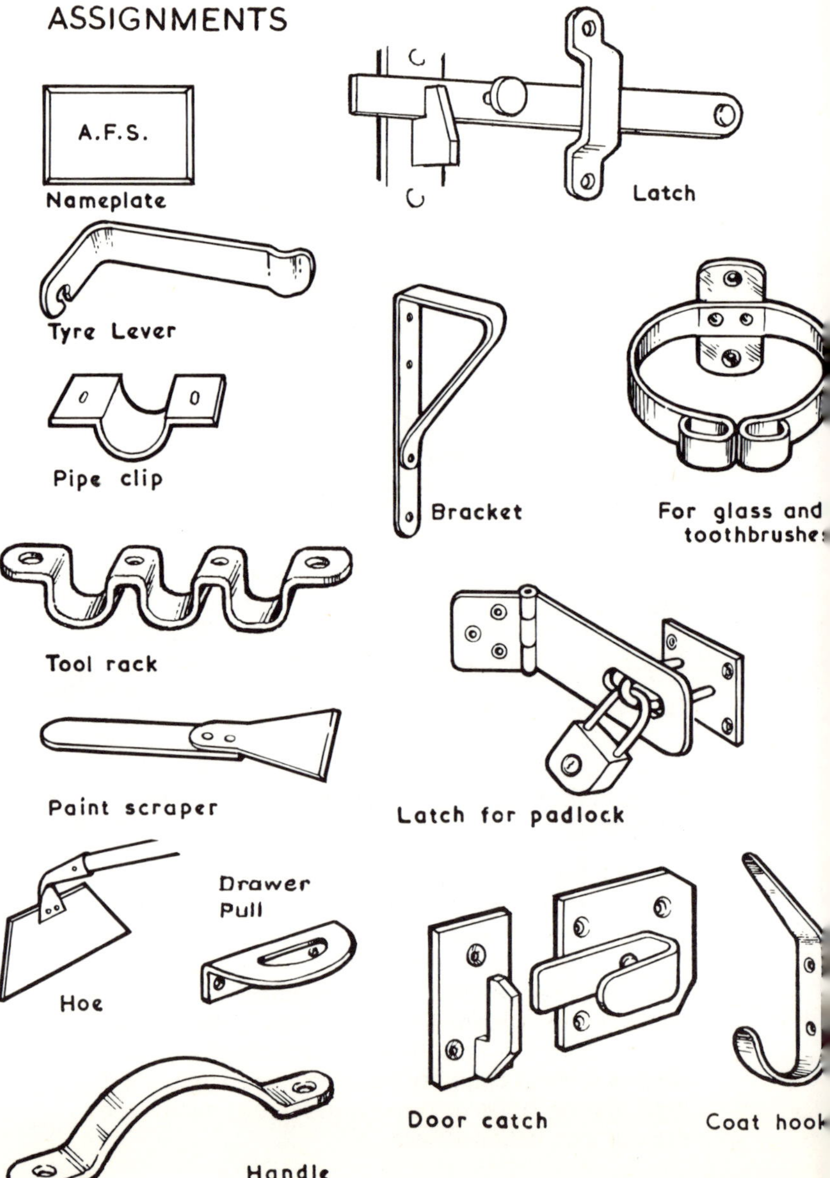

Plate 3. **Kitchen Equipment**

Kitchen tool set and rack. Made of stainless steel, satin finish, by George Wostenholm & Son (Sheffield) Ltd., and designed by S. Fowler

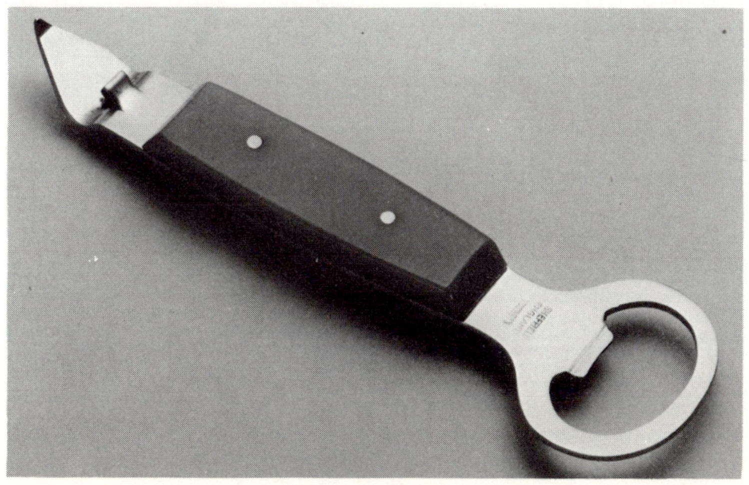

Can and bottle opener. Designed and made by Needham, Veall & Tyzack, Ltd., Sheffield, of stainless steel with a coloured perspex handle, black, pink, red or green

Plate 4. **Contemporary Handles**

Above: Pull or push door handle made of aluminium, finished silver anodised or black nylon covered. Designed by Roger Peach
Right: Elbow action pull handle for hospital use made of bronze, brass or aluminium rod finished bright or satin chromium plate, bronze metal antique or anodised aluminium. Must be fixed at the correct height. Designed by Roger Peach
Below: Door lever handle manufactured as a hot pressing from aluminium and satin anodised. Designed by Robert Welch

(4) Tool rack. The drawing is only a suggestion. This could be an excellent design brief as the kind and number of tools decides the shape and size of the rack and this offers a wide variety of exercises.

(5) Paint scraper. The scraper suggested is made from two pieces of metal, a rigid handle which must be easy to hold and a thinner blade which will bend slightly and can be sharpened by bevelling. You can decide the material, the sizes and the method of joining the two pieces.

(6) Hoe. Several types of hoes can be designed but there is only one suitable material—mild steel. The one shown has a flat blade with a piece of tube flattened at one end riveted firmly in position at the back of the blade. Work with sloping sides or ends like the blades in (5) and (6) are set out with centre punch and scriber, cut and filed to the line and tested with a rule for straightness as shown on p. 25.

(7) All kinds of handles can be made all sizes for all kinds of purposes out of many materials from flat, round and square sections. The handle illustrated is made of strip aluminium—150 mm × 20 mm × 5 mm—bent so that there is room for the fingers between the door and the handle. Look at the handles opposite.

(8) This drawer pull is made of brass strip 100 mm × 60 mm × 4 mm bent along its length with a suitably shaped grip hole which was drilled and filed to shape.

(9) The suggestion shows a simple construction for a rigid bracket from strip mild steel but its size will depend on its use.

(10) The use of the glass and toothbrush rack is obvious but several wire circles will have to be tried on suitable glasses before the actual size can be decided. As it will probably be fixed in the bathroom aluminium alloy is recommended as a suitable material.

(11), (12) and (13) are latches or catches. There are all kinds all around us but only simple shapes which can be made from strip are given here.

(14) The hook is a fine exercise in design. What is going to hang on it should determine the size and shape and must affect its material e.g. pure aluminium would probably be too soft to support heavy coats best; aluminium alloy might be suitable; and its use would affect where it is going and how it will be fixed.

5

Fitting—Cutting (Saws and Sawing)

Sawing. Metal is cut with a hacksaw which is a narrow hardened steel blade fixed rigidly in a metal frame. Hacksaw blades for hand use are usually 12 mm wide and 250 or 300 mm long, and are made of high-speed steel or a less expensive alloy steel, e.g. low tungsten steel which can be made flexible and practically unbreakable. High-speed steel gives maximum blade life and speed of cutting and is particularly suitable for cutting very hard metals. Hard blades are more rigid and therefore better for quick accurate cutting, but flexible blades are less likely to break so are recommended for general work, especially in school. Popular saw teeth sizes are 18, 24 and 32 teeth to 25 mm, 18 for medium-hard and soft metals to prevent clogging of the teeth, 24 for hard, and 32 teeth for thin metal, as at least three consecutive teeth must always be in contact with the material. In spite of metrication the teeth of hack saw blades are to be described and categorised by the number of teeth to the inch for several years although 25 mm may be used instead of the inch, e.g. 18 teeth to 25 mm. The blade is fixed in the frame with the teeth facing forward so that it cuts only on the forward stroke. The saw should be used with long steady strokes, about 60 per minute, and the work must be firmly secured. The left hand must hold the back of the frame above the blade to avoid any danger of the hand being injured by the vice jaws or vice clamps.

Hacksaw Frames are usually adjustable and there are several differently shaped handles, but fixed length frames are more rigid.

HACKSAWS

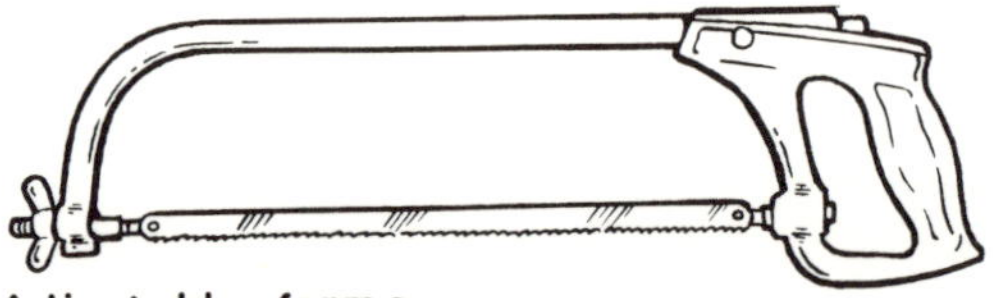

Adjustable frame

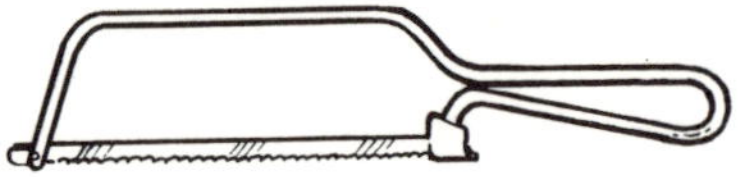

Junior

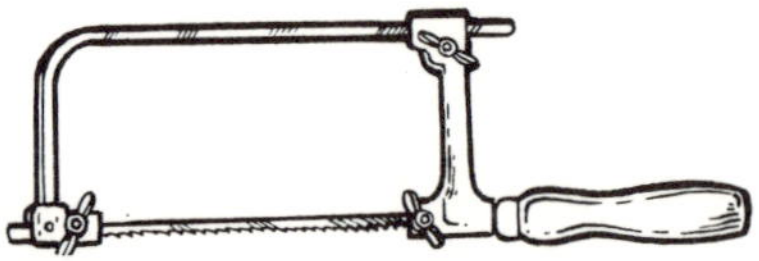

PIERCING SAW

ABRAFILES

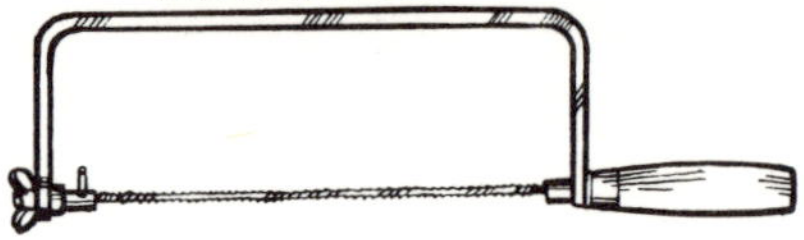

Solid frame

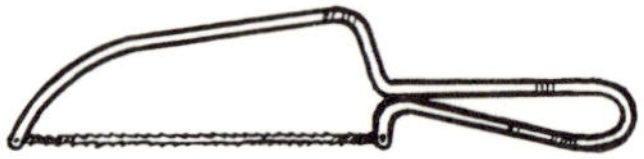

Junior wireback

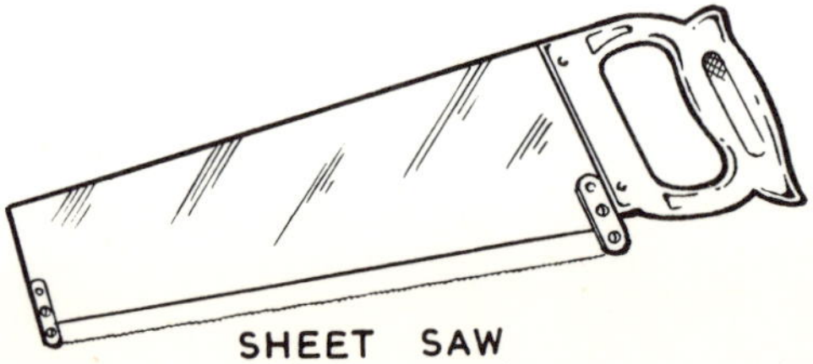

SHEET SAW

Junior Hacksaws are strong and useful. The blade is 150 mm long and 6 mm wide and it fits in a spring tension frame.

Piercing Saws are used for very fine work, especially by silversmiths. Piercing is the cutting, often of decorative patterns, from the inside of thin metal. When piercing, or cutting inside circles in beaten metalwork, as in removing the middle from the base for a coffee pot (*see* p. 93), the saw is used vertically with the teeth pointing downwards and with the work on a piercing table (*see* p. 35) which has a vee cut in front to allow for the free passage of the blade. The saw is fitted in the metal by drilling a hole, loosening one end of the blade and passing it through the hole in the metal, afterwards refixing it in the frame.

Abrafiles are thin flexible round files fitted in saw frames and are used for piercing but not for fine delicate work.

Sheet Saws cut all types of sheets including metal and are fitted with removable hacksaw blades 300 mm × 32 teeth.

Assignments

Much work can be left from the saw especially piercing. Setting out a letter so that when completed essential parts do not fall out is a good and useful exercise. The bracket and wallhook involve sawing out, filing and bending thin metal while the calipers also include hinge-riveting with possibly the making of washers. The drawer handle should be another design brief. Thick metal is shaped by cutting and filing after drilling (*see* p. 40), and the shape of the blackplate can be varied. Alternatively, the handle could be forged—a piece of thick metal bent to shape after heating.

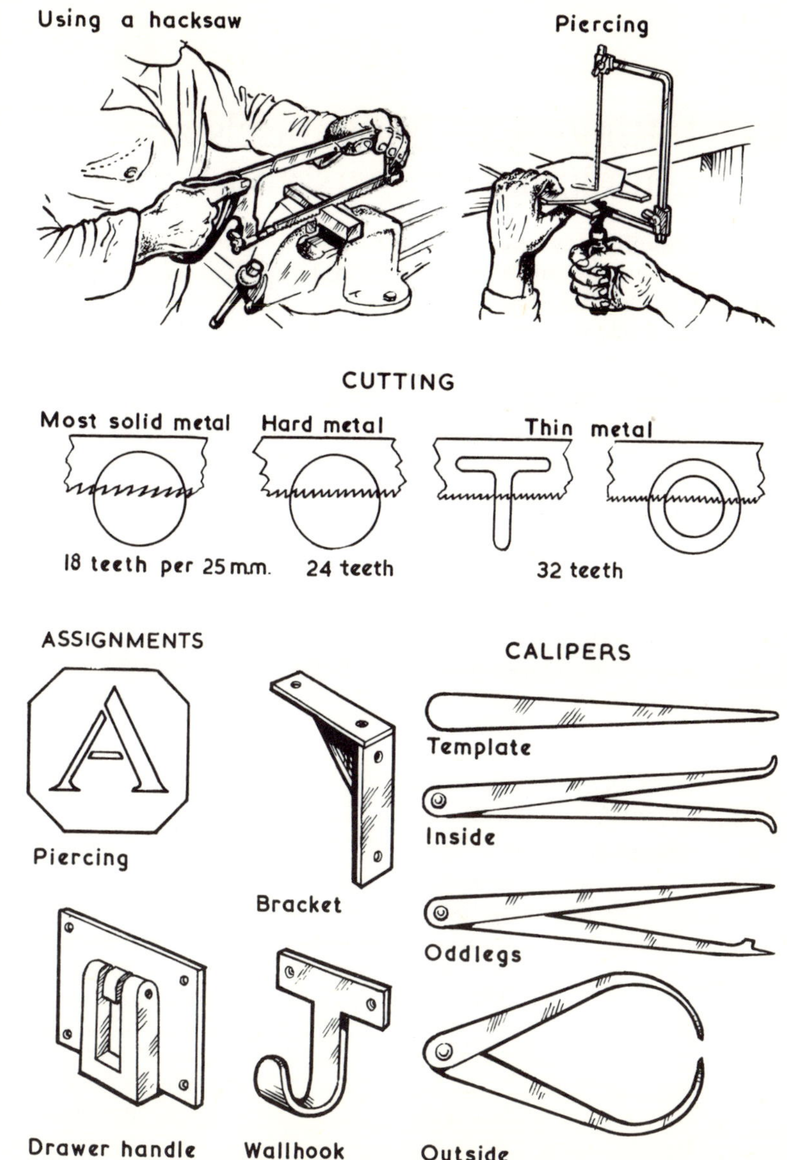

6

Fitting—Cutting (Chisels and Chiselling, Scrapers and Scraping)

Chiselling is an old and inaccurate way of cutting metal, but in some circumstances it is still the best and quickest method. The flat cold chisel, the best known metal chisel, is used for chopping out, shearing and chipping.

Chopping out is cutting sheet or plate metal when tinman's snips, guillotine or saw cannot be used. When chopping out holes it is advisable to drill holes on the waste side of the line. This helps to avoid distortion and is essential when cutting slots as on the bevel shown opposite. The chisel is ground accurately on both sides of the cutting edge, a cutting angle of 60° being correct for mild steel, 65° for cast steel and cast iron, 50° for brass, and less for softer metals down to 30° for zinc, and the metal must be rested on a firm bed, e.g. a cast iron block or the anvil. The chisel should be held vertically near to the head and struck with a hammer of convenient weight—500 g is suitable in schools. The hammer should be held near the end of the shaft, about one quarter of the way down. It is better to cut from both sides, beginning the second side when the chisel marks begin to show through.

Shearing is used to cut narrow strips from metal 1 mm to 4.5 mm thick. The metal is held securely in the vice, the cutting line level with the vice jaws and the part to be removed just above. The chisel should be held so that it is at an angle of 45° to the work, both vertically and horizontally; when it is hit with a hammer the cutting action is similar to that of a pair of shears. Shearing is also a method of removing a piece of metal between two saw cuts, as in making the spade rack and hinge as shown on the opposite page, when the chisel is held at right angles to the work so that it cuts straight across the vice.

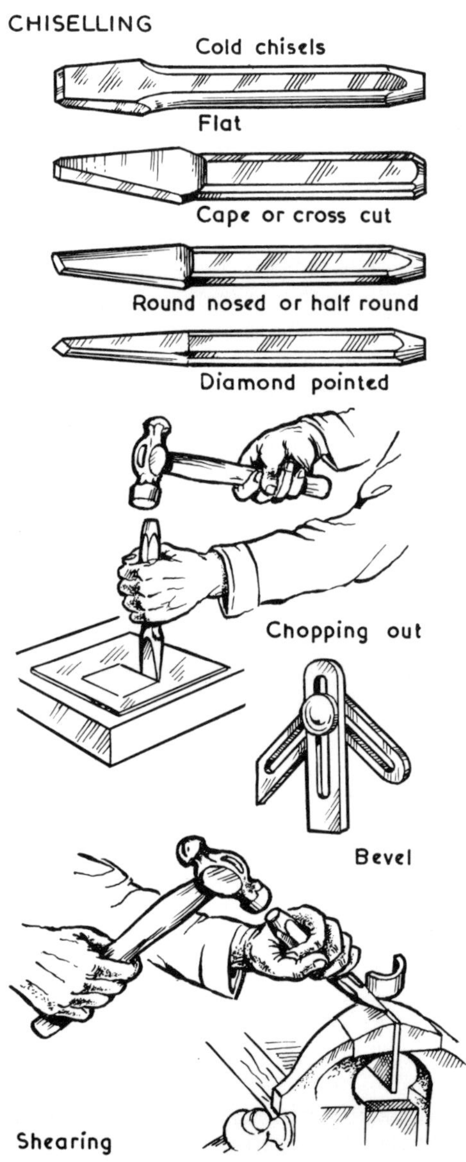

Chipping reduces the thickness or width of a block but, today, grinding, milling, and shaping machines have made this hand process largely unnecessary. The surface is first cut with a cross-cut chisel to form a series of narrow grooves of the required depth; then a flat chisel is used to remove what is left of the original surface down to the level of the bottom of the grooves, and the new surface is finished by scraping.

Chisels are made of cast steel or alloy steel, e.g. nickel chrome, with the cutting edge hardened and tempered and the body left normal so as to withstand the heavy blows and lessen jar. Some are made of silicon manganese alloy steel, which is tough enough to stand up to heavy cutting but soft enough to be sharpened by filing. The flat chisel is the general purpose cold chisel. A cross-cut or cape chisel is used to cut grooves such as oil channels and keyways, as well as for chipping. The end of this chisel is narrow, with the cutting edge slightly wider to prevent the body binding in the groove. A round-nosed or half-round chisel is for cutting half-round and curved grooves and for rectifying a misplaced centre punch mark when commencing drilling. A diamond-pointed chisel is used for cleaning out corners and cutting small grooves, and can also be used to correct faulty centring.

The head of a chisel should be maintained ground to its correct shape and the burrs caused by hammering must be removed. If left, pieces may break off and injure a bystander, or the hammer may slip off an irregular head and harm the worker.

Chisels are used to break riveted joints by removing the rivet head and cutting through rusted bolts. Small rivets are sheared with a flat chisel, but large rivet heads may have to be chipped away with a cross-cut chisel.

A Shearing Machine or **Guillotine** is a form of bench shears with two hardened steel blades, operated by a long lever which closes the top blade against the side of a fixed bottom blade to cut sheet metal which is too thick to be cut with

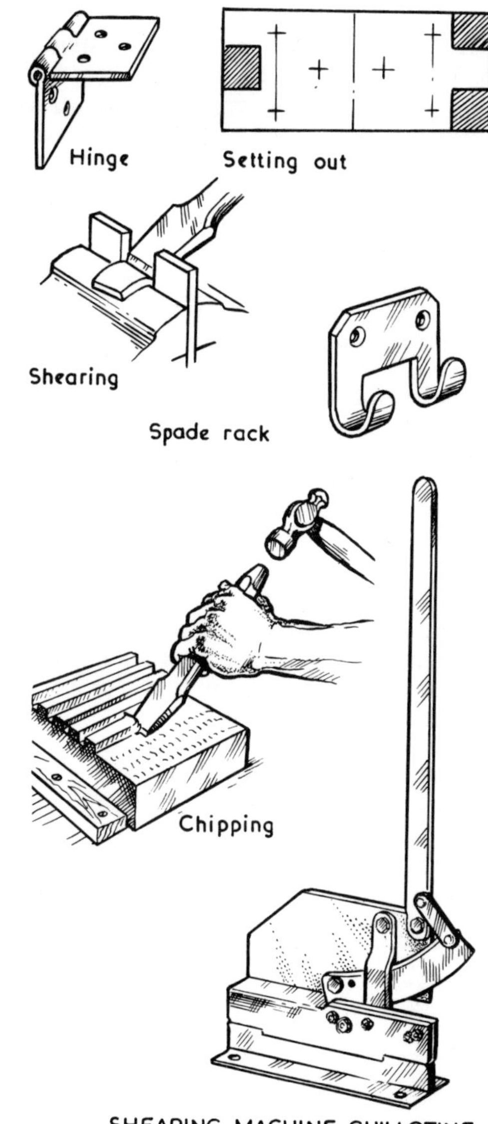

SHEARING MACHINE-GUILLOTINE

snips (p. 79). It cuts with a scissor-like action and must be fixed securely on a bench or heavy stand, so that long strips or large sheets can be cut. The long handle must be fixed safely, usually in an upright position, when not in use. If this machine is used carelessly, metal may be bent, buckled, and distorted beyond correction, and good metal is spoilt when the cut is allowed to continue further than necessary.

Scrapers are for scraping away small amounts of metal to produce dead flat surfaces, as for surfaces plates or the perfect fitting of two like-shaped surfaces as when fitting bearings. They are hardened steel blades, often being made from old files, and are in various shapes, the three illustrated being most used. The flat tapered scraper has its cutting edge on the end and is used for flat surfaces. The curved half-round scraper is sharpened on two edges and is used on hollow surfaces such as bearings, while the three square or triangular scraper, for small curved work, is sharpened on three sides.

Scraping is a difficult operation: it is necessary on high-class work, e.g. machine tools, and is done successfully only after much practice. Surfaces to be scraped are rubbed on a surface plate or on the master surface with which the new surface must "make" or fit, and which has been previously coated with marking blue. Rubbing will show the high spots which must be scraped down, and then the surfaces must be tested again, and scraped again until both surfaces are covered completely with blue. The scraper must be sharpened every few minutes.

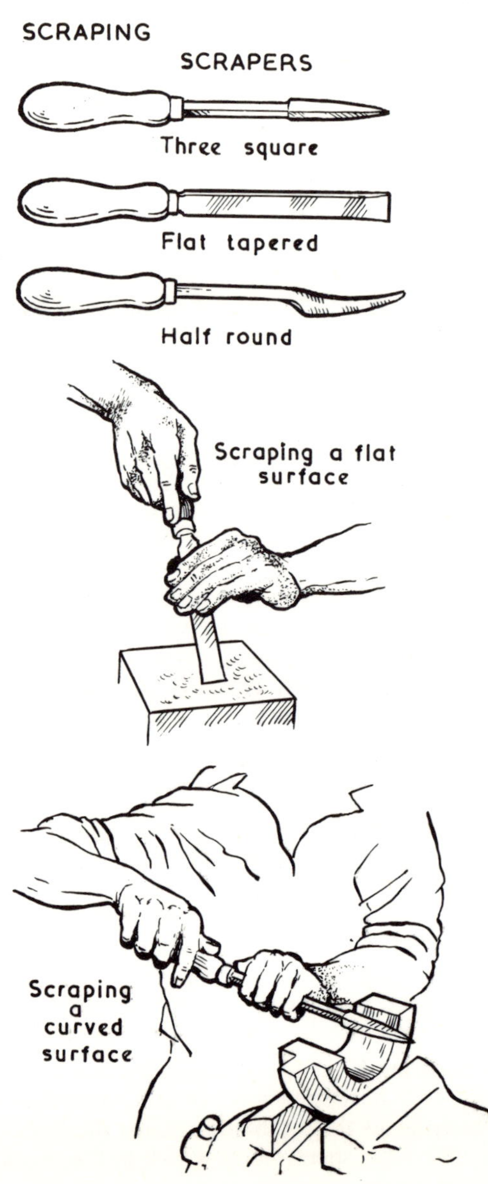

7

Fitting—Setting Out

Scribed lines and Punched Dots. Setting out, or marking out, is a fundamental preliminary process in metalwork. Usually the surface of the metal is scratched with the hardened point of a scriber and the metal is coloured so that the scratches can be easily seen. It can be wiped with copper sulphate solution which gives a very fine copper plating or it can be coated with one of the proprietary brands of marking-out liquids, usually bright blue. If the surface is rough, as on castings, it can be covered with chalk or even whitewash. Scribed lines are sometimes emphasised by a series of light centre punch dots or pops. This is often necessary on curved work (as on the drill stand overleaf) when it is advisable to use an automatic spring punch, which gives an impact of between 5 and 10 kg without the use of a hammer. When filing to a scribed line the line disappears, but if the line is centre popped, half of the punch mark remains. However, this may look unsightly on small work. When lines are scribed parallel to a true edge e.g. centre lines, lines for a series of holes or scribing to width (see overleaf), jenny calipers are used.

Combination sets are special marking-out tools which consist of four units. One of these is a rule which fits into the other three, one to form an engineer's square, another to form a protractor for setting out angles and the third to form a centre square for finding the centre of round metal bars (*see* p. 61).

Setting Out. For most simple exercises a true edge or side is essential. It can be obtained by filing but if square-edged strip metal, e.g. bright drawn mild steel, is used, the sides, i.e. the long edges, have been rolled true. One end must be filed true and tested with an engineer's square as shown on p. 25. Then the metal is marked to length, scribed, as

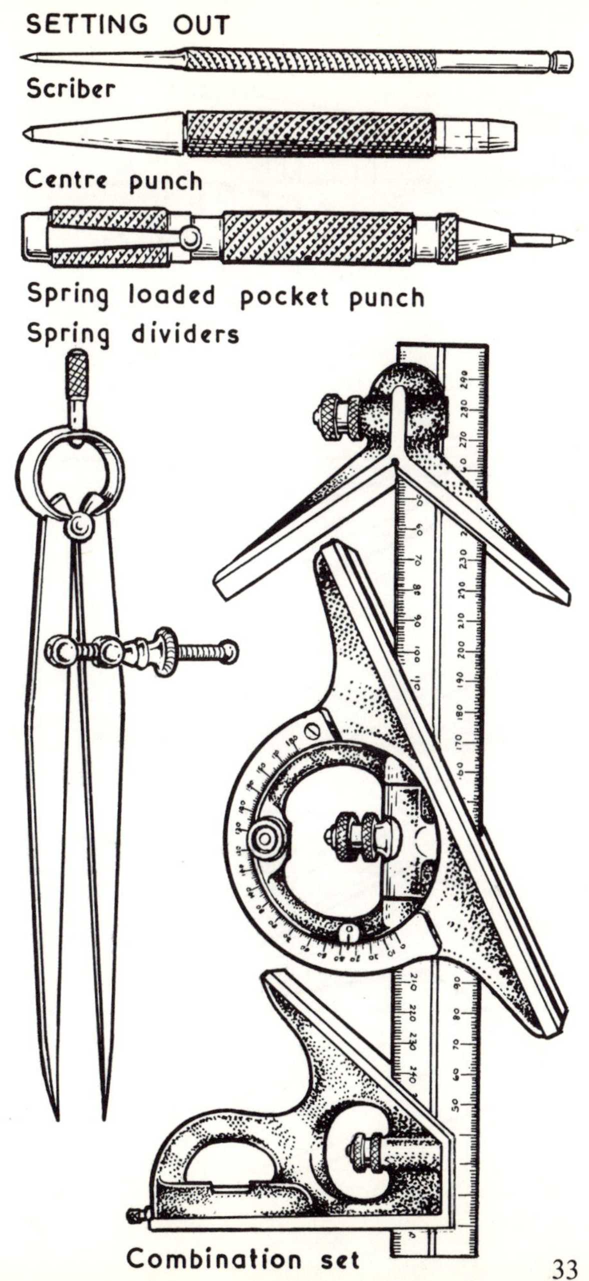

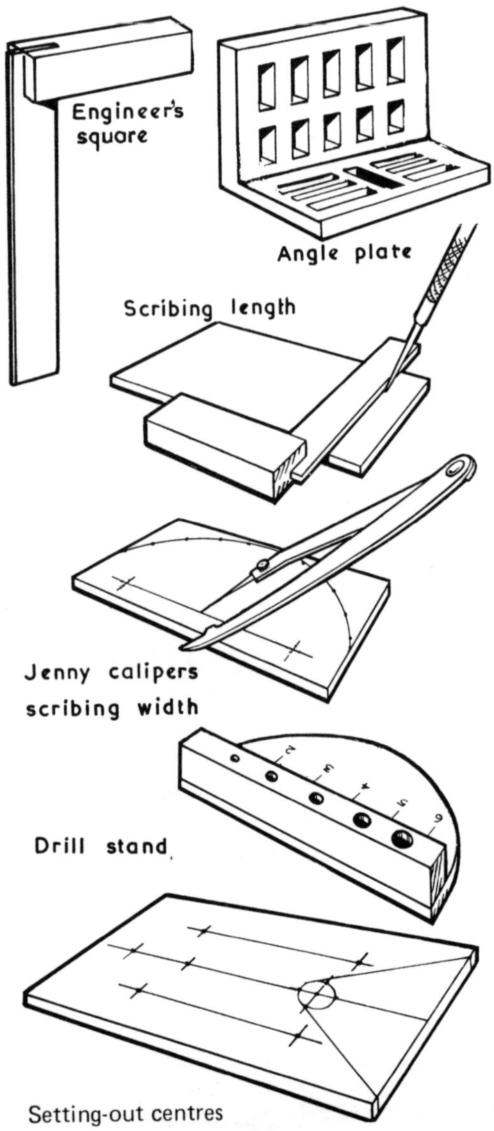

shown overleaf, sawn if necessary, and then filed to the line. If it has to be prepared to width the metal is measured, scribed and filed to width after it has been filed to length. Filed surfaces may be tested with a rule or square but can be tested more accurately on a surface plate. Marking out blue is spread on the surface plate so that when the filed or machined surface is rubbed on it the high parts can be easily detected. Centres of holes are indicated by scribed lines crossing at right angles and by a centre punch mark at the intersection. Large circles are scribed with spring dividers and centre dots are added at the intersections of the circumference with the right-angled centre lines.

The **surface gauge** when used on the **surface plate** provides an accurate method of marking out which should be practised in the school workshop, especially on large work. Uprightness and squareness of ends can be tested with a square on a surface plate as shown opposite, testing the ends of the router body. Lines parallel with a true edge or surface can be scribed with a surface gauge while the edge or surface is resting on the surface plate. A horizontal centre line for the rivet holes for joining the clamp to the body of the router is scribed in this way. Similarly thin metal can be scribed if it is held vertically against the side of an angle plate while both are resting on a surface plate.

Vee blocks and **clamps** are used on a surface plate to mark the ends of round stock and the sides as for keyways. They are shown opposite finding the centre of a bar. The scriber of the surface gauge is set as near as can be judged to the desired centre and a horizontal line is scribed. Then the bar is turned through 90° and another line is scribed; this is repeated twice to produce a small quadrilateral within which is the centre. If necessary, diagonals can be scribed across the square and their intersection will mark the centre. Jenny calipers can also be used to mark the centre of a rod (*see* p. 61).

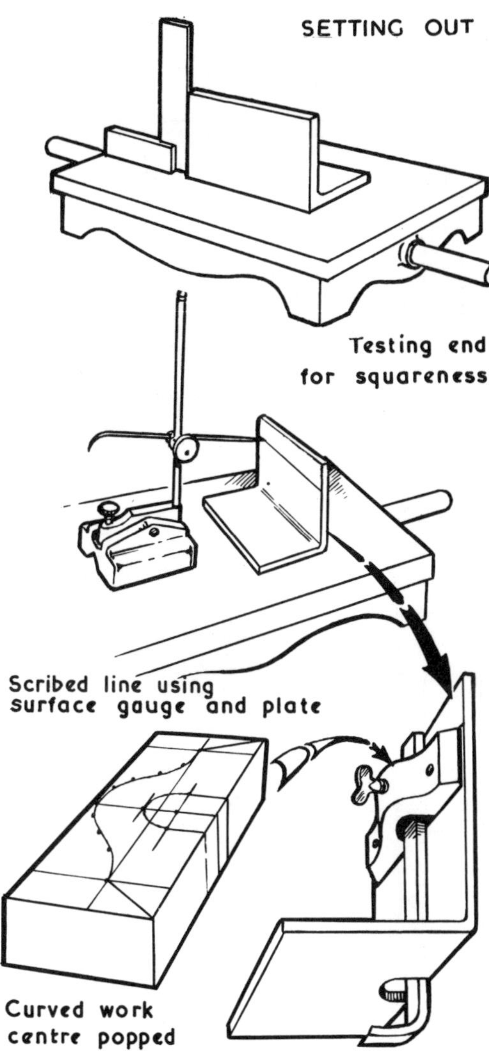

Setting out on Castings. An excellent test for school metal-workers is the machining of castings and this involves special problems in setting out. The surfaces are rough so they must be whitened with chalk or whiting and it is most important that setting out and machining should begin on the correct surface, the one from which all subsequent setting out and machining are organised. This is called the datum face. The casting illustrated is the body of a machine vice; the datum face side is the underside and this must be machined accurately before the ends or sides can be trued and before the centre of the hole for the screw can be set out. Castings often have odd and awkward shapes, and such equipment as buttons, wedges, small jacks, parallel strips, and other pieces of metal all accurately machined, may be necessary to set up the work accurately on the surface plate so that it can be scribed with precision. Such jobs may be bolted to an angle plate which rests on a surface plate for setting out previous to machining on a lathe, in which case it may be bolted to a face plate, or on a shaper or milling machine.

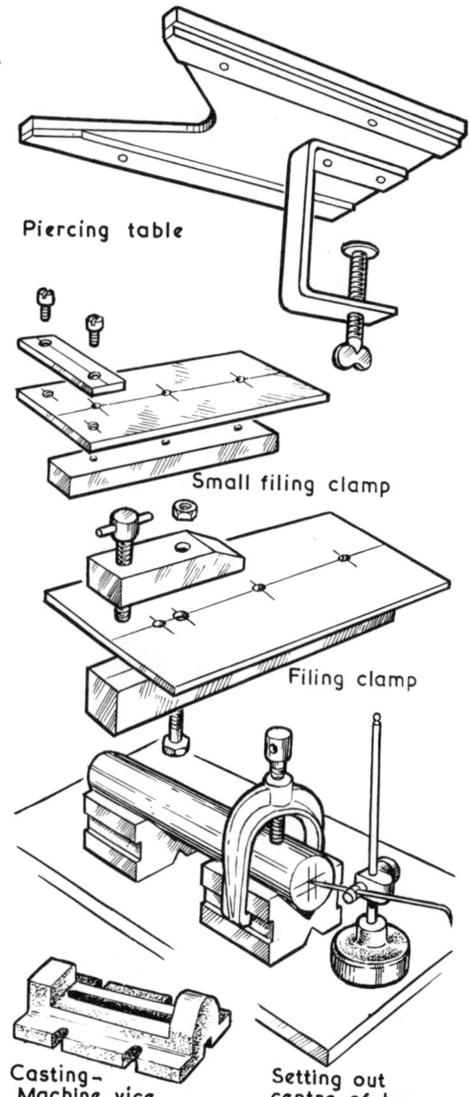

8

Fitting—Drills and Drilling, Reaming

Drills. Most school workshops have drilling machines and the most popular drill is the twist drill. It has two helical grooves which extend along its working length. Theoretically, the slope of the helix should vary with each type of material being drilled. Quick sloping helix drills are made for drilling copper, aluminium and other soft metal, and slow helix drills for brass and bronze. These grooves are important: they form the cutting edges at the bottom of the drill and allow the swarf to move upwards and the coolant to flow downwards. Twist drills are made with parallel and taper shanks. In school, drills up to 13 mm diameter are usually parallel and larger drills have taper shanks. The former are used in a self-centring drill chuck held by jaws, usually three, which are tightened around the drill with a chuck key. The chuck fits on the parallel end of the arbor, the other end of which has a morse taper and fits up into the taper sleeve in the spindle of the drilling machine. Taper shank drills can be obtained up to 100 mm diameter (600 mm long) and there are six, No. 1 to No. 6, morse taper shanks. They fit directly into the spindle sleeve which is made to one of these standard morse taper sizes. When the taper inside the spindle and that of the drill are not of the same size, an adaptor, which has a different internal morse taper from that on the outside, can be used. The drill fits tightly in the sleeve and turns with the spindle of the machine. The flat tang at the end is for ejection only. There is a slot in the machine spindle corresponding to the position of the tang through which a drift is pushed to loosen the drill. The drill must not be allowed to fall on to the drill table or a concrete floor, as this might spoil its end.

DRILLING I

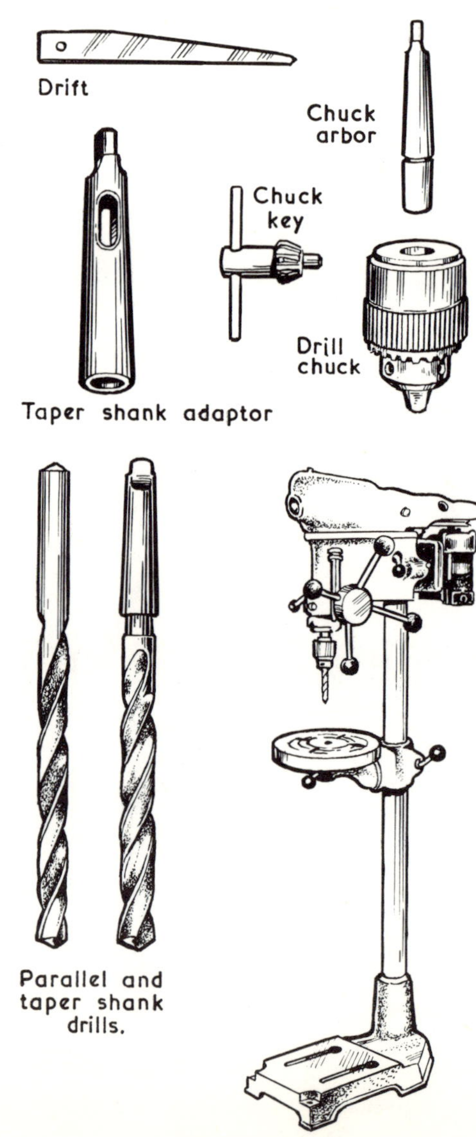

Drill Sizes. There is now only one recommended system of measuring drills—Metric—0.3 mm (straight shank) up to 100 mm (taper shank). In the smallest sizes the drills increase in size by 0.025 mm.

Speeds and Feeds. The speed at which a drill revolves and the feed, the rate of entry into the metal, depend on the drill, the material being drilled, the depth of the hole, the quality of finish required and the effectiveness of the cutting fluid. A high-speed steel drill can be used at twice the speed of one made from plain carbon steel on the same material, and brass can be drilled at five times the speed of cast steel. The peripheral speed for drilling manganese steel is very slow, 3–4 m per minute; for cast steel it should be 15 m, mild steel 30 m per minute and brass up to 75 m per minute. The peripheral speed is the speed of the circumference of the drill; thus, cutting at 10 m per minute, a 10 mm drill is turning at nearly a thousand revolutions per minute and a 1 mm drill ten thousand per minute. A 20 mm drill cutting mild steel should revolve at approximately 500 revolutions per minute and the feed should be 120 mm per minute, whereas the feed for a 10 mm drill should be approximately 200 mm per minute. Information on speeds and feed can be obtained from tables and charts supplied free by the drill manufacturers.

Lubricant and Coolant. Although some metals, e.g. copper, brass and cast iron, can be drilled dry, the drill should not be allowed to get too hot. Most metals need a coolant whilst being drilled. A good cutting fluid, e.g. soluble oil (*see* p. 67), will cool both the work and the drill, and lubricate the surface of the chips and the outer edges of the drill.

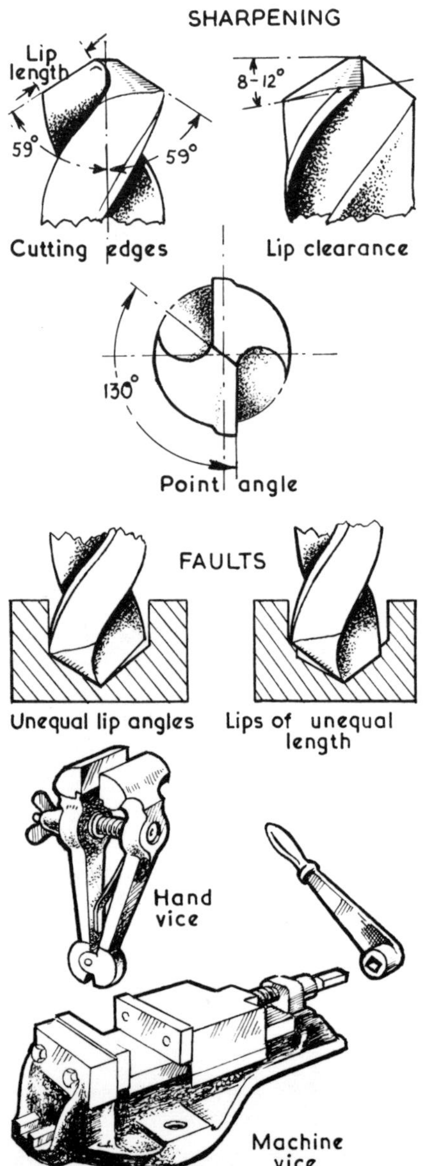

Grinding Drills. Drill points are usually ground at an inclusive angle of 118°, and 8° to 12° clearance is desirable. Drills should be resharpened by machine, but it can be done by hand and, when this is necessary, a new drill should be copied. The lips must be equal in length and have the correct clearance behind the cutting edge. Otherwise the drilled hole will be oversize and the cut surface rough. Sometimes the point of a drill must be ground thinner because the web thickness increases towards the upper end of the flutes to increase strength and rigidity, but this should be done on a specially shaped grinding wheel of the correct grit and grade. Grinding needs a continuous supply of coolant, or none at all. Dipping the drill into a can of coolant at odd times during grinding may cause local cracking at the point.

Drilling. When drilling, the drill needs a start which is provided by a small indentation at the centre of the hole made with a centre punch. This is essential and it also serves to locate the drill. For a large hole, say more than 10 mm, a pilot or lead hole saves time and reduces wear on the larger drill. The diameter of the pilot hole should be a little larger than the drill point so that when drilling the larger hole all the pressure is exerted on the actual cutting edges of the drill, and, as a drill will always follow a hole that is already drilled, the cutting efficiency of the drill is increased. Work must be firmly supported and rigidly held while drilling: it must never be held in the hand. The action of the drill may jerk the work out of the hand, and hands can be badly cut by revolving metal. Whenever possible a machine vice should be used. It holds the work securely and can be placed or bolted accurately on to the machine table. Thin metal is held in a hand vice with the metal supported on a block of hard wood so that the drill can pass through the metal cleanly without damaging the drill or the drill table.

Countersinking and Counterboring. Countersinks are used to shape the top of a drilled hole to take the taper head of a rivet or screw so that they may be set flush with the surface of the metal. There are several forms of countersinks with a tool angle of 60° or 90°. The smaller countersink illustrated has a parallel shank which fits into the chuck of a machine or hand drill, and the taper shank countersink fits directly into the taper sleeve of a drilling machine or lathe spindle and is used for heavier work. When the end of a drilled hole is drilled to a larger diameter, so that a square shoulder is formed inside, the operation is called counterboring and can be drilled with a counterbore or step drill; in school a larger drill is often used. Work is often drilled in the lathe and the centre drill, a combined drill and countersink, is used in the lathe for centring work (*see* p. 61).

Reaming after drilling provides extremely accurate holes and can be done by hand or machine. Machine reamers have taper shanks and should be used at half the drilling speed, but the feed can be twice as great. Reamers have left-hand helical or spiral flutes as illustrated, but hand reamers often have straight flutes.

They all taper slightly for a short portion of their length so that they can enter the drilled hole. Reamers are better worked upright, with oil, but can be used in a lathe and should always be turned in a clockwise direction whether entering or leaving a hole. The hole should be drilled accurately with a well ground tool 0.4 mm to 0.5 mm under size for holes up to 14 mm diameter, 0.75 for 0.75 mm holes over 14 and under 32 mm and 1 mm smaller for holes above 32 mm in diameter for machine reaming but the allowances should be approximately half that for hand reaming when the reamer is turned with a tap wrench. Reamers are made 1.5 mm to 50 mm in diameter and they increase by 0.5 mm up to 25 mm dia. and by 1 mm from 25 to 50 mm diameter. They must be handled carefully because they are expensive and the cutting edges of the long flutes chip readily if they are allowed to roll against each other. Reamers should be wrapped in paper and be kept in boxes.

DRILLING 3

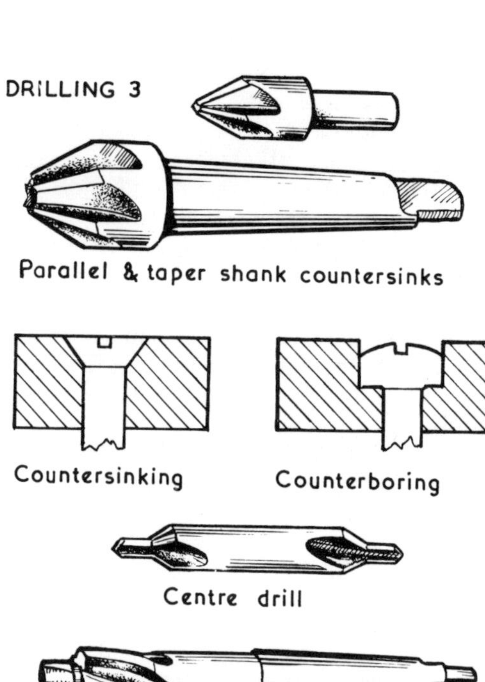

Parallel & taper shank countersinks

Countersinking

Counterboring

Centre drill

Counterbore drill

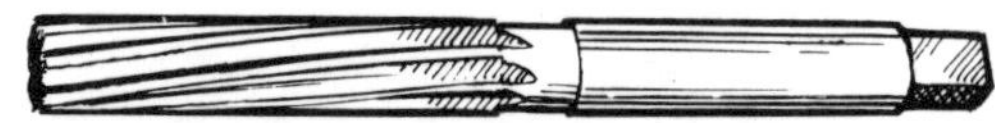

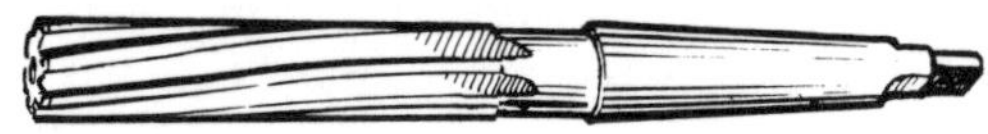

Hand & machine reamers

Assignments

Drilling is an essential operation and is involved in all the jobs suggested. The escutcheon, number plate and teapot stand are all decorative and could be made of attractive non-ferrous metal and pierced (*see* p. 29). In school, however, it is much easier, when shaping inside edges, to drill out as much as possible, cut out the rest with a chisel or abrafile and file to finish. In any case, holes must be drilled for fixing and for inserting the saw blade or abrafile. The bracket is made from 2 mm mild steel with the sides bent at right angles and a triangle drilled out, chiselled and filed. The dovetail gauge might be of strip aluminium, 35 × 2 mm, and the two accepted dovetail angles are 1 in 6 and 1 in 8. Stainless steel 3 mm thick is suitable for the lamp bracket and mild steel, 120 × 35 × 5 mm for the spanner. Two holes are drilled, filed to shape and the jaws must be case hardened (*see* p. 111). Bright mild steel 20 × 3 mm is used for the bevel and the slots are cut by drilling, chiselling and filing. The body is formed by riveting two outside strips on to a smaller inside piece all the same width and thickness. A screw and wing nut can be purchased but the knurled nut illustrated should be turned. The screwdriver is made from 30 × 9 mm cast steel with holes drilled and filed hexagonal and the end hardened and tempered to a blue colour. The frames for the vee block and gee cramp are both shaped the same way and are of mild steel 12 mm thick and perhaps 80 × 50 mm, but the vee block frame must be made to fit the vee blocks made previously. The screw, it might be turned and filed, has a knurled head for hand tightening and an Allen socket so that it can be made more secure (*see* p. 47).

6 mm Drill
12 mm Drill
9 mm

G-cramp

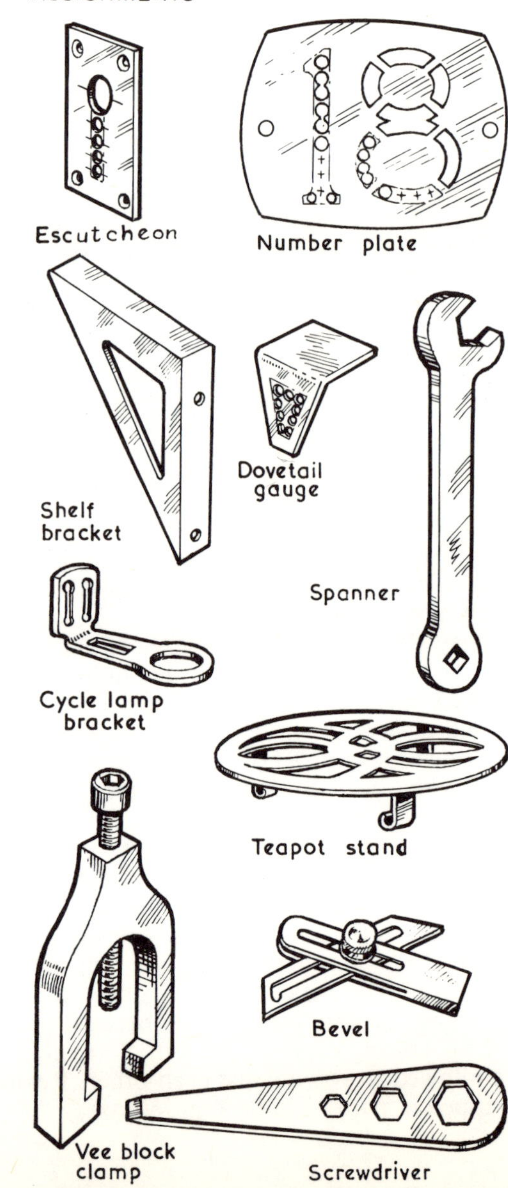

9

Fitting—Rivets and Riveting

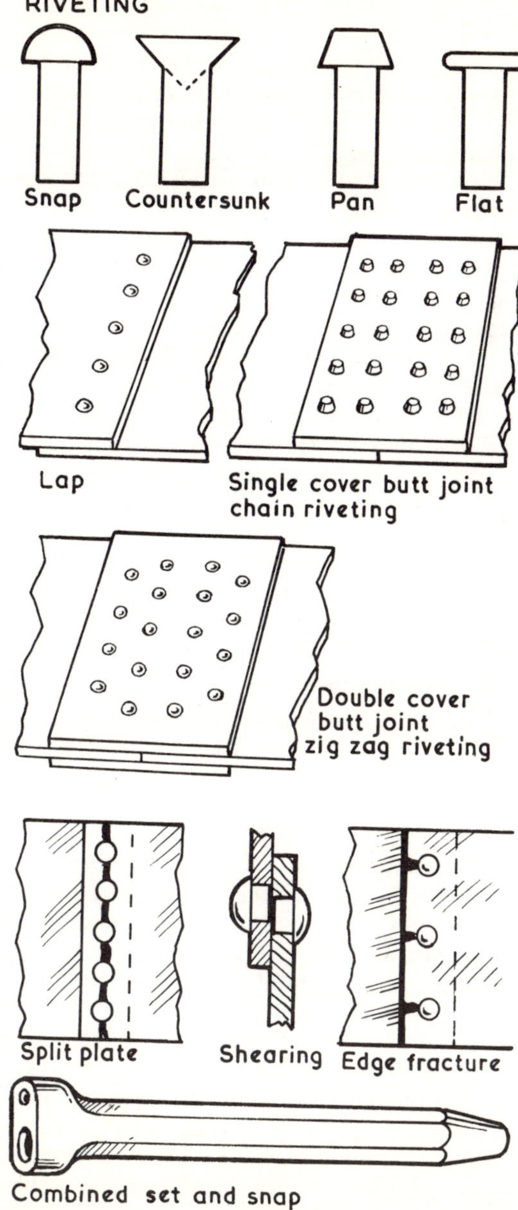

Rivets have been used to join metals for thousands of years: they are used in boiler making, in joining girders for buildings and bridges, and in shipbuilding. Riveting is a permanent method of fastening which has been largely superseded by welding, but it is practised considerably in school workshops. Rivets are short malleable metal rods with a shaped head on one end and are generally made of mild steel, copper, brass or aluminium. The hemispherical shaped head, snap or cup head, is the popular shape, but there are the countersunk rivets for flat riveted surfaces, pan heads which are usually of non-ferrous metal and used for sheet metalwork, and the flat head rivets which are tinned rivets suitable for tinplate work. The dimensions of rivet heads are standard, dependent on the diameter of the rivet. The length of a countersunk rivet is its overall length but other rivets are measured from the underside of the head.

Riveted Joints. There are three shapes of countersunk heads having contained angles of 60°, 90° and 120° and, when riveting, the countersunk hollow should be of the same shape and size as the rivet head. This may be difficult and flush riveting may be more successful using snap head rivets; the snap head can be hammered into the countersinking and the size and shape of the recess are not so important. Riveted joints can overlap or be butt jointed with cover plates, straps, on one or both sides and the rivets can be in straight lines along and across, as in chain riveting, or staggered, zig-zag. The diameter of the rivet should be one and a half times the thickness of the plates to be joined, and correct spacing is very important. There must be at least twice the rivet diameter between rivets and one and a half diameters between the rivets and the edge of the plate. Common weaknesses in riveting are (1) splitting along the line of rivets due to their being placed too close together, (2) shearing due to holes being slightly out of line, (3) tearing beyond the holes when they are drilled too near the edge.

Riveting. Metrication has produced a wide range of standard metric sizes for rivets but the small rivets used in schools are likely to be 3, 4, 5 and 6 mm in diameter. A combined rivet set and snap is generally used in school riveting and its size must match that of the rivet. The set is a cylindrical hole of the same diameter as the stem of the rivet—and the snap is a hollow of the same size and shape as the rivet head. The holes are drilled, any burr is removed, the rivet is placed through the holes, and the job is arranged so that the rivet head rests on a firm bed with a piece of soft metal to protect it. The anvil serves excellently for the firm bed. The rivet set is placed over the end of the rivet and hammered to force the plates closely together, and then the rivet end is hammered over and trued to shape with a rivet snap. It is helpful to work in pairs, one holding the work with the rivet head resting in one snap which is held upside down in the vice while the other does the riveting. In this method the snap underneath serves as a "dolly". To form a snap head the amount of rivet protruding above the metal should be one to one and a half times the rivet diameter and for flush riveting it should be three-quarters the diameter of the rivet. If the rivet is too long, it will bend when hammered, thus spoiling the joint and preventing the end being correctly shaped. Rivets should be annealed and, in industry, they are used hot where the holes are often punched and the riveting carried out by hand machines.

Assignments with Rivets

The hook, the bracket and the utensil rack should be studied as design briefs—what are they to carry? How large? What material? Where and how are they going to be fixed? Most of the articles use snap head rivets, hammered flat into countersunk hollows and filed flush on the back, but some, the utensil rack, the rake, the stand and the hammer do not have separate rivets. These are **end riveted or spigot riveted,** i.e. the pieces to be riveted have rivets turned on the end of the metal or filed to shape with a hand file. Beginners can fix the metal in the vice with the rivet length above the jaws, place a washer over the metal end so that the vice jaws are not damaged and file sideways to form a rivet and shoulder. Alternatively these spigots rivets can provide early turning exercises but they must be annealed before riveting. The plant stand is made of strip metal, two rings being bent, brazed and riveted to the three legs. The plant pot is made of tinplate, conical and painted in a bright colour, different from the stand. The hook and utensil rack are of aluminium alloy and as aluminium and its alloys cannot be soldered in the usual

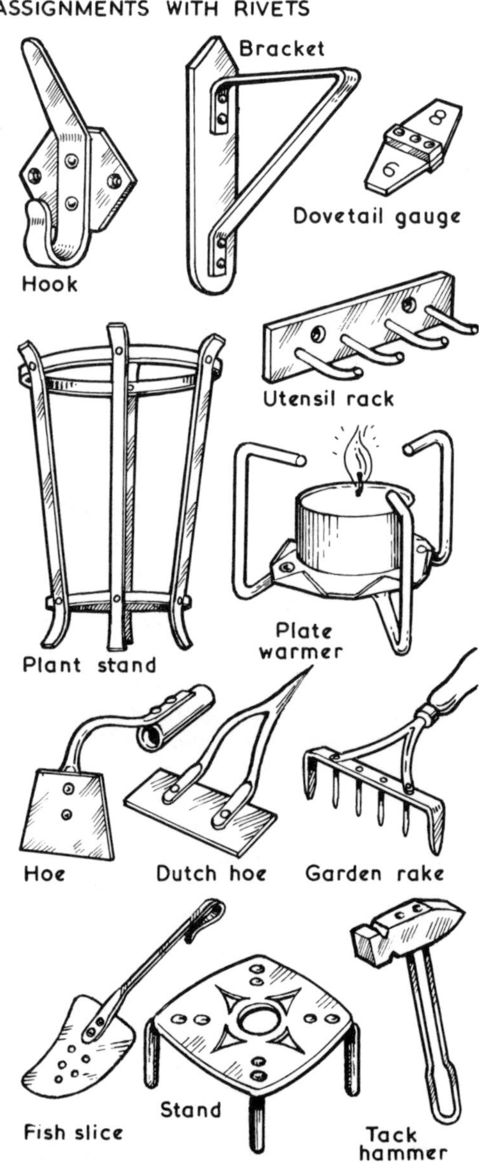

way it is easier to rivet them in schools. The plate warmer is an interesting exercise and simple to make. The legs must be of the same shape and size, so a bending jig is essential. The ends of the legs are hammered flat and riveted to the plate which carries a night-light.

Both hoes have forged stems riveted to the blade but in one case the stem is riveted to a short piece of tube while the other stem has one end split for riveting and the other end forged to a tang. Alternatively a piece of 10 mm round mild steel could be bent double and welded and forged to form the tang. The rake has a similar tang. The fish slice could be of stainless steel using thin cold rolled 0·5 mm steel for the blade. The kettle stand has mild steel legs bent flat at one end and riveted with snap head rivets to a brass, copper or gilding metal top decorated by drilling or piercing. Alternatively, the legs might be twisted or turned to shape and spigot riveted to a steel top. The handle of the tack handle is of 6 mm round mild steel bent to shape around a former, riveted over and brazed into holes drilled in the hammer head. The treacle tin billy-can is for camping and the sheet iron fitting must be riveted to the side of the tin, for a soft soldered joint would melt. The handle is of 4 mm round mild steel. The smallest lamp has three 6 mm mild steel legs spigot riveted to the metal plate to which the fitting for the light holder is silver soldered. The tall reading lamp has 10 mm × 5 mm legs joined by curved 10 mm × 3 mm rails. This idea might be adapted for a tiered cake or fruit stand or, made larger and with more rails, for a saucepan stand or a decorated stand for fruits or savouries at a Christmas party. The third lamp has 6 mm × 3 mm strips riveted to rings of the same metal and into a 3 mm thick brass plate which is supported on three ball-headed screws, screwed and soft-soldered to the brass base.

The hat and coat racks consist mainly of 6 mm round mild steel with coloured wooden knobs. The smaller rack has the rod flattened and riveted to the back plate, while the zig-zag rack has triangular pieces brazed on to the corners for fixing to the walls, and to which the three extra pegs are spigot riveted. The jardiniere is a riveted trough of sheet iron in a riveted iron frame. A similar trough, larger and semicircular in section could be a log basket. The milk bottle holder is to hang on the door or stand on the step. It is made from 10 mm × 3 mm mild steel with a sheet iron bottom.

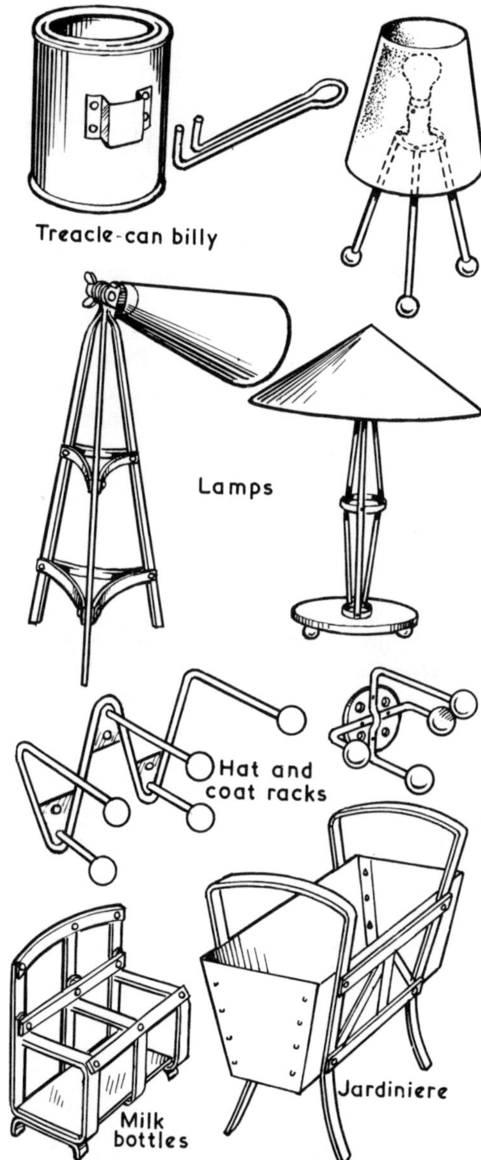

10

Fitting—Screws and Screwcutting by hand

Screw Threads. Screwing is the method most widely used for joining together metal parts which may have to be taken apart. The screw represents an inclined plane around a cylinder, and screwing depends on the gradual movement of two inclined planes, one upon the other, the nut upon the bolt. As well as for fixing and holding parts together, screws are used to give movement as does the screw of a vice, a cramp or the lead screw of a lathe. There are several forms of screw threads but the vee and square threads are by far the most common, the vee thread being best for strength and the square thread for movement. Metrication has brought about great changes in our screwthreads. Apart from the changes in dimensions Whitworth, the 55° standard vee thread is, after years of continual use (*see* p. 162) being phased out as is the more recent ISO (International Organisation for Standardisation) Unified Screw Thread and they are being replaced for general purposes by the ISO Metric Screw Thread Coarse Series. It is very similar to the Unified Thread as it has the same profile, 60°, but is not interchangeable owing to the difference between English Imperial and Metric sizes. This thread lies half way between British Standard Whitworth (BSW) and British Standard Fine (BSF) and is the one referred to in metric drawings, e.g. M12 refers to an ISO metric thread, course series, of 12 mm diameter unless any other indication is stated. This screw will have a pitch of 1.75 mm. More recently a "Fine Series" has been introduced and a 12 mm screw in that series will have a pitch of 1.25 mm and be indicated as M12 Fine. The clearance drills are 1 mm larger for the smallest screws, up to 2.5 mm diameter, and 2 mm above the thread size for all others. The recommended tapping drill sizes stated above give a 75% depth of thread, which is acceptable for all general purposes.

Normally the ISO Course Series will be satisfactory for all school requirements. One advantage of this series in school is that the tapping size drill can be obtained from subtracting the pitch from major diameter. Thus for a 16 mm diameter screw the pitch is 2 mm and the tapping size is 14 mm.

ISO Metric Thread—Course Series

Diameter	2	2·5	3	4	5	6	8	10	12	16	20	24
Pitch	0·4	0·45	0·5	0·7	0·8	1·0	1·25	1·5	1·75	2·0	2·5	3·0
Effective Diameter	1·74	2·208	2·675	3·545	4·480	5·530	7·188	9·026	10·863	14·701	18·376	22·051
Tapping Drill	1·6	2·05	2·5	3·3	4·2	5·0	6·8	8·5	10·2	14·0	17·5	21·0

ISO Metric Thread—Fine Series

Diameter	8	10	12	14	16	18	20	22	24
Pitch	1·0	1·25	1·25	1·5	1·5	1·5	1·5	1·5	2·0
Effective Diameter	7·350	9·118	11·188	13·026	15·026	17·026	19·026	21·026	22·701
Tapping Drill	7·0	8·8	10·8	12·5	14·5	16·5	18·5	20·5	22·0

Although BSW and BSF will soon become obsolete the Whitworth thread form is, for the time being, maintained for pipe threads. It is obvious that a pipe can be screwed only by a fine thread which will not cut through the walls of the tube, so a special thread is essential. There are coarse, fine and pipe threads in the American National Screw forms.

BA Threads (British Association) for small screws are still being used for electrical fittings. They are described by numbers, No. 0 (6 mm) to No. 25 (0.25 mm) although BA screws smaller than No. 12 (0.79 mm) are seldom used. Nos. 2, 4, and 6 are in common use.

Square Threads are used when quicker movement is required than is possible with single vee threads especially on lathes, cramps and vices.

Acme Threads give easy movement and are easier to cut than square threads. They are used on the lead screws of some lathes. When such screws are metric they may be described as trapezoidal.

Buttress Threads are used when screws have to resist a force always acting in the same direction as in a vice and they allow very easy movement in the other direction as in quick release vices.

The **Crest** of a thread is the prominent part of the thread whether it be internal or external.

The **Root** of a thread is the bottom part of the groove.

The **Core** is the minimum diameter of the screw.

SCREW THREADS

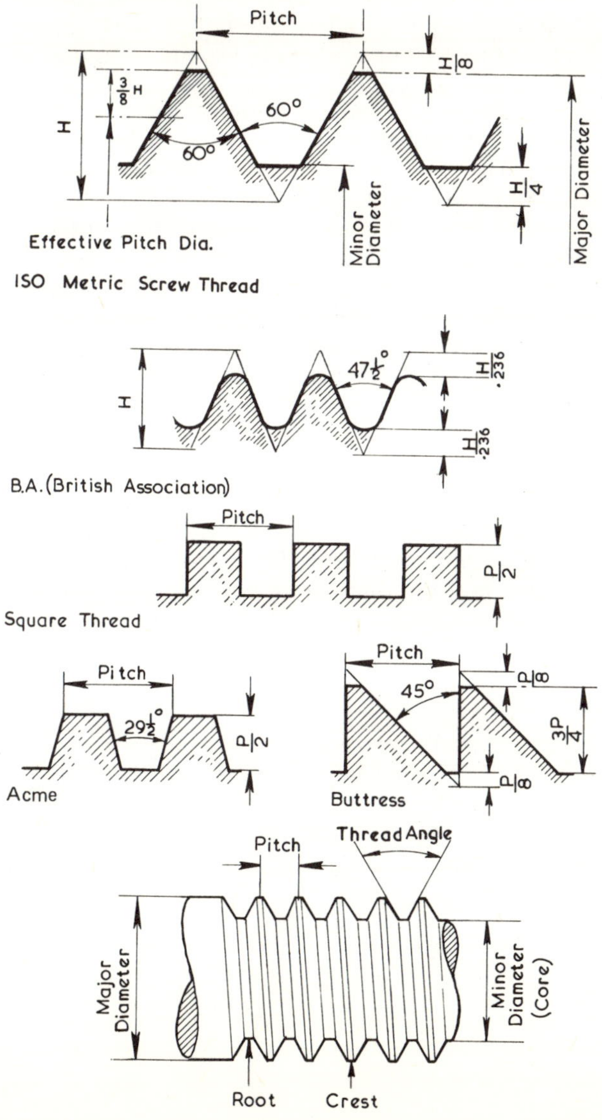

ISO Metric Screw Thread

B.A.(British Association)

Square Thread

Acme

Buttress

The **Pitch** of a screw thread is the distance, measured parallel to its axis between a point on one thread form to the corresponding point on the next thread form. For convenience this is usually indicated as the distance between the crests. Most screws have a single thread running continuously around a central cylindrical core forming a single helical curve. This is a single-start thread. Sometimes a quicker movement than that given by a single-start thread is required. Such screws have two, three or more threads running around the core so that the slope is twice, three times or several times as great and the nut will move twice, or more times as far in one turn. The pitch, the distance between the crests, is not altered if the thread is double, treble or multiple start.

The **Lead** of a screw thread is the distance it advances axially, which is the distance the nut moves, in one revolution. On a single-start thread the lead and the pitch are identical; on a double-start screw thread the lead is twice the pitch, on a treble-start thrice the pitch and so on.

Nuts and Bolts provide the best known use of screw threads, especially on machines and engines, on cycle parts and on Meccano parts, which have to be taken to pieces and reassembled frequently. They are made from many different materials, depending on how and where they are being used. Black mild steel nuts and bolts are used for general work, bright mild steel for accurate work and high-tensile steel where stress, strain and weight (needing thinner bolts) are the main factors. Stainless steel should be used where hygiene is important, e.g. food machinery and medical instruments, and titanium and aluminium when lightness counts. Silicon bronze, monel metal and aluminium bronze nuts and bolts are made to resist corrosion. Today there are extensive methods and applications for plating and coating, tin, zinc, cadmium palladium, rhodium, even silver and gold, all being used on nuts and bolts. Nuts and bolt heads are usually hexagonal or square with a chamfer to remove the top sharp edges, but carriage bolt heads are circular with a domed top. Hexagonal nuts take up less room than square nuts and a spanner is easier to use on a hexagonal shape. Bolts are screwed only for that part which is likely to receive the nut. Washers, made to standard sizes, are usually placed between the work and the nuts. Lock nuts which are thinner than standard nuts are used to prevent the main nut loosening, e.g. by vibration. Both nuts are screwed down tightly with the main nut on the outside. Then the lock nut is turned back with a thin spanner against the main nut.

Screws. When it is not possible for the bolt to project on both sides a screw, or a set bolt, is used to hold the two parts together. The screw passes through the first part and screws into a tapped hole in the other, usually the main part. The threaded hole must be long enough to allow for a small gap beyond the end of the screw. Screws are described by the shape of their heads. The normal length of a countersunk screw is its overall dimension, but most other screws are measured from the underside of the head.

Plate 5. **Perspex Chair**

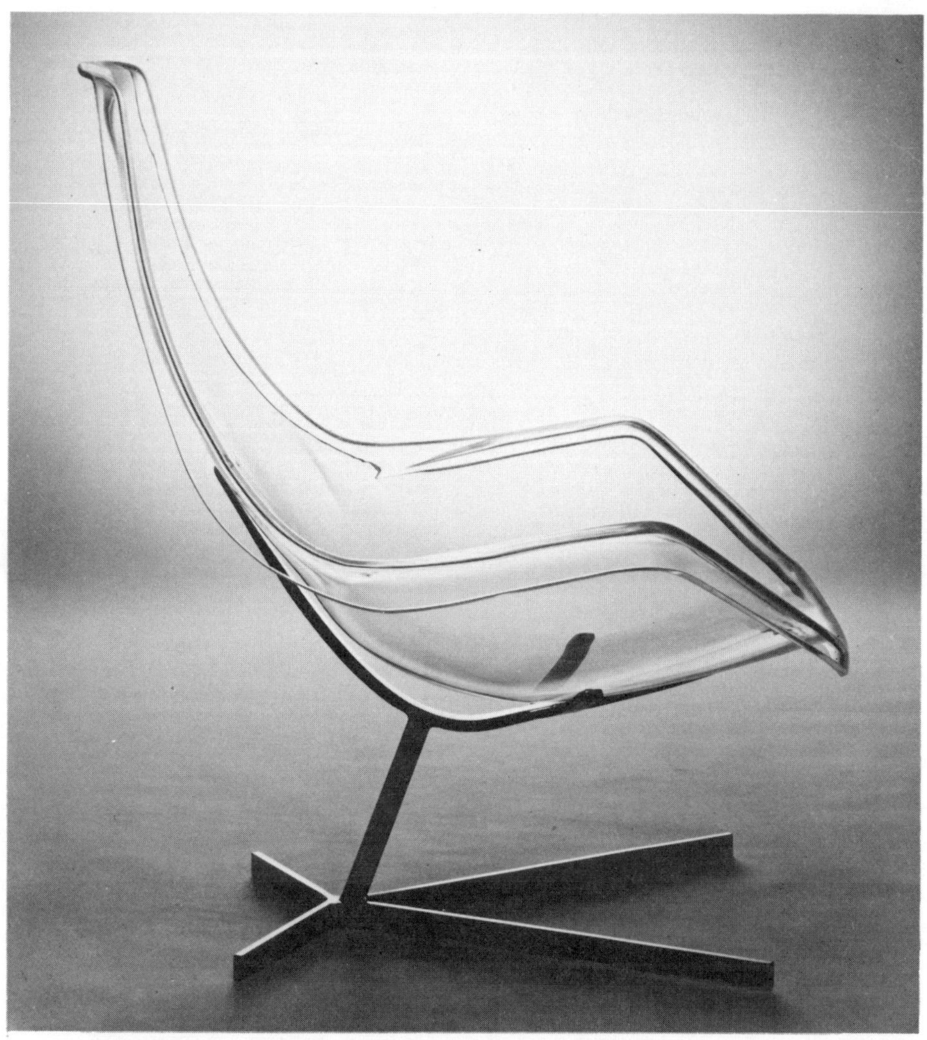

Designed and made by Peter Holte, Farnham, Surrey. Framework of mild steel

Plate 6. **Hanging Chair**

Frame of mild steel rod nylon coated in black or white, seat of nylon or leather lashed to frame by means of PVC tubing through brass eyelets. Suspended by a nylon chain with nylon coated screw hooks. Can be used with a stand, which is not shown, and indoors or outdoors. Designed and made by Rupert Oliver of Croydon

Studs. When machine parts have to be continually separated and a bolt cannot be used or when one part has to be fixed to a soft metal body, such as aluminium, a stud is used. A stud is a short length of a rod screwed at each end with a plain portion between. One end, the fast end, screws into the body of the machine. The second machine part is placed over the stud and a nut is screwed to the other end of the stud. If a screw were used, there would be a tendency for the tapped portion of the hole, usually in the main part of the work, to strip or wear, owing to the constant removal of the screw. It is much easier and cheaper to change the stud which wears at the loose or nut end than to repair a stripped hole in the main part of the assembly.

Set Screws are used to fix parts together, such as a pulley to a shaft or a handle to a spindle, so that they turn together. The most common set screw is a **Grub Screw,** a headless screw with a screwdriver slot but small socketed and square-headed screws, are also used as set screws. **Socket Screws,** have an octagonal recess in the head and are called "Allen" screws. They are turned by hexagonal metal bent at right angles to form a wrench and often called an Allen key. Allen screws are now being extensively used in engineering as set screws and grub screws. Sometimes as set screws they have a countersunk head or a round knurled head which can be tightened by hand before final tightening with an Allen key.

Self-tapping Screws are a very important recent development, especially in sheet metalwork and are being used in rapidly increasing numbers. Two important kinds are those with a coarse tapering thread which can be pushed in with a press or driven in with a hammer, and standard screws with a slot cut part way into the end of the thread down the screw. These cut as a tap does and are screwed in with a screwdriver. Both types are used successfully on steel, brass, aluminium, zinc die castings, plastics and even cast iron.

Taps. Vee threads can be cut by hand or machine as on a

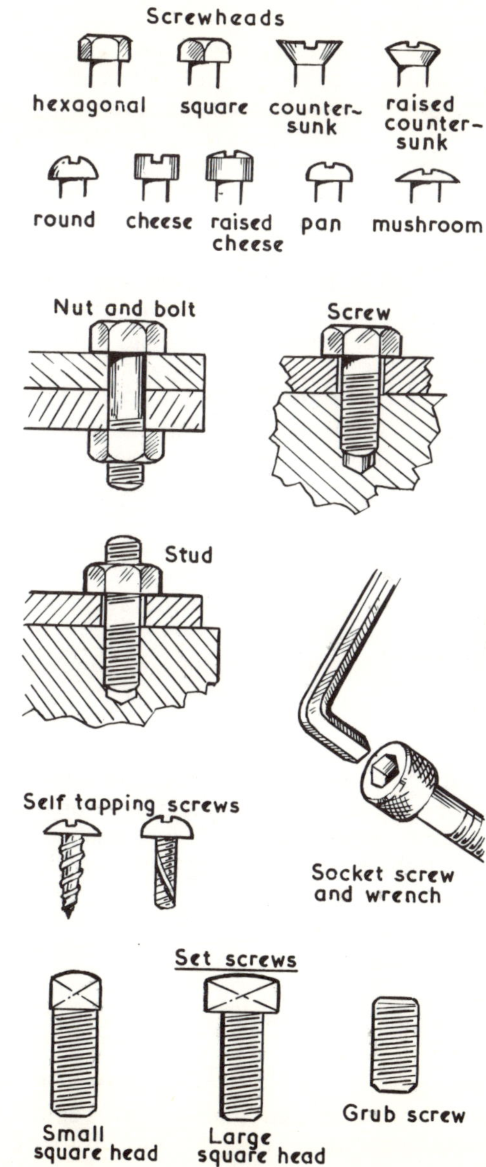

lathe. Industrially, they can also be mass produced by grinding and rolling. Taps and dies are the hand tools. Taps which are used to cut internal threads are screws with three or four flutes cut down the side to provide cutting edges. They can be obtained in sets of three, a taper tap to enter the hole easily and to begin the thread, second tap which has a little less taper and a little more thread, and the plug or bottoming tap which has a full thread throughout. Before tapping, a hole equal to the diameter of the core of the screw must be drilled. This size can be obtained from drill tables. If it is a through hole the taper tap will go right through and make a full thread but if extreme accuracy is required it should be followed by a plug tap. When a hole does not go right through it is called a blind hole and it is far more difficult to tap, especially if it is a shallow hole. It must be drilled a little deeper than the depth of the required thread. Often the taper tap will not cut at all and sometimes only the plug tap can be used. Taps must be applied carefully. They must be kept upright and turned forwards and backward by a tap wrench which fits over the square section at the top, half a turn forwards and a quarter back, to break off the chippings and prevent them jamming and breaking the tap. Taps are made of cast or high-speed steel. They are very hard and break easily. When a tap breaks in use, especially if it is in a blind hole, it is difficult to extricate. If it cannot be held and turned with pliers, it can be annealed and drilled out, or removed with a tap extractor. This has flutes like a tap, with three or four fingers, according to the number of flutes, which can be pushed down into the flutes and tightened by screwing down a collar so that the tap can be screwed out.

Tap Wrenches are usually adjustable. Two types for small taps are shown and one for large taps. A fixed tap wrench with three square holes is shown on p. 108. *See also* p. 50.

Dies are the hand tools used to cut external threads. They are of two kinds, circular one-piece split dies and two-piece rectangular dies. They fit into holders of different types

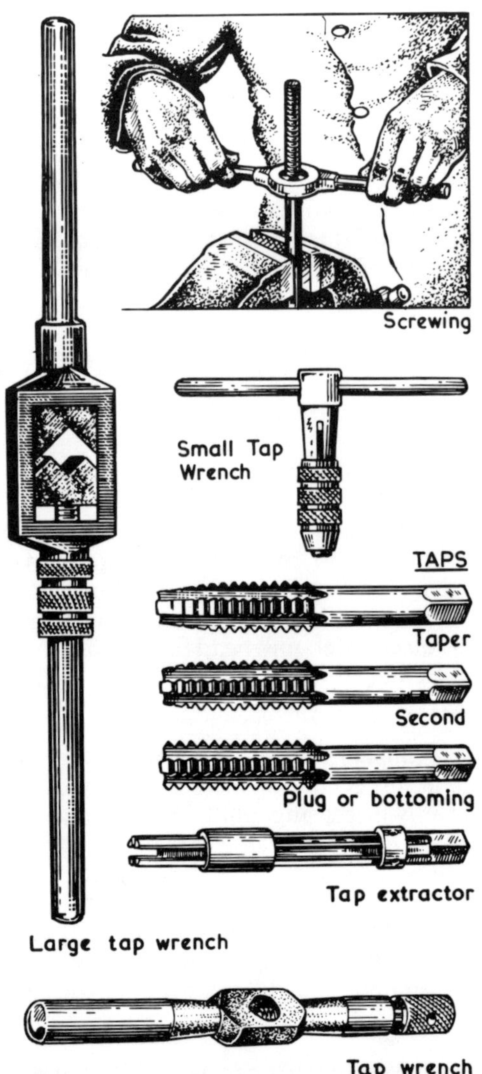

called stocks, and both are adjustable. Two-piece dies are used for heavy work but the circular split die fitted into a die stock of the correct size is used in school. The die must be fitted in the correct way. On one side the thread is cut away slightly, bell-mouthed, and this must be the underside. Otherwise it will be extremely difficult to start the thread. The size and description of the thread are usually marked on the upper side of the die and this side must fit against the rebate in the die holder. If the die stock is used upside down, the die will be forced out. The dies are slightly adjustable but the taps are of a fixed size: hence the hole or nut should be threaded first. There are three screws in the side of the die holder. The die should be so arranged that the position of the centre screw, usually the longest screw, fits into the split in the die so that when this screw is tightened, it screws into the split and opens the die. The two outside screws, two small grub screws, screw on to the outside of the split and tend to close the die. The three screws should be adjusted until the die will cut a thread which fits the previously threaded nut. It is very important that the die should be held and used horizontally so that the screw will fit at right angles to the surface containing the internal thread. Most screw-threads are right handed i.e. they are tightened by turning to the right, clockwise, and are made by turning the taps and dies clockwise but left handed screws are made and used for special circumstances, e.g. when two screws, one right and one left handed move in opposite directions as in a wire strainer. Thin oil should be used as a lubricant when screwing and tapping, especially on mild steel.

Die Nuts are accurate and of fixed size. They are used to true rather than to cut threads.

Die Plate. This was used by gasfitters on brass tubes cutting a shallow thread about 1 mm pitch on tubes 6 mm to 16 mm in diameter.

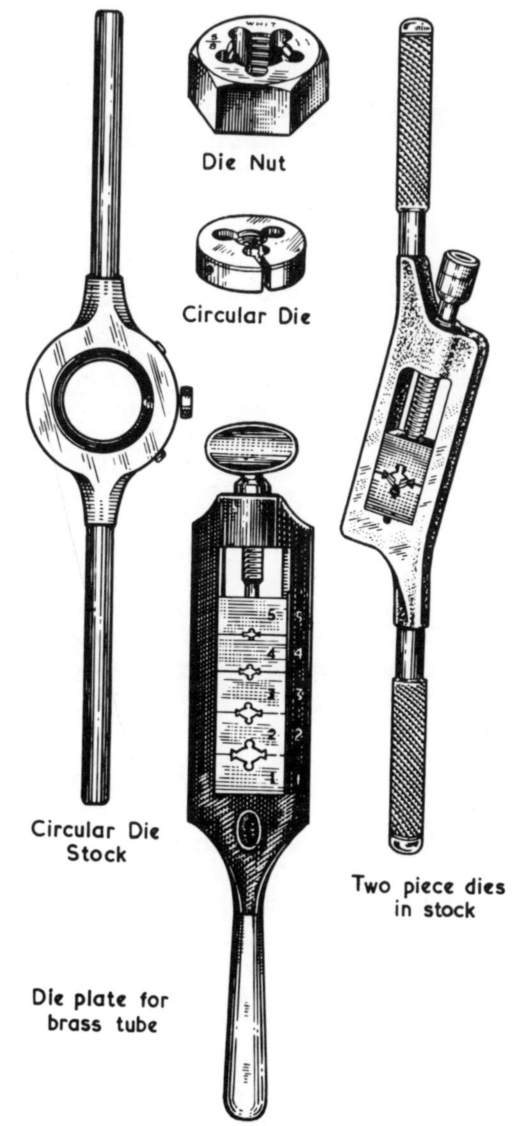

Die Nut

Circular Die

Circular Die Stock

Two piece dies in stock

Die plate for brass tube

Assignments with Screws

Three drawer handles, of brass, gilding metal or nickel silver, are among the exercises. One is solid and chamfered. It could have filed decoration. Another is made from tube with part filed away and a flat piece silver soldered on, and a third is made from rod, with silver soldered collars to fit against the drawer fronts. The first two with single screws, must have location pins to prevent the handle from turning. The other exercises are mainly of mild steel. The toolmaker's clamp has both screws on one side so that in use it can be rested on the bench or on a surface plate. The screws are screwed and brazed into the lower jaw. The large nuts are of brass and can be filed octagonal, or can be turned and knurled. The inside faces on the clamp must be true and they should be case hardened. Two or three pairs should be available in the school workshop. The handles of the tap wrench should be tapered and can be turned circular or filed square from 8 or 10 mm round or square mild steel. The screws, 4, 5 or 6 ISO metric must be shouldered and they work from opposite sides, each passing through a clearance hole and screwing into the far jaw. Tap wrenches to be useful for school work should be between 150 and 250 mm long. The screw clamp is used in the vice to hold screw threads tightly so that the ends of the screws can be cut or filed. That shown is 125 mm long and 25 mm wide and 10 mm thick with a clear 16 mm hole drilled in the end. The other holes are tapped 4, 6, 8, 10 and 12 ISO metric course series; they could be 3, 4, 5, 6 and 8 if that were more convenient for the work in hand. The clamp is cut down the middle to meet the large hole and the knurled headed screw screws into one side against the other side to keep the cut open.

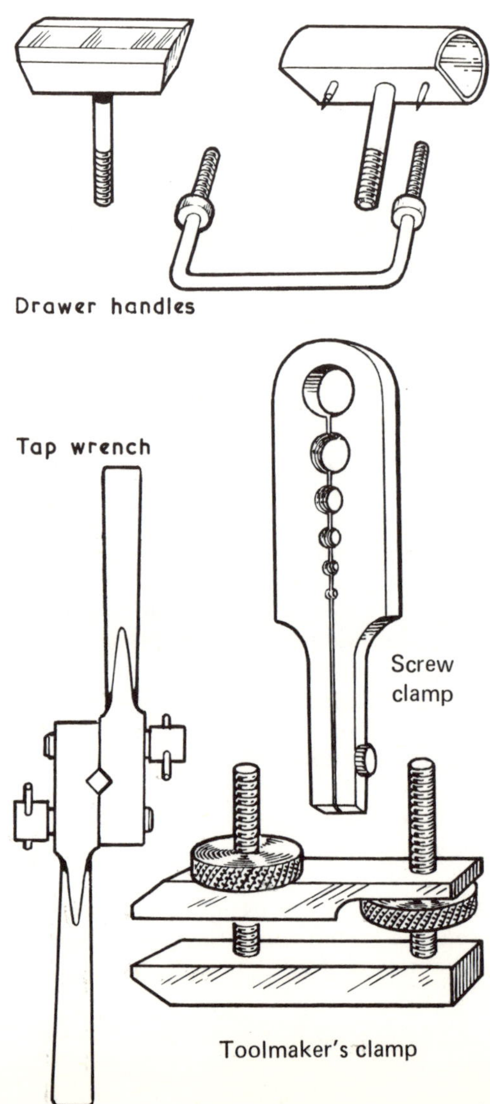

Adjustable Spanners. Ordinary spanners have already been made but five adjustable spanners are suggested here as assignments which depend on screw threads. In each case the size of the material and parts will depend on the size and use of the spanner. Those suggested here are between 100 mm and 200 mm long in the order shown. The body of the smallest (1) is shaped from the solid, 10 mm thick with a 6 mm hole drilled through it and filed rectangular in the upper half so that the jaw will not twist. The screw ϕ 5 mm, is brazed into the top jaw. The screw of the second spanner (2) is ϕ 6 mm and is part of the top jaw which is cut from 6 mm mild steel. The bottom jaw of the same material has a sleeve of 1.5 mm mild steel riveted around it. Spanners (3) and (4) also have sleeves riveted to their lower jaws. In (3) the screw is ϕ 6 mm but flats are filed on each side to make it 5 mm thick, the same thickness as the body, and it is brazed into the top jaw which is 8 mm thick. The end of the ϕ 6 mm screw of spanner (4) is filed circular, ϕ 4 mm, tenoned or spigoted and brazed into the bottom jaw and the guide is riveted and brazed on to the 6 mm thick body which is part of the top jaw. The last spanner is larger and more difficult to make. The lower jaw has a vertical groove cut on each side, and the screw which is part of the top jaw is slotted down the middle to fit over the body and into these grooves. In each of these spanners the body must be cut away for the knurled nut which can be made of brass.

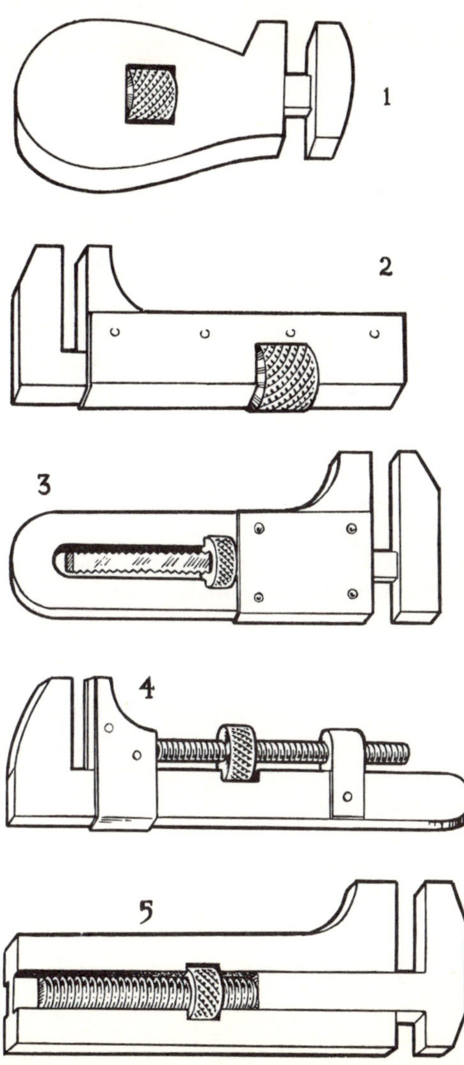

11

Lathework—Parts of a Lathe and Processes

The lathe is one of the oldest tools and has been used for more than three thousand years, firstly for making wood circular and later for the shaping of metal, but today there are many different lathes used for all types of shaping of many materials. Students of metalwork need some experience of machines and school workshops are usually equipped with centre lathes. This is a simple lathe originally evolved to hold metal between centres so that it could be made circular by turning, but it soon had many more uses. Other kinds of lathes, all important developments of the centre lathe, are capstan lathes, turret lathes, copying lathes, automatic lathes and special purpose lathes. In industry some lathes are set and controlled electronically.

The school lathe is designed for the operations mentioned below and must be easy to handle, rigid in construction, efficiently driven and economical in upkeep. Lathe operations in the school workshop are turning (including taper turning), facing, drilling, boring, parting, knurling and sometimes screwcutting.

Parts of a Lathe. Basically the lathe consists of an accurately machined horizontal bed, supported on legs or standards, on a cabinet or on a bench. On the bed, to the left, a headstock is fixed in position; to the right there is a tailstock which can be secured in any workable position and between them is a tool rest which is usually part of a movable carriage. Simple training lathes, consisting only of these essential components and on which the tool is moved by hand wheels, are now made to teach the basic lathe processes.

The Bed must have a true surface so that the tailstock and the carriage fit accurately, move smoothly and are in alignment with each other and with the headstock. It must remain true, and be strong so its cross section must be sufficient to withstand the pressures and the shocks of heavy work. The overall length of the bed is one of the important sizes used when describing a lathe. Other important dimensions are the distance between centres, the maximum length of material which can be worked in the lathe, the height of the centre above the bed, and the "swing", the maximum radius and the maximum diameter of material. Large lathe beds have a "gap", i.e. a short removable section near the headstock which enables metal of greater diameter to be worked. The Boxford lathe, as illustrated, can take material 225 mm in diameter. The bed is 1065 mm long and work 560 mm long can be turned between centres. This lathe can be obtained with a short bed, 915 mm, or a long bed 1.2 mm long, and these hold metal 400 mm and 700 mm between centres. The lathe is shown bolted on to a cabinet and it has a 0.5625 kW electric motor in the bottom of the left hand cupboard. It is a popular lathe in school and is suitable for all the operations described in this book.

The Headstock usually has a hollow spindle. On the Boxford lathe rods up to 20 mm diameter can be passed through the headstock and worked upon without having previously been cut up into short

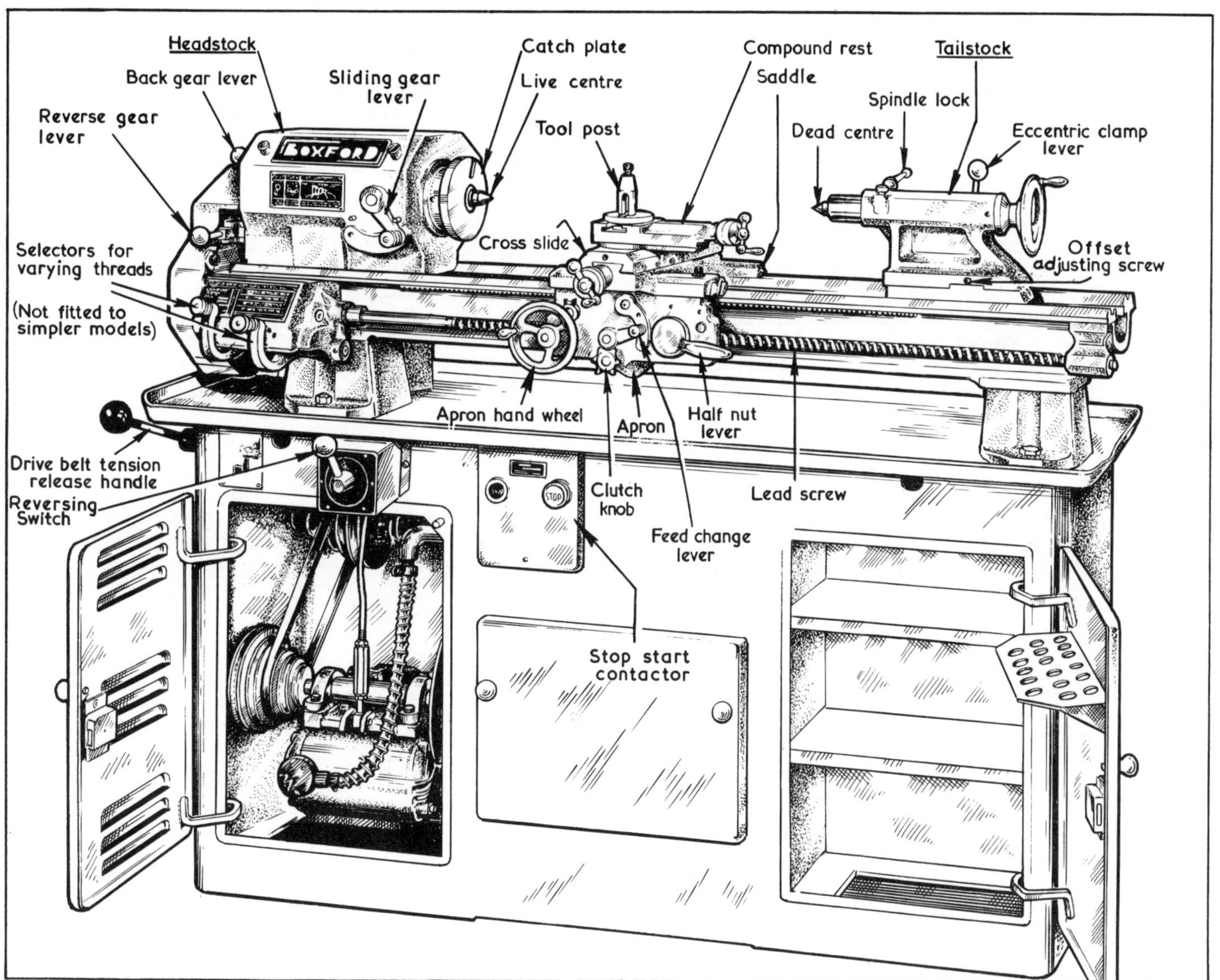
Headstock
Back gear lever
Reverse gear lever
Sliding gear lever
Catch plate
Live centre
Tool post
Compound rest
Saddle
Tailstock
Spindle lock
Dead centre
Eccentric clamp lever
Cross slide
Offset adjusting screw
Selectors for varying threads
(Not fitted to simpler models)
Apron hand wheel
Apron
Half nut lever
Drive belt tension release handle
Reversing Switch
Clutch knob
Lead screw
Feed change lever
Stop start contactor
BOXFORD
STOP

pieces. The nose end of the spindle has an outside diameter of 38.1 mm and is screwed to take the screwed fittings which revolve the work, e.g. catch plate, face plate, and chucks. It has an internal morse taper, No. 3 in this case, in which a centre or drill can be fitted. Gear wheels, called change wheels, are fitted on the left hand end of this headstock to connect the headstock spindle with the lead screw which drives the carriage for automatic or power feed and screwcutting.

The countershaft driven by the 0.375 or 0.56 kW electric motor on the Boxford lathe carries a cone pulley of five different sizes which connected by a belt to a similar cone pulley on an intermediate shaft above gives five possible speeds. There is an extra pulley on the intermediate shaft connected to a pulley on the headstock spindle to drive this at speeds of 210 to 1400 revolutions per minute. As this lathe is fitted with back gear, five additional lower speeds (40 to 270 revs. per min.) are available as indicated on the plate fixed to the headstock and shown opposite. The headstock diagram shows the main pulley as it is normally used—with the back gear out.

Back Gear

To engage back gear the knob of the sliding gear lever must first be moved to the left and this disengages the sliding gear by moving the large toothed wheel to the right, so separating this wheel from the main pulley which is normally connected to the toothed wheel by metal pins—see diagram opposite. Then the back gear lever, which controls the back gear shaft, is pulled forward and the two gear wheels fixed on this shaft engage with the two on the headstock spindle. The drive is transmitted from small gear wheel **W** which revolves with the main pulley **V** to larger gear wheel **X** and wheel **Y** both on the back gear shaft, then back from wheel **Y** to the large gear wheel **Z** which is keyed to the headstock spindle. New lathes are being made so that back gear can be connected by the simple movement of one lever on the headstock.

All-Geared Headstock

Many lathes have the cone pulley inside the headstock, but most of the large modern lathes have an all-geared headstock so that a number of speeds can be obtained by moving gear levers instead of moving the belt on cone pulleys, and with all-geared headstocks back gear is unnecessary. Generally, however, the motor is connected to the headstock spindle by a belt drive.

INSIDE OF HEADSTOCK SHOWING BACK GEAR

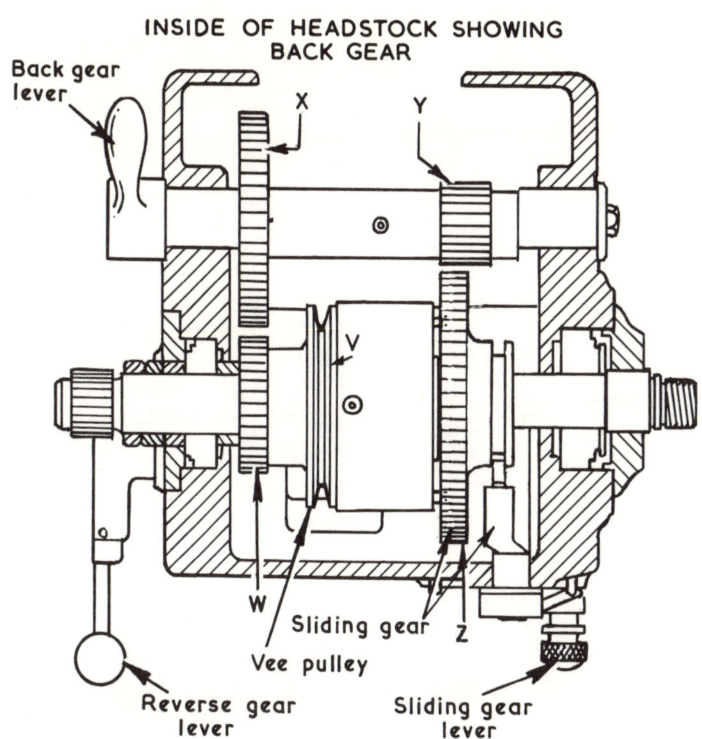

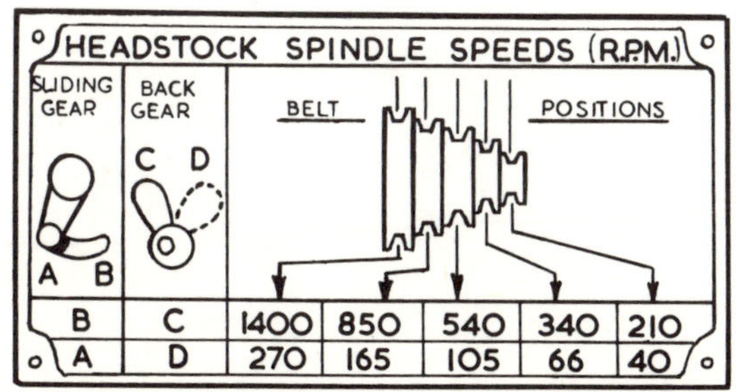

HEADSTOCK SPINDLE SPEEDS (R.P.M.)

SLIDING GEAR (A, B)	BACK GEAR (C, D)	BELT POSITIONS				
B	C	1400	850	540	340	210
A	D	270	165	105	66	40

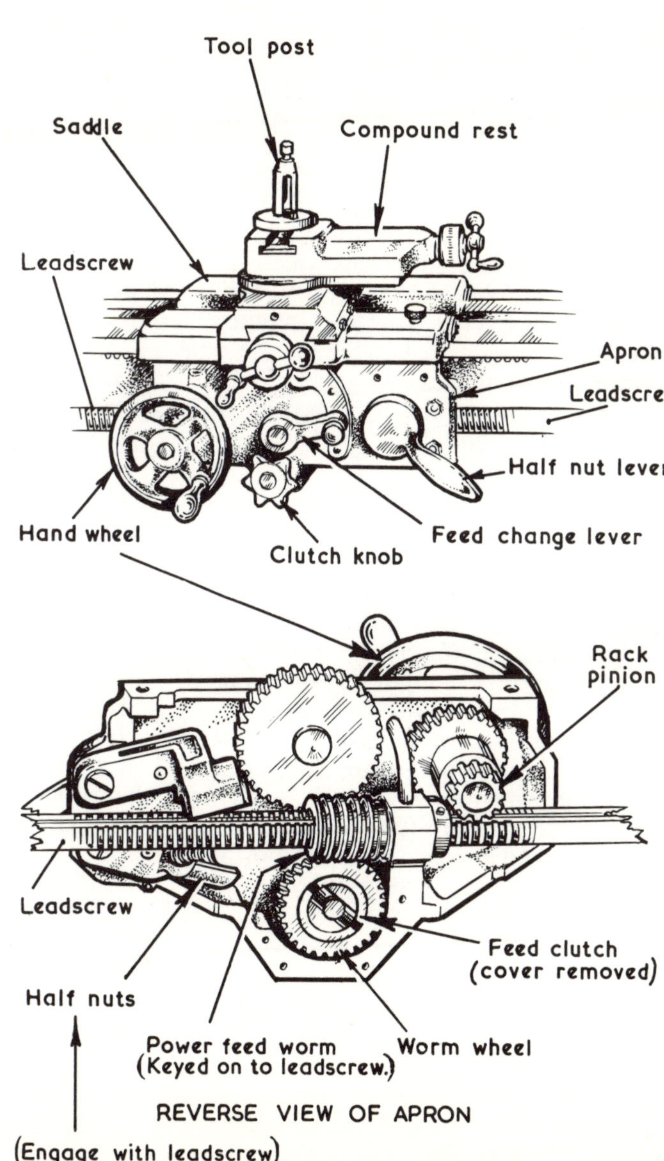

REVERSE VIEW OF APRON

The Tailstock, occasionally called a loose headstock or poppet, has a hollow spindle which is moved backwards and forwards by turning the hand wheel at the right. The other end of the spindle has a tapered hole, No. 2 morse taper on this Boxford lathe; the taper in the headstock is usually larger than that in the tailstock, which takes a centre, a drill chuck, a large drill or a machine reamer. The tailstock spindle often has a dimensioned scale graduated in millimetres and marked off in tens which is particularly useful when drilling holes of fixed depths. Drills and centres are automatically ejected from the spindle when it is turned back to zero as indicated on the spindle scale. The spindle is locked in position by the spindle lock and the Boxford tailstock is clamped to the lathe bed by an eccentric clamp tightened by moving the clamp lever.

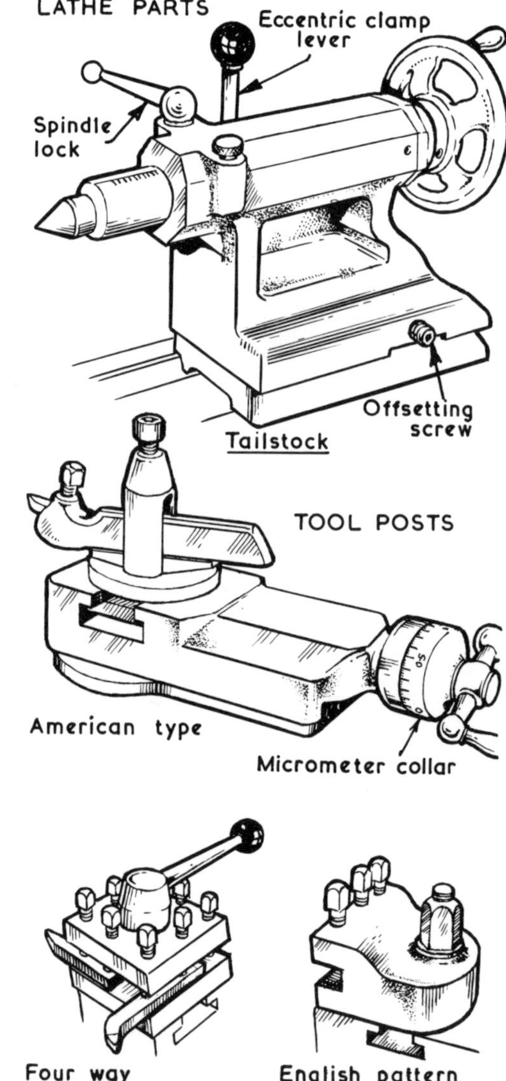

The Carriage moves along the lathe bed. The saddle of the carriage rests on the bed and carries the cross slide which moves across the bed, and the compound rest, upon which the tool post is fixed. The compound rest or compound slide is fitted across the cross slide normally parallel to the lathe bed. Beneath it, on the cross slide there is a scale graduated in degrees, and the compound rest can be swivelled around so that the tool can be fed to the work at any angle as when taper turning. The apron fits over the front of the bed below the saddle covering part of the lead screw, and on it are the hand wheel which moves the apron, the feed change lever with its three positions (up for longitudinal feeds, down for cross feeds and a central neutral position), the clutch to operate both automatic power feeds, and the half nut lever which is for screwcutting and which cannot be used unless the feed change lever is in its central neutral position.

The Toolpost shown on the lathe is of the American type favoured when toolholders are used. It has at its base a ring and a rocker which is curved underneath, boat shaped, and can be tilted to raise or lower the tool point, thus enabling adjustments to be made quickly; but it must be noted that the movement of the rocker affects the tool angles for cutting.

The English pattern toolpost is a simple tool clamp, while the four-way toolpost, which is used considerably in industry, can hold four tools at once, each of which can be easily and quickly applied to the work. It is particularly suitable when several tool operations have to be carried out on the same job.

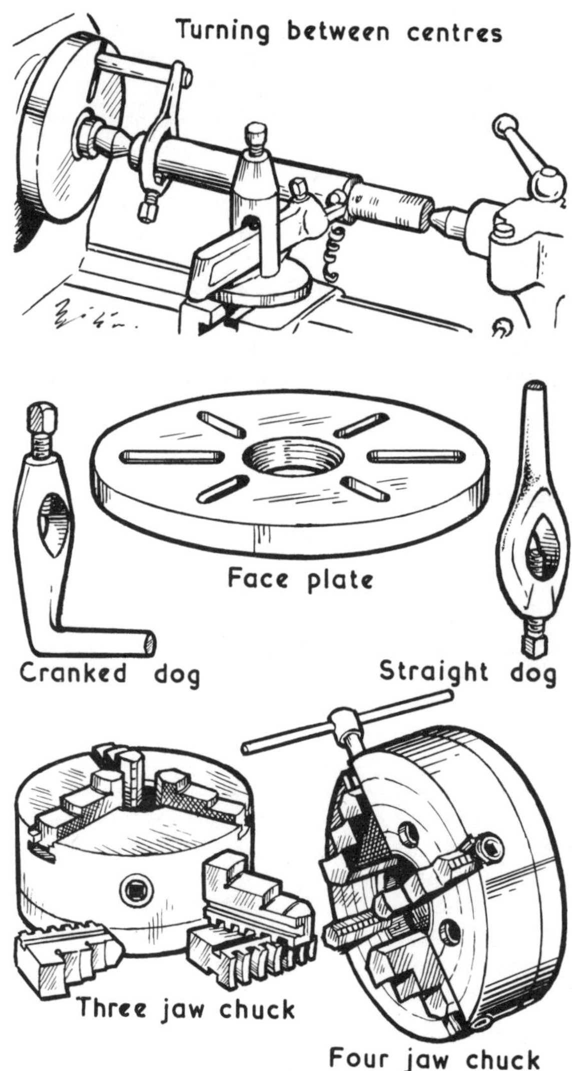

Turning Between Centres can be practised when the Boxford lathe is fitted and arranged as illustrated. This is a simple method of turning bars of moderate diameter. The ends of the work are centred so that it can be supported by the centres but it is obvious that the bar cannot be turned unless special provisions are made for revolving the bar. A screwed peg or bolt is bolted in the slot in the catch plate and this turns a carrier or dog which is clamped on to the end of the work. The carrier can be straight or bent tailed, in which case the tail fits in the catch plate slot, so dispensing with the peg. The carrier prevents a cut being taken all the way along the bar and after part of the work has been turned, the bar is reversed with the carrier fixed to the turned end. Although this method represents the basic principles of turning it is not good for beginners as few articles are made between centres and it is wasteful if practised only as an exercise. Turning 2 mm from a 16 mm diameter bar reduces the diameter to 12 mm and so removes nearly half the metal, a considerable loss especially if the bar is of any length. Chuck work is better for early exercises as turning, facing and taper turning can all be practised on the same job. The chuck is convenient for small work and it is the usual means of holding work for drilling.

A Chuck is a rotating vice and the two main lathe chucks are the 3-jaw and 4-jaw. These are used considerably, especially when the material is short and does not have to be supported at the other end by the dead centre. 3-jaw chucks are self-centring, are used for circular and hexagonal work and are very convenient in schools as they are easy to use. The jaws all move at the same time as they fit on one flat spiral thread or scroll which is turned by the chuck key. Unfortunately the thread soon wears and the action is not very accurate, so it is difficult to replace work accurately once it has been taken out of the chuck and it is practically impossible to reverse work accurately. Work is usually gripped on the outside but the jaws are not reversible and a set of inside jaws is supplied with each 3 jaw chuck so that work can be held internally. On a 4 jaw chuck the jaws move independently and are reversible (*see* p. 57). The concentric circles machined on the face are to aid in approximately centring circular work as it is placed in the chuck.

Face Plates

Another method of holding work on a lathe for machining is clamping it to a face plate. A face plate is similar to a catch plate inasmuch as it is of the same shape and fits directly on to the spindle nose. For the same lathe the face plate is usually larger than the catch plate. It can be very much larger. Face plates are used to hold odd-shaped jobs e.g. castings which are too large or too awkwardly shaped for a chuck, or when the location of the part to be machined makes other methods of holding difficult or impossible, for example, boring a deep hole in one corner of a large casting of irregular shape. A face plate has several slots and holes for the bolts or clamps which hold work to the plate. Sometimes special fixing brackets or frames are made for securing work to the face plate. Some jobs are best machined when they are fixed to an angle plate which is bolted to the face plate. This method is particularly helpful when holes have to be drilled or bored parallel to an already accurately machined surface. For this operation the work and angle plate might be on one side of the face plate, in which case some kind of balance weight, e.g. a heavy piece of metal, possibly lead, would also have to be fixed to the face plate, opposite the angle plate, for counterbalancing while turning (*see* p. 63); otherwise severe vibration will be created.

Care of Chucks and Face Plates. These, and catch-plates will run out of true if their main internal thread and the thread on the nose spindle are not maintained in good condition. Threads and shoulders on the spindle nose and in the chucks and plates must be wiped clean immediately before use to ensure that they are free from dust, filings, turnings etc., and they should be inspected regularly. It is most important that chucks, faceplates and catch plates are screwed on carefully and that they should not be allowed to drop on to the lathe bed when they are being removed. Craftsmen make sure that their arm is underneath while unscrewing and in school it is a wise precaution to place a piece of wood across the lathe bed in case of accidents. When storing chucks etc. the internal screw and the shoulder should always be uppermost. These chucks must be fitted accurately to backplates which can be screwed on to the nose of the lathe spindle as is the catch plate shown on the Boxford lathe on p. 53. There are many kinds of chucks, some of which are made for special purposes and in industry magnetic and pneumatic (compressed air), chucks are becoming increasingly important.

Plate 7. **"Undulation" Table**

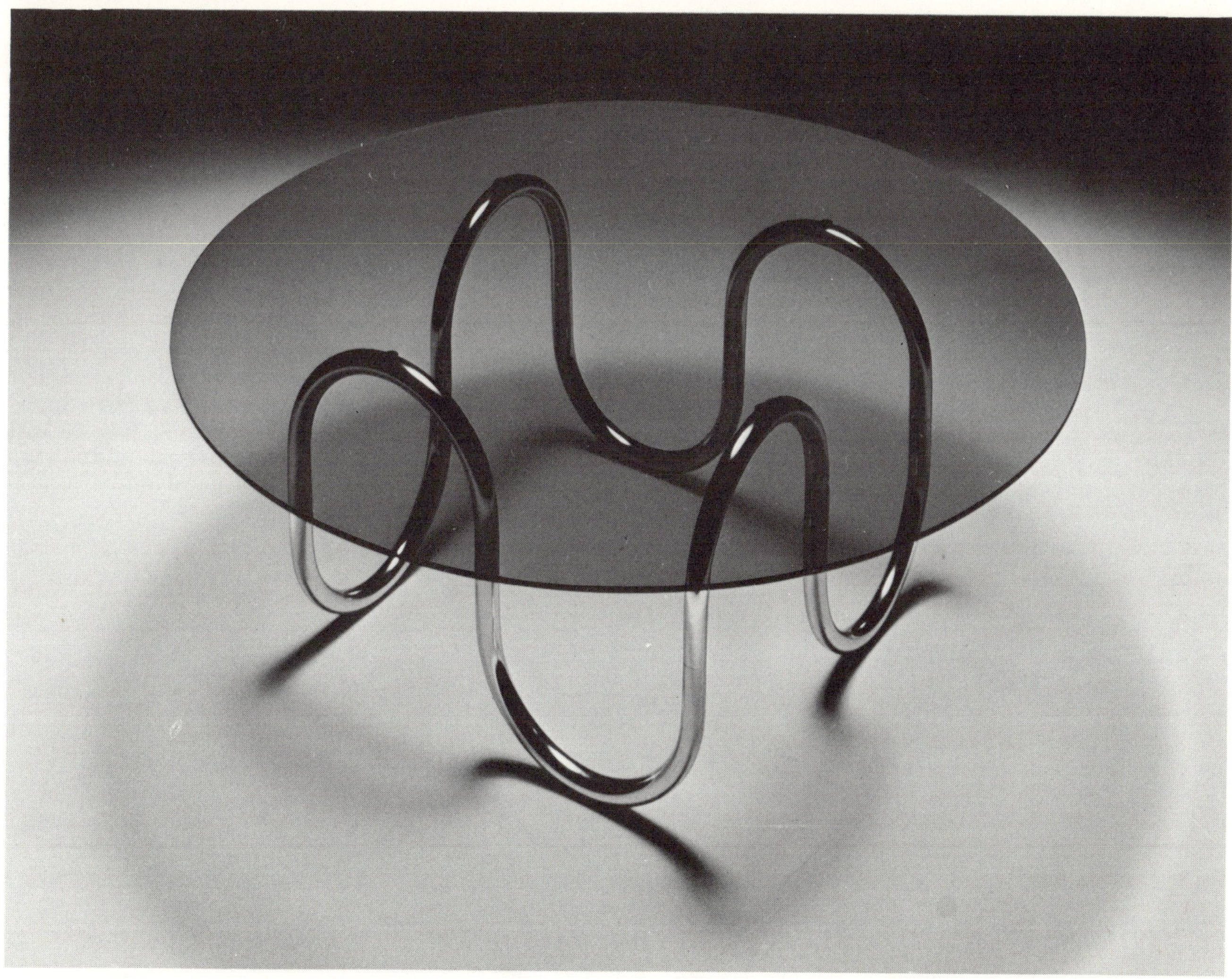

Undulating framework of polished aluminium or mild steel with a white epoxy resin finish and the top is of smoked glass. Knock-down construction. Designed by Frank Wardle and made by Vono Ltd., of Tipton

Plate 8. **Tables**

Left: Coffee table designed by Arkana Design Studio and made by Arkana Ltd. of Bristol. Base of cast aluminium finished white or polished natural and a top of chipboard faced with plastic laminate with the edges epoxy resin filled, sanded and painted

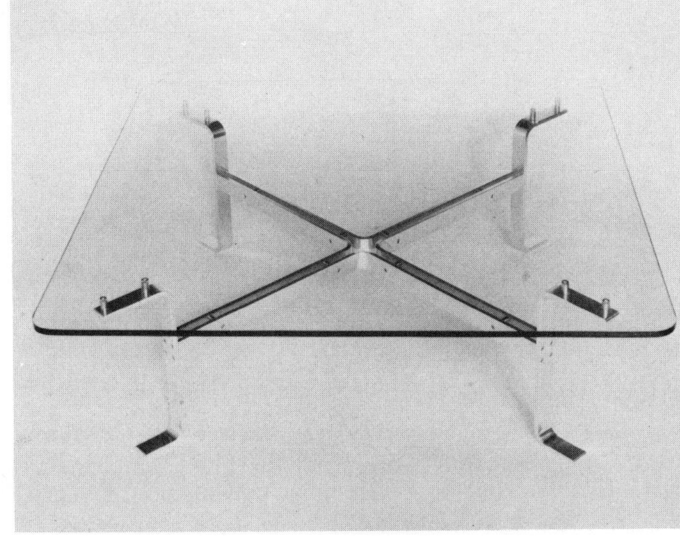

Right: Occasional table designed by William Plunkett and made by William Plunkett Ltd. Heat strengthened anodised and polished aluminium alloy frame sections 37 mm × 18 mm, fixed by countersunk socket screws with a 12 mm plate glass top held by 8 PVC covered shoulder screws

Collets or draw-in collet chucks are used for precision work such as the making of small parts for clocks and watches, typewriters, radios and small tools. They are very useful in the school workshop as alternatives to 3- and 4-jaw chucks, especially when accuracy is very important. They are made very accurately in sets to hold bright bar, round, square or hexagonal up to 20 mm diameter dependent on the size of the lathe. They are like flanged collars, made slightly adjustable by having fine transverse slots cut partway down their length and they screw inside a collet bar or drawbar which is pushed through the hollow headstock spindle from the rear. The nose piece is screwed on to the spindle threads, the hardened closing sleeve is placed inside the No. 3 morse taper in the spindle nose, and the collet is inserted into the closing sleeve, the pin in the sleeve engaging in the slot in the collet. The collet is closed on to the workpiece, which must be reasonably true to size as there is little more than a tenth of a millimetre for adjustment, by screwing the drawbar on to the collet.

Collets grip the work securely along its length so that there is no slip while turning. Their special advantage is that work can be fitted easily, quickly and accurately. Moreover, they are particularly useful for holding square metal such as, for example, the end fitment of a hacksaw which must have one part square and another turned circular so that it can be screwed (*see* p. 77), or for turning the end and the taper of a centre punch. Octagonal metal fits into a square collet but hexagonal metal needs an hexagonal collet. The closing sleeve is removed by unscrewing the nose piece.

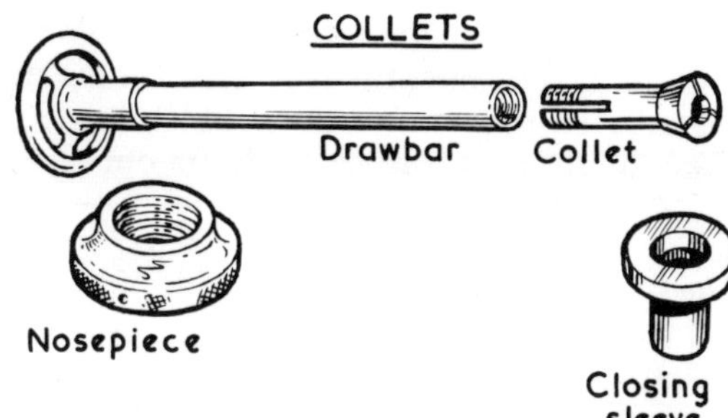

Setting up Work in a 4-Jaw Chuck

When setting up work in a 4-jaw independent chuck or on a face plate it can be tested for accuracy with chalk, with a surface gauge, or with a dial test indicator. A piece of chalk held against one of the outside surfaces while the work is revolved slowly indicates the parts which are furthest from the centre. A surface gauge held on the lathe bed or the carriage is a little more accurate than chalk and is suitable for rough castings. A **dial test indicator** is the best tool when the work has a smooth surface as the dial is graduated to read to 0.02 mm and a high degree of accuracy can be obtained. The dial must be fixed to a rod or bar which can be held in the tool post but an improvement is to have a rod in a magnetic base which can be placed anywhere on the lathe. There is a knob or stylus

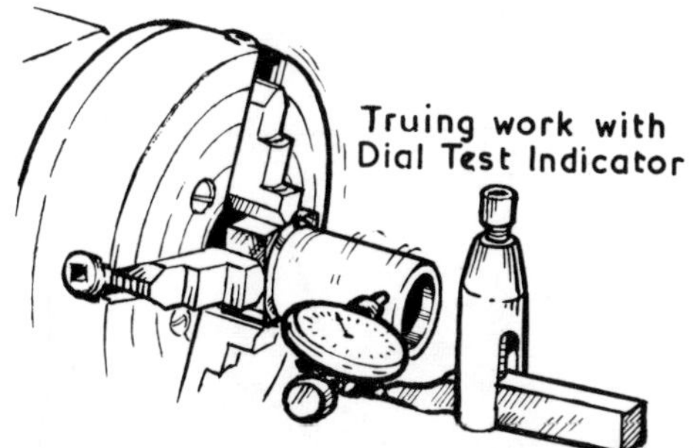

outside the dial and as the work moves touching this stylus the amount of movement is registered on the dial. It must be remembered that the work should be moved only one half the amount that it is shown to be out of true, that is, half the measurement on the dial.

Revolving centre

A Lathe Centre is ground to an angle of 60° and the body is tapered to one of the standard morse taper sizes. The headstock centre, called the live centre because it revolves with the work, is made of soft steel so that it can when necessary easily be ground to shape. The dead centre which fits in the tailstock spindle is specially hardened and is often made of high speed steel marked with a turned groove to identify it. This centre does not rotate but the work rotates upon it so causing friction which is reduced considerably when a revolving centre is used. The **revolving centre** is of great help in school as it minimises the difficulty of worn centres and of adjusting the centre, whether it is too tight or too loose, and lubrication is unnecessary. A half centre allows the lathe tool to work up to the centre of the work as when facing, or turning small diameters.

Fixed steady

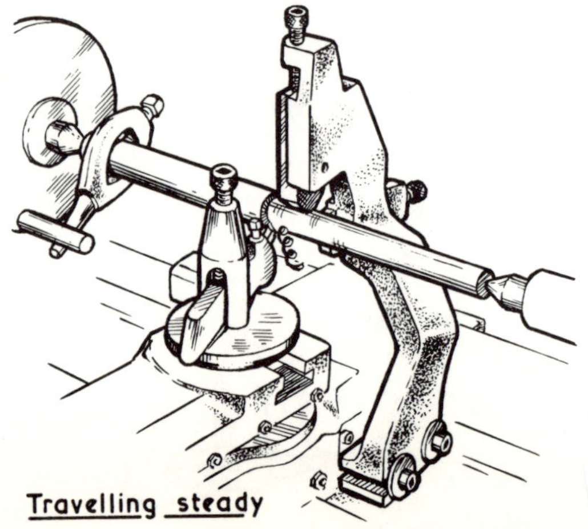
Travelling steady

Steadies are used to prevent the work springing away from the cutting tool when long shafts are being turned or long screws cut. A **travelling steady** is attached to the saddle of the lathe and it travels along with the tool. It has jaws which are adjusted to press lightly against the work just behind the tool so as to counteract the pressure of the tool. Sometimes a **fixed steady** is fitted to the lathe bed and this is particularly useful when the end of a long bar is to be drilled or turned and a tailstock cannot be used. The fixed steady is then set up at the end of the bar, usually while the bar is between centres, and this steady has three adjustable jaws which are arranged so that they grip the work but allow the bar to revolve. Then the tailstock is moved away. The top part of a fixed steady, that part with the upper jaw is hinged so that it can be more easily set up.

Centring. There are several different methods of finding the centre of work for turning: (1) by scribing from the outside with odd leg calipers, (2) with a centre square with which lines are scribed across the end of a bar, setting the square in different positions, or (3) with a cup or bell punch the conical part of which fits over the end of the bar and locates centrally the punch which is struck with a hammer. These last two methods should be used only if the work is fairly round. A fourth method in which a surface gauge is used on a surface plate is described on p. 35 dealing with setting out. Circular work which can be held in a 3-jaw chuck or collet is usually centre-drilled direct without preliminary centring. A centre drill (*see* p. 39) is a combined drill and countersink, double ended, with a parallel body which serves as a shank, and it is used for centring work for turning or grinding. It is held in a drill chuck in the tailstock and as centre drills are expensive and break easily, they must be used carefully. Make sure that the centre drill is securely held and in line with the axis of rotation of the work; start slowly, feed slowly and withdraw frequently to remove chips. Ideally the workpiece and the drill should revolve in opposite directions but on a lathe the centre drill remains still while the work revolves. Centre drills are made in several sizes with body diameters between 3 and 20 mm and the maximum diameter of the drilled centre hollow should not be more than 3 mm for rods up to 25 mm and 5 mm for work up to 100 mm diameter.

Drilling in the Lathe. This is often convenient, especially when the hole is centrally placed in circular work, or before boring, or internal screw-cutting. Small drills are held in a drill chuck the arbor of which fits into the taper bore of the lathe tailstock, whereas drills of more than 13 mm diameter having taper shanks can be inserted direct or with an adaptor socket into the tailstock. The work is usually held in a chuck or collet and the drill is applied by turning the tailstock handle. Heavy work may be bolted to the carriage, in which case the drill is fitted into the headstock spindle and the feed is applied by moving the carriage. Drilling must be preceded by centre drilling and large holes need pilot holes, small holes drilled to act as guide for the larger drill and to help it cut more freely.

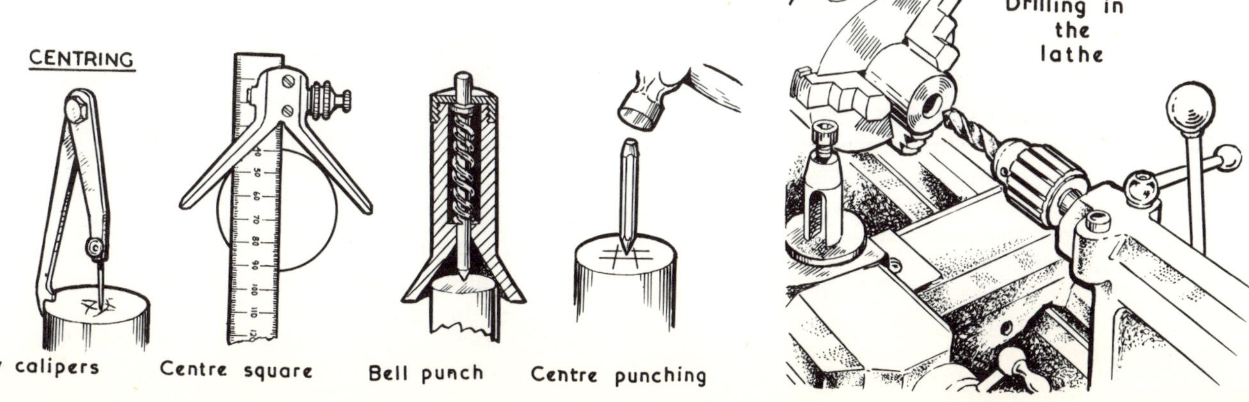

Jenny calipers   Centre square   Bell punch   Centre punching

Turning, in its broadest sense refers to all work carried out on the lathe with the normal lathe tools but specifically it means longitudinal cutting on the outside of cylindrical work. For all kinds of turning, the first cut should be deep enough to get below the surface of the metal especially if it is cast iron which always has a hard skin. A tool which just grazes the outer surface in spots will be dulled in a comparatively short time. On a heavy lathe a 10 mm cut is common practice but when using a Boxford lathe in schools the depth of cut should not exceed 1 mm for roughing or 0.25 mm for finishing cuts. The cut is started by hand but then the power or automatic feed should be engaged except for very small surfaces. The tool should cut continuously. The best way for beginners, and the only possible way on the simple training lathes, is by turning the wheels on the carriage by hand. One wheel at a time is turned, the large front wheel for longitudinal feed and the ball handled top wheel for cross feed; both hands must be used together on one wheel to achieve a smooth and continuous action. It is difficult, however, to maintain the necessary steady movement, and screwcutting lathes have change wheels, gears, on the left of the lathe which can be adjusted to give a continuous automatic movement of the tool, a power feed, longitudinal for turning and transverse or cross for facing and parting. On the Boxford lathe this is operated by a worm wheel shown on the illustration of the inside of the apron (p. 55), which is driven by a spline, the longitudinal groove in the lead screw. The worm wheel is engaged with the lead screw by turning the clutch knob after the feed change lever has been set in its correct position, top for longitudinal and bottom for cross feeds. On many lathes, especially the large ones, there is a separate splined shaft fitted below the lead screw called a feed shaft which provides a slow motion suitable for power feed independent of the lead screw. Smaller screwcutting lathes, on which the lead screw is not splined, supply the longitudinal power feed through the change wheels as for screwcutting but with the lead screw turning much more slowly. Power cross feed is not possible on such lathes.

Facing is truing surfaces across the lathe, e.g. machining the ends of bars or shoulders or the faces of work held in a chuck or on a face plate. The tool should be brought up to the work by moving the carriage which should then be locked in position and the feed is controlled by the cross slide, by hand or automatically. The depth of cut is adjusted by the compound rest. Facing the end of metal is a good test for the height of the tool. If correct, the tool will cut cleanly across the end; otherwise a pip will be left.

Boring is the operation of turning an internal surface, the truing and enlarging of holes. The cutting tool is a boring tool made in one piece or a tool bit fitted in a boring bar. Boring bars are of several kinds, including small bars which fit inside a spring box, and large bars which are used between centres or between a chuck and the tailstock centre. Solid tools and small boring bars are held in the tool post while the work is fixed in a chuck or on a face plate, but for large work a boring table is fixed to the carriage in place of the cross slide and compound rest, so that the work can be bolted to this table and be bored by a tool bit fitted in a revolving boring bar. When boring short tapers the compound rest is used. Boring is not the drilling of holes.

Plate 9. **Lamps**

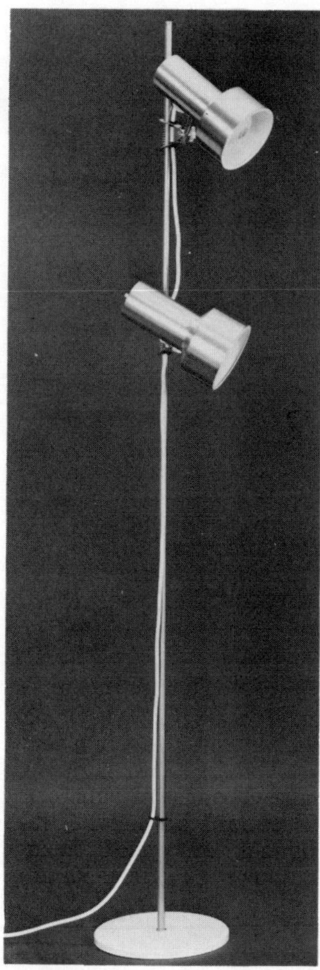

Adjustable standard lamp. A mild steel chromed stem on a heavy round base with aluminium shades; also available in white. Designed by New Dimension Product Development Team and manufactured in Denmark

Adjustable desk lamp—made of aluminium with a weighted base and finished satin aluminium, brass or coloured copper. Designed by G. Furst and J. D. Fradenham and made by The Modern Lighting Company, Watford

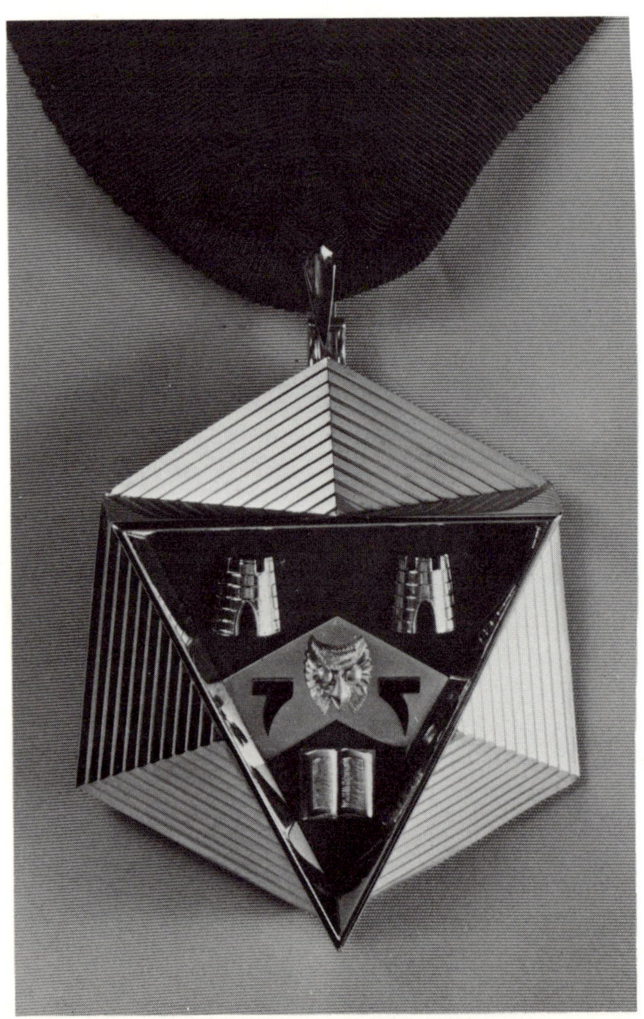

Ceremonial badge in yellow and white gold and enamels made for the Aberdeen Advocate. Designed by Alex Styles and made by Garrards

Pepper mill in silver with case diamond decoration designed by Anthony Elson and made by Davis & Elson Ltd. of London

Parting Off is the severing of pieces by cutting straight across the metal, but a parting off tool is also used for cutting grooves and for squaring shoulders. It must be narrow at the end with clearance on each side and it must be mounted accurately at centre height and at right angles to the axis of revolution. The narrow front of the parting tool breaks easily if jarred so there must not be much bearing play or backlash in the lathe; the work must be held firmly, usually in a chuck, as parting cannot be carried out between centres, and the tool should be firmly fixed with a minimum of overhang and as near to the chuck as possible. The feed should be continuous and swarf must not be allowed to collect so that it jams the tool.

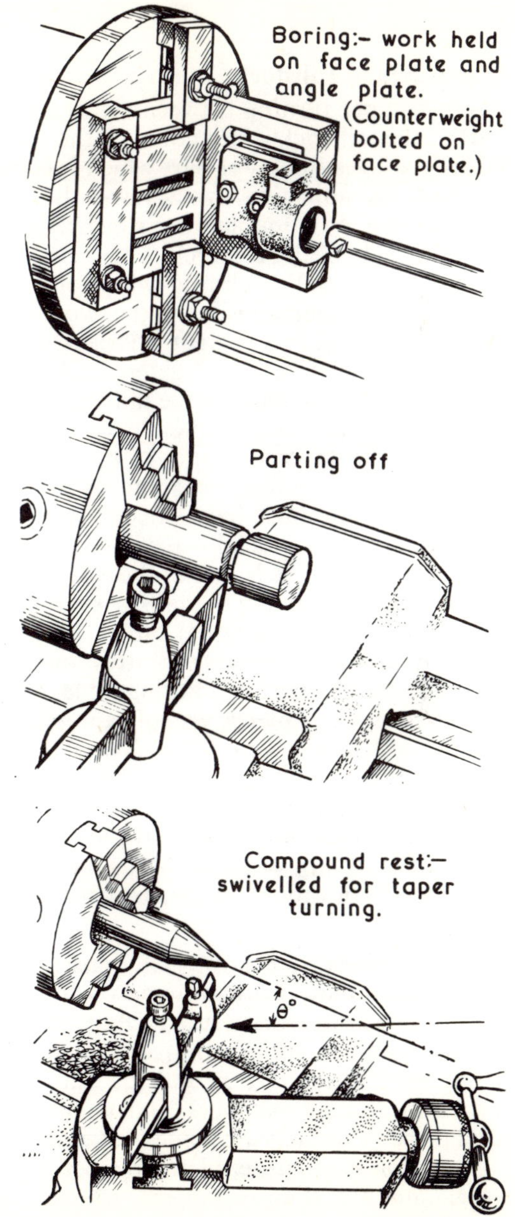

Taper Turning is the turning of tapered work. When the taper is on the outside it can be carried out in four ways: (1) by using a form tool with its front edge ground at an angle to the work for very short tapers; (2) by swivelling the compound rest and feeding the tool at an angle to the lathe bed, (3) by setting over the tailstock centre so that it is out of alignment with the headstock centre, using the feed in the ordinary way, and (4) by using a special taper turning attachment which on the Boxford lathe is fitted to the rear of the saddle with a bracket clamped to the lathe bed and is connected to the back of the cross slide. The compound rest is used, generally without a tailstock centre, for short tapers with considerable slope, or too much slope for other methods. It is the simplest method for beginners who can set the rest to the required angle and machine the taper by turning the top feed screw by hand. In school the tool can be fed its maximum traverse and the carriage locked in position with the tool safely clear of the chuck. Then the tool is screwed back so that the necessary cuts can be made and with such safety precautions the risk of damage is minimised—but the tool must be set correctly and heavy cuts should be avoided. This is the easiest method for small work.

Offsetting the Tailstock

When taper turning between centres, the upper part of the tailstock which contains the spindle can be moved over the lower part which is clamped to the bed, by adjusting two screws, the offsetting screw (*see* p. 56), and another similarly placed on the other side of the tailstock. The eccentric clamp should be partially released when offsetting the tailstock and, after adjustment, the two screws must both be tightened to prevent sideways movement, and the eccentric clamp tightened. The taper is determined by the amount the tailstock body is set over and this depends on the difference in the diameter of the tapered work. If the metal to be turned is to taper from ϕ 25 mm to ϕ 15 mm the tailstock centre must be set over 5 mm, half the difference, because metal is removed all round i.e. 5 mm each side. The length of the work is not considered when offsetting the tailstock. This method cannot be used for internal tapers unless a long boring bar is fitted between centres and the work bolted to the carriage or a boring table. Millimetre per centimetre is a metric way of expressing tapers. A taper of 1 mm in 2 cm is 1 in 20 and if this taper has to be machined on a shaft 200 mm long, the diameters at each end of the tapered shaft will differ by 10 mm so the tailstock centre must be moved over half of 10 mm = 5 mm. Metric tapers can also be expressed in ratios, 1 in 20, or percentages, 5%.

Lathe Mandrels. It is not usually possible to turn tubular or hollow work between centres, but this can be done if the work is fitted tightly on a cylinder called a mandrel. If the mandrel runs true, the hole in the work will run true and the outside can be turned as though the work and mandrel were a solid piece. Mandrels are made in standard sizes of high carbon steel hardened and tempered to lessen wear, and are slightly tapered so that they fit tightly into the hole which must be oiled to prevent seizure during turning.

Micrometer Collars (dials) are fitted on the cross feed and on the compound rest of most lathes (*see* p. 56). They are marked in graduations representing a 0.025 mm, i.e. four divisions equals one tenth of a millimetre so that the depth of cut can be gauged accurately. The graduated collars are fitted separately from the shaft and handle and, by releasing the set screws which fix them in position, they may be set to zero. This is particularly useful when cutting screws as the depth of the thread is very important. Friction dials are now fitted to all Boxford lathes and can be set to zero by simply turning the knurled rim of the dial.

Lathe Tools vary considerably. The shape and size of the cutting edge, including the tool angles, are dependent upon the job to be done, the metal to be cut and the finish required. They are made of steel, usually high speed steel, or of a hard non-ferrous mixture, cemented carbide cutting alloys, of which tungsten carbide is the best known. These cutting alloys are expensive and brittle so they are made as tips and brazed on to a plain carbon steel body. The tips are made by sintering—mixing powdered tungsten and carbide with cobalt, which acts as a binder, and subjecting the mixture to heavy pressure in special tool-shaped steel moulds. Good cutting edge support is necessary, otherwise the carbide will chip, and clearance angles are reduced leaving just sufficient clearance to allow the tool to cut freely. Tungsten carbide tools will cut at high speeds but need special grinding wheels for sharpening. Solid cast steel tools can be forged to shape and hardened and tempered but they must not be

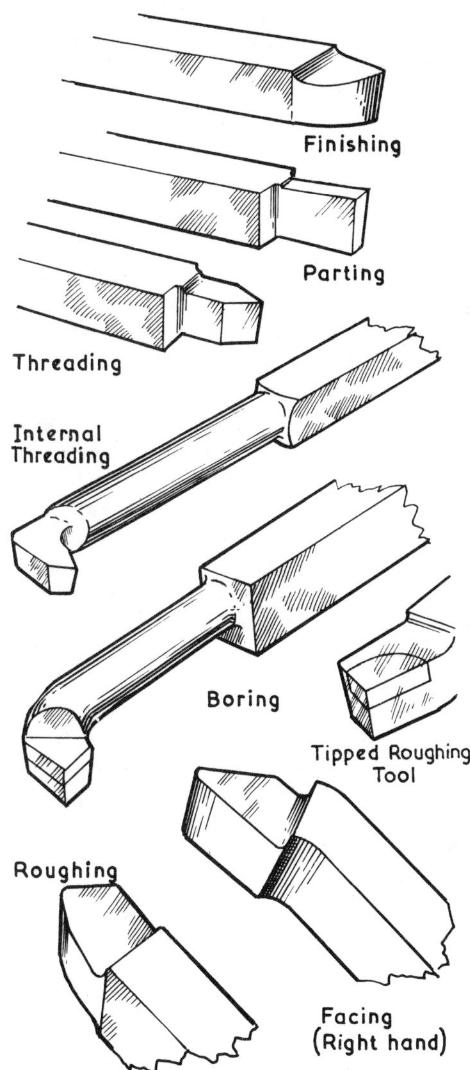

allowed to get hot, so high-speed steel, which as its name suggests can be used at high speeds, is used considerably for lathe tools today and is suitable for school work. High speed steel lathe tools are of two kinds, those with H.S.S. cutting ends welded electrically on to low carbon steel shanks, and tool bits made entirely of H.S.S. and used in toolholders. Tool bits, unlike lathe tools, are purchased square ended and ground to shape by the worker. They may be rectangular in section for parting tools, or round for use with boring bars, but are usually square in section, varying in size from 20 mm × 3 mm diameter for small boring bars to 150 mm and 25 mm square for heavy turning. Toolholders are straight or bent, to the left for facing or for right hand shoulders and to the right for left hand work. There are over fifty standard shapes of butt-welded tools but those used for the operations recently described are the most important.

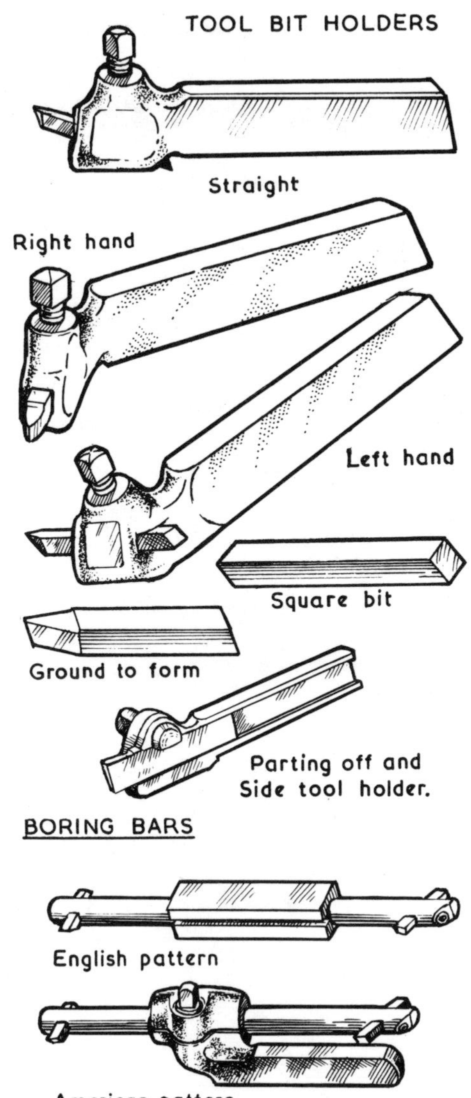

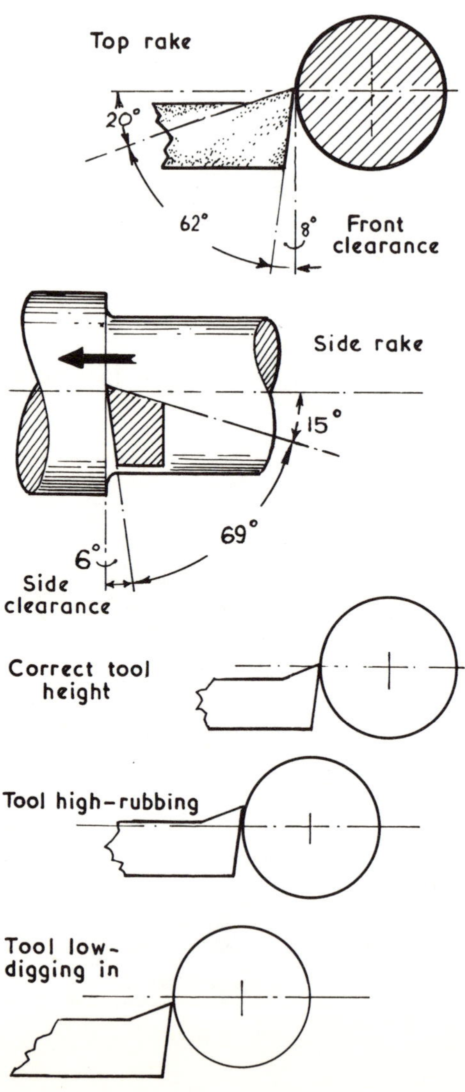

Tool Angles

A parting tool makes a forward, straight cut, acting in one direction only, so there are only three tool angles: top rake 0–30°, cutting angle 50° for soft metals to 87° for very hard cast iron, and front clearance 3–10°. These three angles must equal 90° so for hard cast iron the tool angles would be 0° (no top rake), 87° and 3° for clearance. When turning, however, a lathe tool generally moves sideways so more tool angles, side rake and side clearance, must be considered. Clearance angles ensure contact between the actual cutting edge of the tool and the work, but they must not weaken the cutting edge or reduce the support at the cutting edge any more than is necessary. The cutting angle, or tool angle, is known by experience or by experimenting with the metal to be turned, and then the rake can be estimated: tool angle+rake+clearance=90°. The tool angles illustrated are suggested for cutting mild steel. Tool bits are held in a sloping position so the slope affects the angles and must be allowed for when grinding them. Lathe tools should be set to cut at centre height, especially in school work, although slight variations are practised by experienced turners for special purposes. It must be remembered that any change of position affects the working angles; if placed high, the rake is increased and the clearance decreased, and if placed low, the angles are changed the other way. If too high, the tool will rub and will not cut at all, and if too low, the tool edge will dig in and jam instead of cutting.

Generally speaking, a pointed tool cuts more quickly and effectively than a round nosed tool but it leaves a rough surface, so roughing tools are more pointed than finishing tools which are round nosed. In practice no lathe tool should have a really sharp point as it will cut better if slightly radiused by rubbing with a slip stone, and this will make the cutting edge keener.

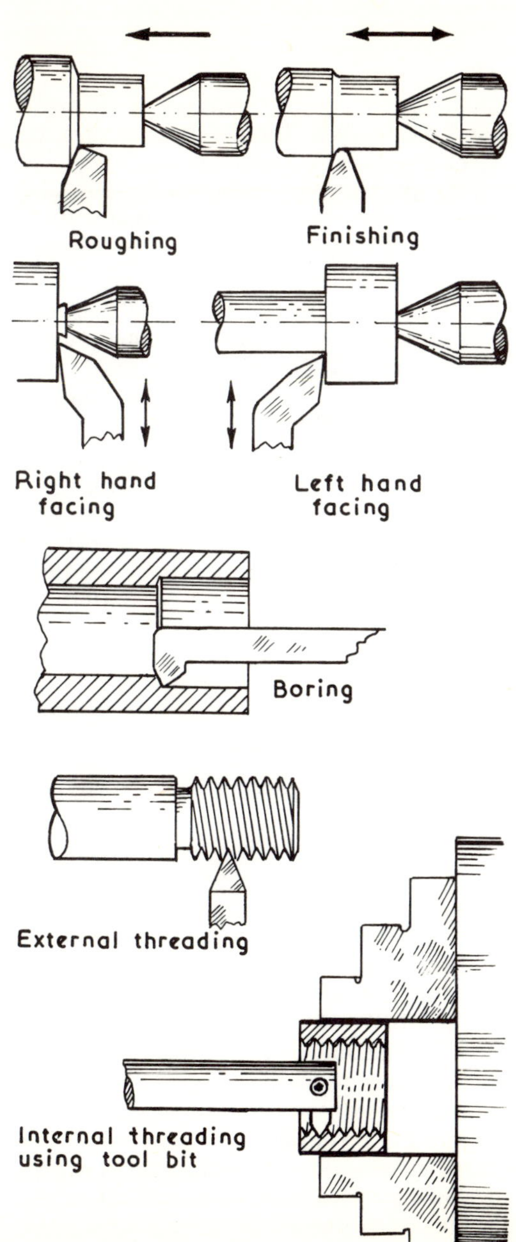

Cutting Speeds, Lubrication and Cooling

The average cutting speeds with high speed tools are approximately 12 m per minute for cast steel, 18 m for cast iron, 25 m for mild steel, 60 m for brass and 100 m per minute for aluminium. These speeds are for roughing and can be increased by a third for finishing. An increase of 50% is possible when a good coolant-lubricant is used. This keeps the work and the tool cool, reduces expansion and so permits higher cutting speeds, and it helps to wash away the swarf, chips and coiled turnings from the cutting point. It lubricates between the tool face and the chip which is being removed from the work, and also between the tool nose and the work, which helps to give a better finish to the work and increases the life of the tool edge. Power consumption is reduced and a good lubricant prevents corrosion of the finished work. These two properties of cooling and lubricating are combined in soluble oil, a mineral oil mixed with various compounds of sulphur and chlorine which, when mixed with water, often about 15 parts of water, is called suds and provides a fluid which can be used in large quantities and is suitable for most school machine work. It is fed to the work by a suds pump, often electrically driven, by a drip can situated above the work or by a brush, but in this method care must be taken lest the brush fouls metal turnings. Cast iron and brass are turned dry; the free graphite in cast iron serves as a lubricant and brass comes away from the tool in small chips without creating much heat.

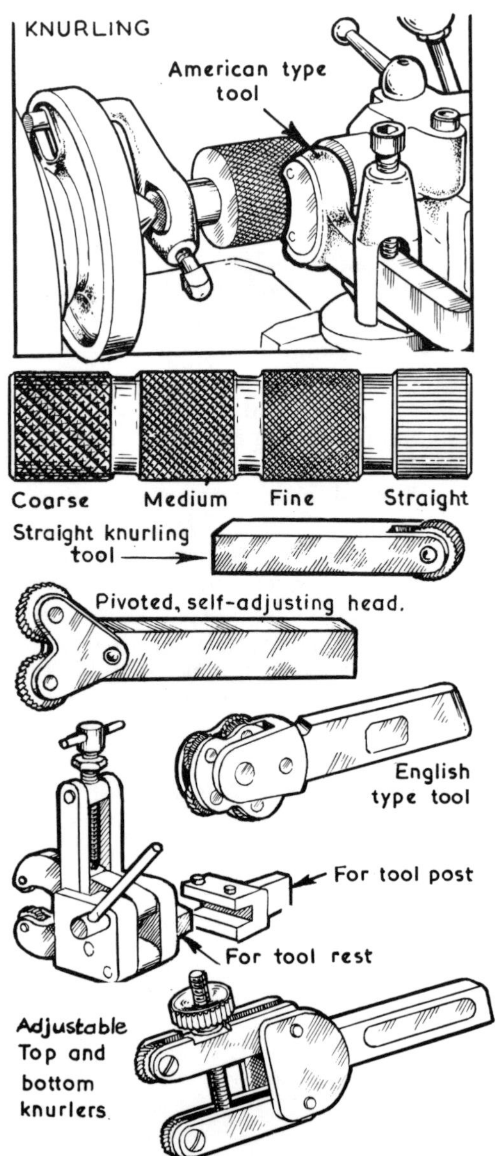

Knurling is indenting a pattern into the surface of the metal usually to provide a finger grip as for the handles of a die stock. Hardened steel wheels with small vee grooves cut in their edges, something like the milled edges of a coin, are fixed in a heavy shanked tool, usually so that they will fit around the work while it revolves very slowly between centres. The tool is applied firmly and must be rigidly mounted as knurling is achieved by forcing the wheels into the metal about 0.05 mm and can be accomplished in one pass. In any case the tool must stay on the work until completion. Considerable pressure is necessary and there is strain on the headstock bearing. Recently improved types of knurling tools have been introduced to relieve this pressure, adjustable tools which tend to squeeze the metal between knurling wheels which may be on each side, or above and below. In knurling both the work and the wheels revolve. There are three accepted grades of knurling, coarse, medium and fine, giving diamond shaped or straight cut patterns.

Measuring and Testing on the Lathe. Calipers are still used to measure and test lathe work, although the ordinary firm joint type has been largely superseded by spring calipers. Micrometers are more accurate measuring instruments and are better tools for use in schools, especially when they are fitted with a ratchet stop, for then they do not depend so much on a sensitive sense of touch as calipers always do. When testing with calipers they must be set to a definite size. For outside calipers one point is placed on the end of a steel rule supported by the finger while the other hand adjusts the other caliper point to the desired dimension. Inside calipers are adjusted similarly, but one caliper point is placed against the stock of an engineer's square which has previously been placed against the end of the rule as shown opposite. When measuring the outside of turned work, the calipers should just slip over, almost by their own weight.

Calipers should never be forced as they are likely to spring and the measurement will not be accurate. Inside calipers should be placed internally as shown by the dotted position on the diagram; then the hand is raised slowly and the calipers finally adjusted, making sure that the points of the calipers are straight across the gap or across the diameter of the hole being measured. Jenny calipers, odd legs or hermaphrodite calipers are set against a rule in the manner described for outside calipers and are used for marking shoulders.

The Micrometer

The main screw of a metric micrometer has a pitch of 0.5 mm so two complete turns of the thimble move the spindle one millimetre. The thimble edge is divided into fifty equal divisions each of which represents one fiftieth of the pitch, 0.5 mm, so each division is 0.5 mm divided by fifty which is

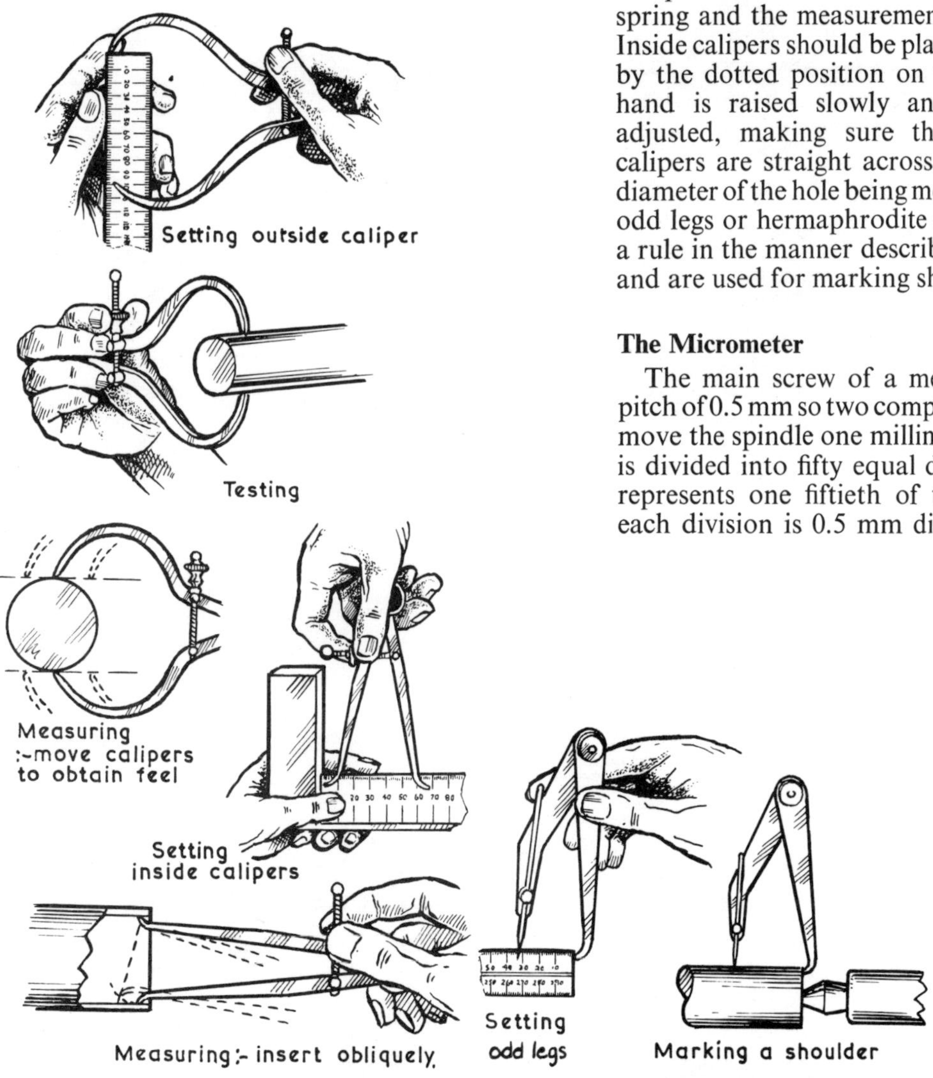

0.01 mm. Hence a movement of one division advances the spindle 0.01.

Each graduation of the longitudinal line along the sleeve indicates one complete turn of the thimble, equals 0.5 mm. Each tenth graduation is numbered as shown representing five millimetres. This micrometer reads to 0.01 mm but some metric micrometers have a vernier scale set out on the sleeve enabling them to give an accurate reading to two-thousandths of a millimetre.

The reading **A** represents 11 complete turns and, because line 28 on the thimble coincides with the longitudinal line on the sleeve, 28 fiftieths $= 11 \times 0.5\ \text{mm} + 28 \times 0.01\ \text{mm} = 5.5 + 0.28 = 5.78\ \text{mm}$. **B** is $13 \times 0.5 + 0.26 = 6.5 + 0.26 = 6.76\ \text{mm}$. The third reading, **C**, can be worked out similarly.

The locknut on the micrometer fixes the setting to prevent it slipping and the ratchet ensures an even pressure—a guard against the heavy handed.

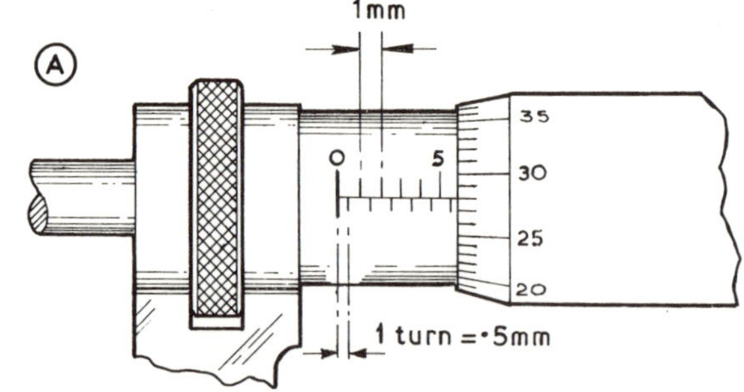

Reading = 5.78 mm

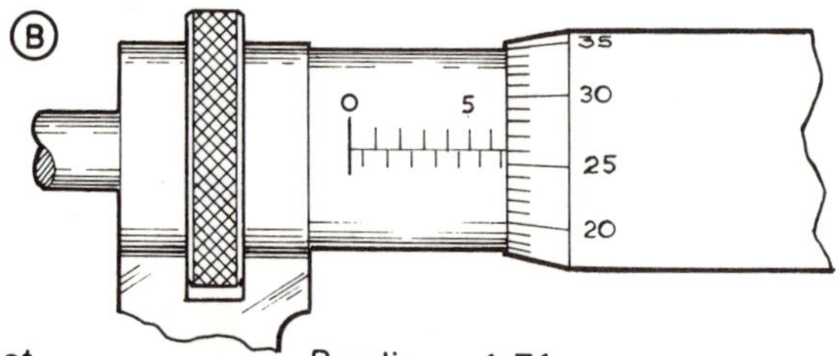

Reading = 6.76 mm

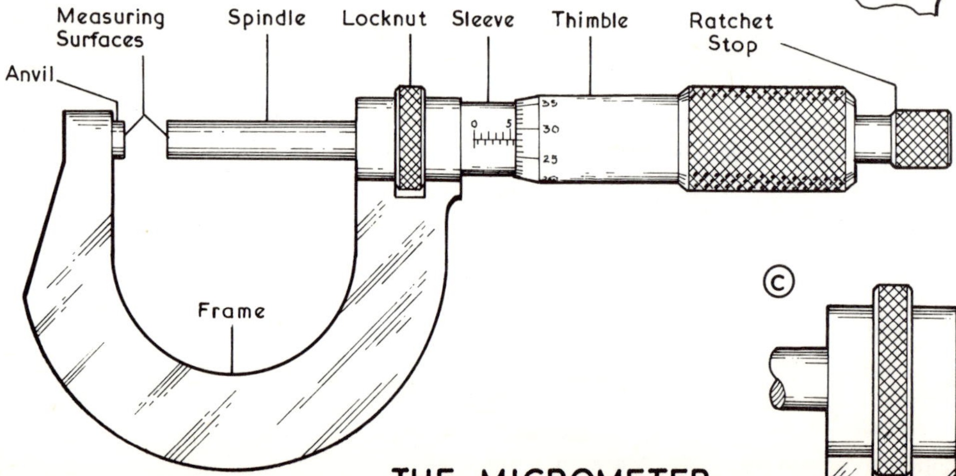

THE MICROMETER

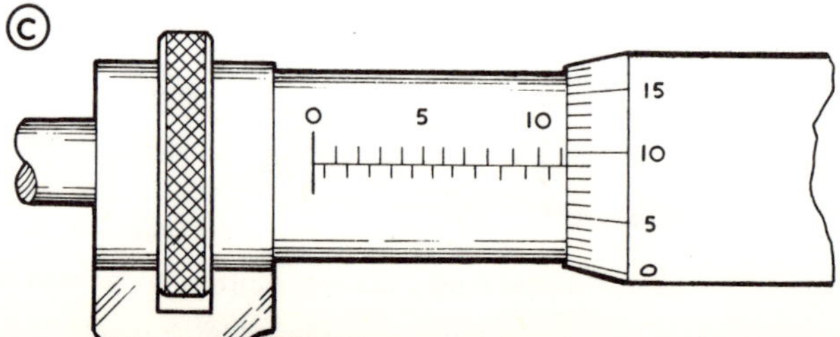

Reading = 11.09 m.m.

Safety

Safety cannot be over emphasised. It must be stressed all the time, hoping that eventually it will be accepted naturally. Dress is important: cuffs must be kept buttoned or sleeves rolled up; there must be no flowing ties or loose wrist watch straps; long hair is dangerous. The work and the lathe tool must be securely held in position and other tools, e.g. drills and files, must not be left on the lathe bed or carriage. The chuck key must be removed from the chuck before the lathe is switched on. Work must not be wiped clean nor tested, measured, oiled or adjusted while the machine is running. Swarf must not be touched—even when the machine is still. Swarf should be moved with a stick of wood—or better still, a piece of 3 mm wire with a ring handle at one end and the other end bent at right angles like a rake to pull the swarf from the machine. If anything jars or catches—or if there are any unusual noises—the machine should be switched off at once. Hands should be kept away from moving parts and handles should not be moved unless their action is fully understood—even if the machine is stationary. The machine must never be stopped with the hand. Although the machine does most of the work, concentration on the job is just as necessary as when carrying out hand tool operations. The operator should always stand at the lathe attentively, and never lean against it. A running machine should not be left. One should walk and never run in a machine shop. Machine tool designers are now striving to produce lathes which are safer for school practice. Interlocking cut out switches are fitted which cut off the motor as soon as a guard is moved or an inspection cover door opened. There are knock-off limit switches which can be set to any position on the lathe bed to prevent power or hand feeding the carriage into a revolving chuck or face plate.

12

Screwcutting in the Lathe

One of the great values of the lathe is its use in cutting many kinds of screw threads. If the cutting edge of a lathe tool is ground to a vee shape (wedge shaped) and is used to cut a round bar which is revolving in the lathe, it will cut a vee groove. If the tool is stationary, there will be one complete groove around the bar but if the tool moves along the bar as the bar rotates, the vee groove will travel around and down the bar, continuously and spirally, to cut a vee screw thread. If the movement of the tool is controlled so that it moves 2 mm for one revolution of the bar, it will move 10 mm for five revolutions of the bar, and if a rule is placed along the bar, there will appear to be one groove every 2 mm although it is realised that the groove is continuous. If the tool is ground to an angle of 60° and if the bar is 16 mm in diameter, the bar can be converted to a 16 mm standard ISO Metric Thread —Coarse Series, pitch 0.5 mm. The two vital factors in screwcutting on the lathe are the shape of the cutting end of the tool and the speed at which it moves in relation to the speed of the work, i.e. the tool traverse longitudinally in relation to the revolutions of the bar, or the distance the tool travels for each revolution of the work.

Tool Movement for Screwcutting. The tool moves with the lathe carriage which is propelled by the lathe lead screw. The carriage is engaged with the lead screw by moving the half-nut lever which causes the halves of a split nut to close around the screw (*see* p. 55). The lead screw is connected to the headstock spindle by the gear wheels (change wheels) fitted on the left hand end of the lathe (p. 74). These gears are changed and arranged to vary the relationship between headstock spindle and lead screw speeds, between the revolutions of the work and the movement of the tool. The lead screw of the Boxford Lathe has a pitch of 3 mm and, if equal change wheels are arranged on the end of the lathe so that spindle and the lead screw revolve at the same rate, a screw thread with a 3 mm pitch can be cut. If the spindle revolves twice as fast the pitch will be 1.5 mm and if at half speed, 6 mm. The change gear wheels can be changed and arranged on this Boxford lathe to cut threads varying in pitch from 0.5 mm to 7.0 mm and the number of teeth on the change gear wheels will determine the metric pitch of the threads to be cut. The change wheel charts (or gear charts) attached on the lathe state the gears to use and how to arrange them to cut the desired thread but this can be worked out mathematically.

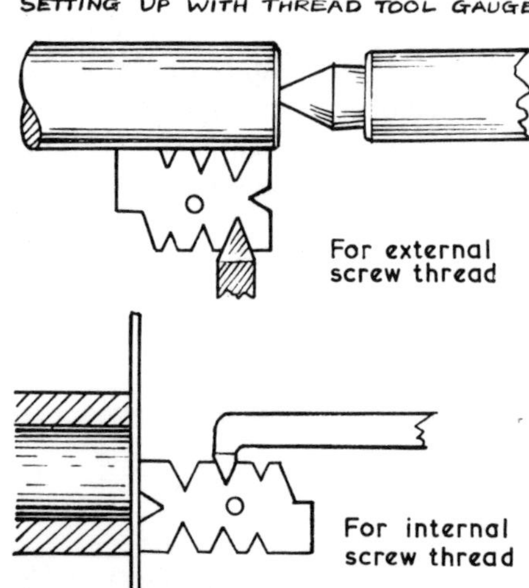

Setting Up. When screwcutting it is always advisable to allow the tool to run out into an undercut as illustrated. This is essential for beginners. The tool or tool bit is ground flat on top without top rake, and for metric threads the point angle is 60°, BA 47.5° and 29° for an acme thread. A thread tool gauge is used to ensure the correct angle and as the angle of the thread will be incorrect if the tool is not set square to the work, this gauge is used for testing the correctness of the position of the tool in the tool holder.

The First Cut. When the lathe has been properly set up, a light trial cut must be taken to test the pitch of the thread, by afterwards resting a rule on the bar and counting the threads in say 10 mm.

Subsequent Cuts. For the second cut the tool can be fed 0.05 or 0.075 mm (two or three graduations on the micrometer collar (*see* p. 56)), and the operation is repeated until a full thread is cut. After each cut the tool must be withdrawn and the carriage returned to its original position. It is essential that the tool always follows the first cut, so sometimes the lathe is reversed after each cut in order to bring the lathe back to the starting point without disengaging the carriage. When the pitch number of the threads being cut is an exact multiple of the pitch number on the lead screw then the carriage can be disengaged from the lead screw and returned to its original starting position by turning the hand wheel. Then the half nut in the carriage can be engaged with the lead screw at random, and the tool will always follow the first cut. When cutting a long screw in which the number of threads is not a multiple of the number on the lead screw, reversing the lead screw is a slow method of ensuring that the

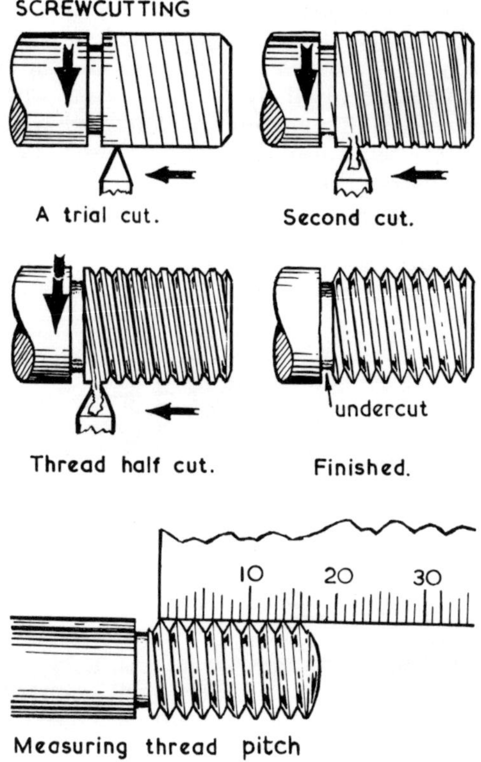

cuts follow each other and can be avoided by marking the position of the carriage at the commencement of the cut with a chalk line on the carriage continuing on to the lathe bed and by chalking marks on the spindle and lead screw gears and by aligning the marks at the beginning of each cut to make sure that every cut begins the same way. Alternatively, instead of marking the carriage and bed, the tailstock body can be moved against the carriage before making the first cut and then the carriage can be moved back against the tailstock for each subsequent cut.

Thread Dial Indicator. A better method is to use a thread dial indicator—a graduated rotating dial above gear wheels which mesh with the lead screw. The dial is revolved by the lead screw when the carriage is stationary but remains still when the carriage is being moved by the lead screw. For each cut the carriage is returned to the correct position and the half nut engaged when the dial is in the right position.

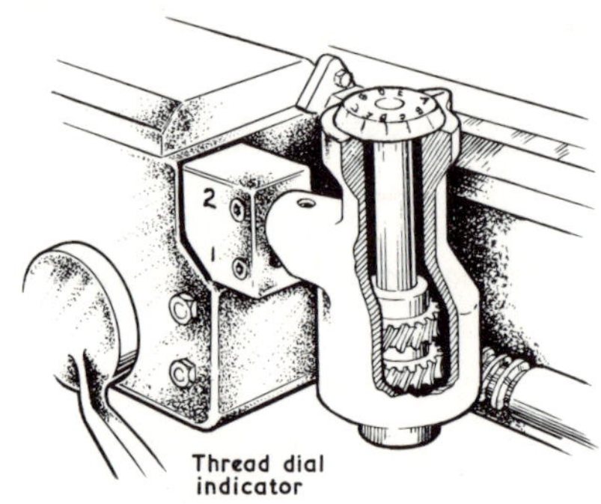

Thread dial indicator

Metric Boxford lathes, i.e. lathes fitted with 3 mm pitch leadscrews must have a metric thread dial indicator which has been specially designed to assist in cutting 20 of the common metric pitches between 0.35 and 6.00 mm. It has a special adaptor block and the dial has nine divisions which are lettered A and two each of B, C, D and E. The adaptor should be secured in the 9 mm hole on the right of the apron and after the lathe gearing for the desired thread has been set up the indicator with the dial showing division A opposite the zero mark is slid into the adaptor and adjusted until the gears mesh. The indicator has two gears 20 T and 21 T and the correct meshing is ensured by fixing the indicator at the right height i.e. by using the hole marked 1 or that marked 2 depending on the thread to be cut and according to the chart supplied with the indicator.

The first cut is taken with the dial at the A position because this is the one position which is common to all threads but for subsequent cuts it may be necessary to engage the half nuts with the divisions oppositely placed, as indicated on the chart for the thread being cut e.g. when cutting 3.5 mm pitch engage on either the division marked A or one of the two marked D. This will ensure that the thread being cut is started in the same position every time.

Simple Train. The formula is as follows: *screw pitch on the lathe lead screw divided by pitch required must equal number of teeth of the lead screw gear wheel divided by number of teeth on the stud gear*. On the simple train arrangement an idler gear connects the stud and the lead screw gears, but an idler does not affect the rotation of the lead screw and a change wheel of any convenient size might be used, but an 80-teeth idler gear is supplied with Boxford lathes for this purpose. When the simple gearing train is used the spacing collar on the lead screw must be placed outside the screw gear as shown. When compound gearing is used the collar can be on the inside, i.e. underneath, or on top of the screw

SIMPLE TRAIN CHANGE GEAR

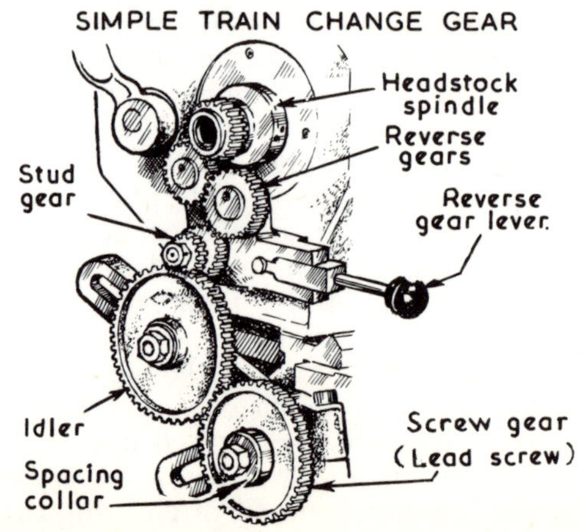

gear—(see illustrations). The size of the screw gear depends on the size of the teeth to be cut. On the Boxford Lathe there are two gear wheels between the headstock spindle gear and the stud gear. These are the reverse gears and are operated by the reverse gear handle and the illustration shows how, by lifting the lever the lead screw can be reversed.

Simple Train
1·4-7·0 Metric Pitch

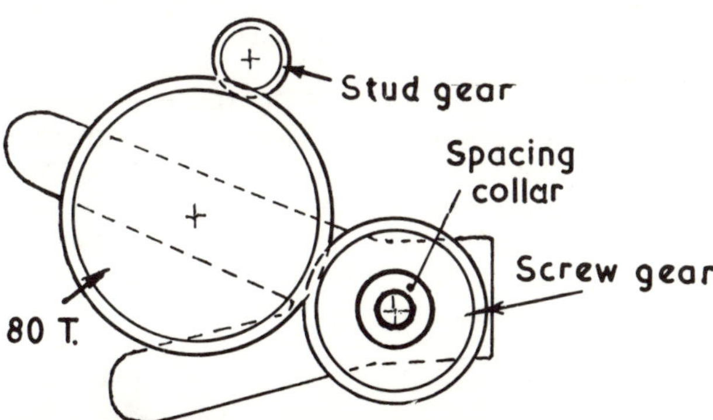

Compound Train. This is used when the desired screw cannot be cut with a simple train. This involves two changes of speed between the stud and the leadscrew gears and is achieved by using a gear change which has two gears fitted and keyed together on one shaft and, if necessary, by placing a spacing collar inside the leadscrew to bring it into line. A simple train always has this collar bolted on the outside of the screw gear. Students usually cut right hand threads, but the reverse gear lever, by cutting out the first of the change gears, reverses the direction of the rotation of the lead screw so that left-hand threads can be cut. The setting up is the same for both but the tool is fed from left to right for left hand threads instead of the more usual right to left as for right hand threads. The work always revolves forward. Many screw-cutting lathes have Norton gearboxes fitted which enable many different screw threads, 48 on the Boxford lathe, to be cut by varying the position of levers on the front of the lathe instead of changing change wheels.

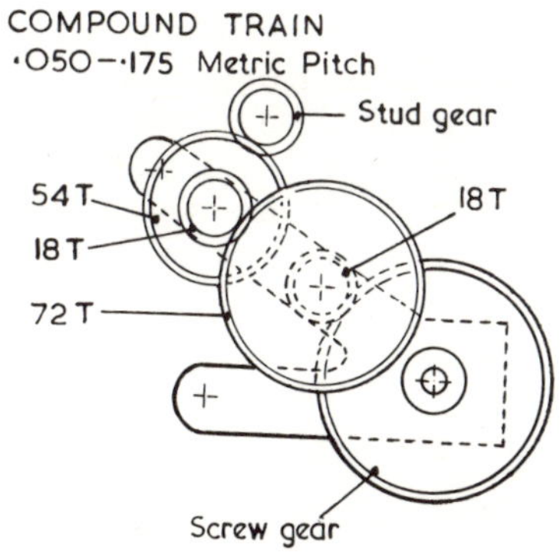

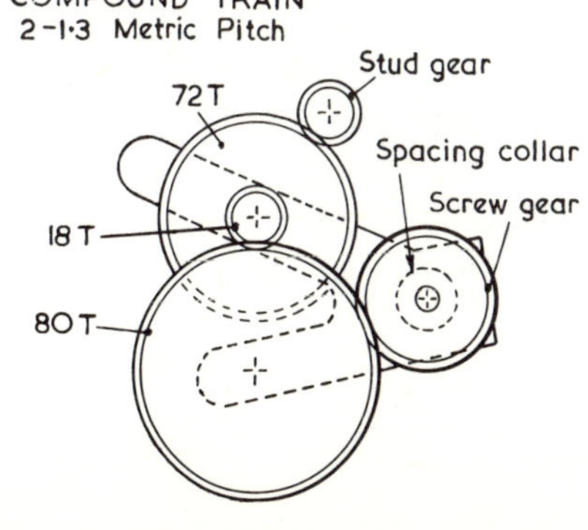

Internal Threads. When cutting these it is especially important that the tool point is set exactly at centre height and that the tool has sufficient front clearance to prevent the heel of the tool from rubbing against the internal thread it has cut. The tool must not be long as there is always a tendency for it to spring or chatter and there must be enough clearance between the width of the tool and the diameter of the hole so that the tool can be backed out without difficulty after each cut.

Testing Threads. All threads should be tested with a screw thread gauge sometimes called a screw pitch gauge and the finished screw should be tested for diameter and pitch with a thread ring gauge or with the nut it has to fit; an internal thread should be a comfortable fit without binding and without play.

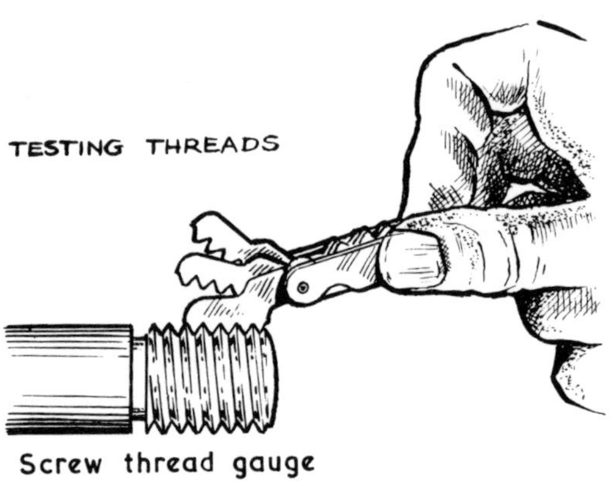

Square Threads. A square thread cutting tool must have the sides of the cutting end ground at an angle to allow for the helical slope of the screw.

Taps and Dies. Threads are sometimes cut with taps and dies while the work is held in the lathe. Some taps have a centre indentation on the top of the square end so that they can be fed into the hole with the tailstock centre while being turned by a tap wrench. The die can be in a die stock and fed by turning the tailstock spindle, or it can be fixed in a special tailstock die holder made to take ordinary dies, as shown. When a rod which has been turned in the lathe is to be screwed by hand, it is easier to start the thread squarely if the thread is started while the work is still in the lathe. The die, fixed in the die holder, is placed at right angles to and in position over the end of the rod. Then the tailstock spindle is applied tightly against the die and the work or the die can be turned slowly by hand and the first few threads will be cut true.

Students must learn to use a lathe before they can work out their own assignments. A good introduction to lathework is spigot turning, turning the rivet on the metal used for the pegs of the rake and utensil rack shown on p. 42. Later, parts of other assignments will provide good turning practice, e.g. knurled nuts for adjustable spanners as shown on p. 51 and hacksaw fittings. There are many ways of making a hacksaw and this makes a very good design brief, but this turned fitting will always be needed and the handle shown on p. 123 can be made use of. The plumb bob is a safe exercise in taper turning using the compound rest as described on p. 63. Hexagonal mild steel bar is drilled and turned on the lathe for the small screwdriver handle in which the blade is screwed and brazed. The hammer and large screwdriver have cast aluminium alloy handles and the end of their ϕ 6 mm stems are slightly flattened so that they will not turn in their handles or fall through the 6 mm hole in the two-piece mould while the handles are cast around the stems. This two-piece mould is made by drilling and bolting together two similar pieces of mild steel and gripping them in a four-jaw chuck while drilling out the mould. A G-cramp should hold the top together while casting. The handles and the cast steel hammer head which must be hardened and tempered are turned to shape. The door handle could be cast from an ingot made in the same mould but the handle shown is built up from brass, wood, and coloured plastic material screwed together and turned in one piece. Poker and shovel handles could be made in the same way while varying the shape and the materials. Simple tools are always good school exercises and tap wrenches, opposite and on p. 48, offer many interesting possibilities. Die stocks can be turning assignments.

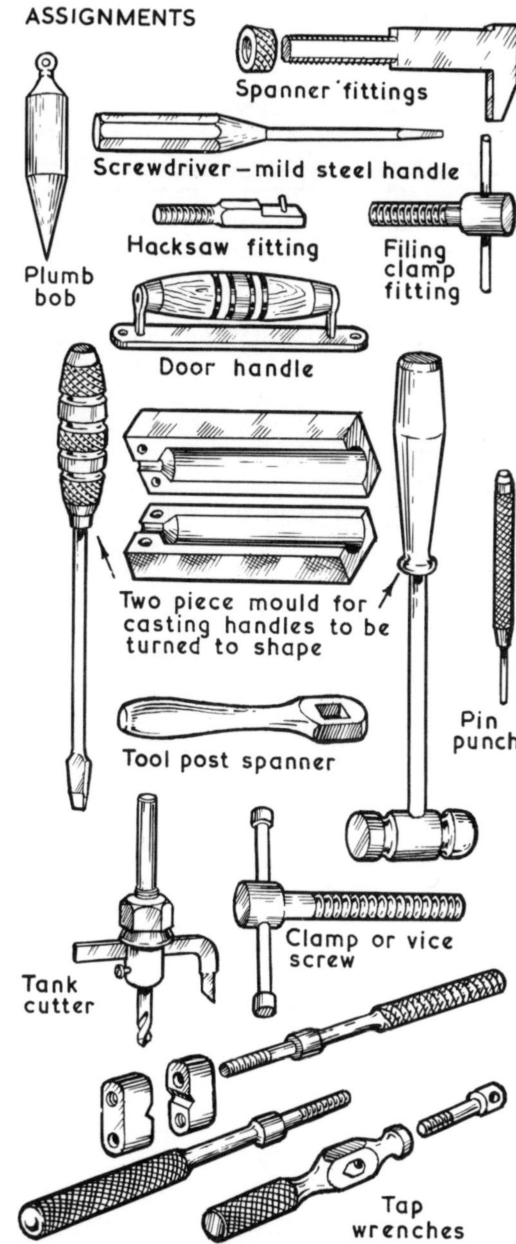

The cruet involves taper turning and could be made of aluminium alloy or stainless steel or brass and wood, possibly teak, turned together by building up the materials on brass tube. In this case the tube acts as the inside container so the taper might have to be modified. The tray could be of aluminium alloy, cast and turned, or of wood. The stock of the marking gauge is aluminium alloy. The weather vane illustrated functions because the upper part is turned and drilled to rotate on a point which is turned on the lower part. An alternative method would be to drill down the upright of the lower part, fit the arrow on to thinner material, the end of which is turned to a point, or it could be rounded and a ball bearing dropped in the hole in the lower part. Oscillating engines are always popular and involve various fittings and turning processes. The frame of the vertical steam engine is fabricated while the horizontal frame is cast. One hole is drilled in the cylinder and two in the frame, inlet and outlet, and these coincide alternately with the cylinder port as the cylinder oscillates. These engines should be part of a larger group assignments, part of which would be to see whether, and if so how, the engines would work. A group assignment would be to make a boiler and use the boiler to test and find the comparative efficiency of the same or of several different types of engines.

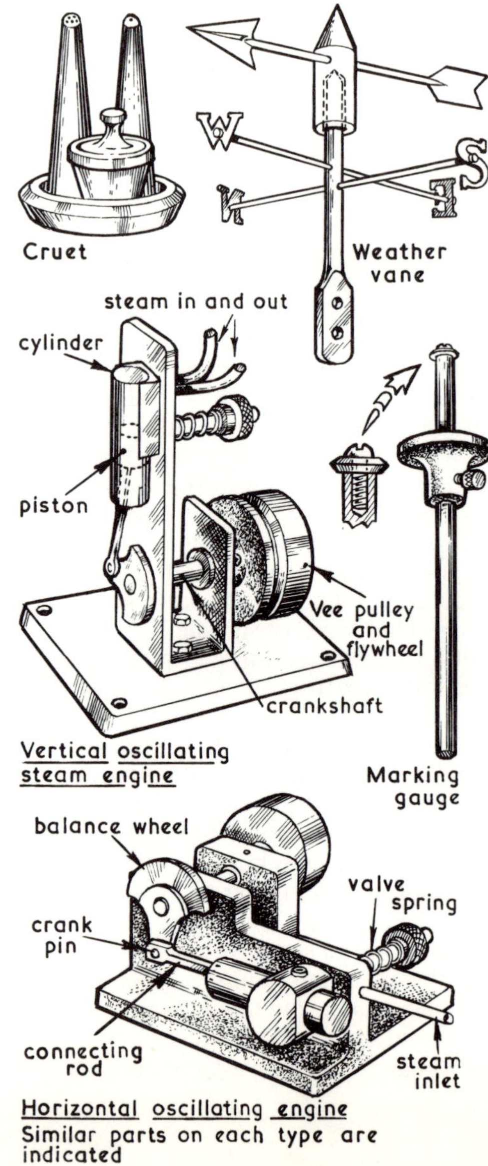

Similar parts on each type are indicated

Plate 11. **Candlesticks**

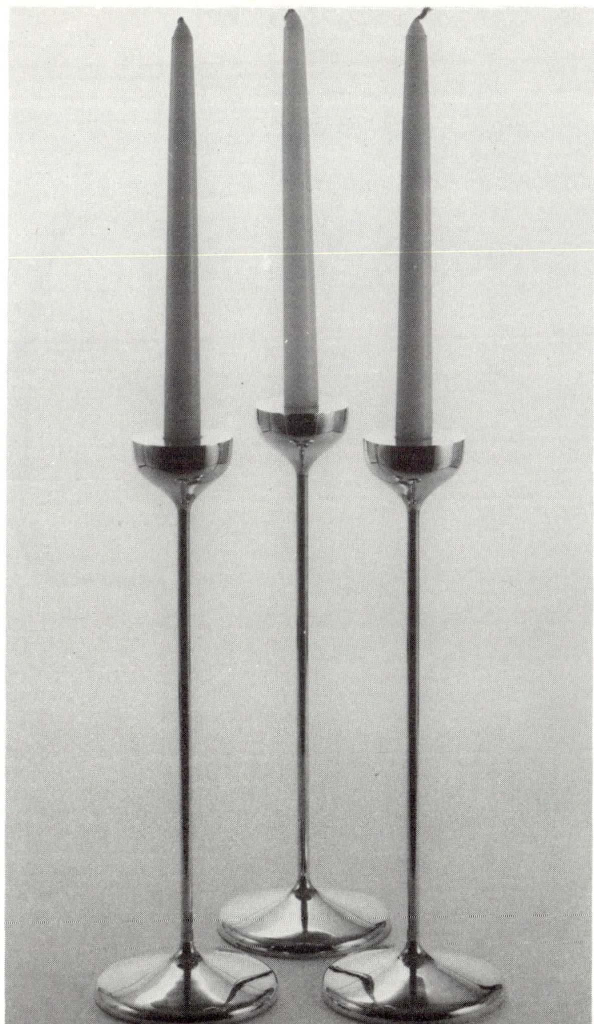

Sterling silver candlesticks by Robert Welch chosen by Mr. Harold Wilson as gifts from his government to Mr. Kosygin of the Soviet Union and to the Prime Minister of Canada

Taper candlesticks with silver gilt filigree frames on forged silver stems by Stuart Devlin

Plate 12. **Metalwork by Robert Welch**

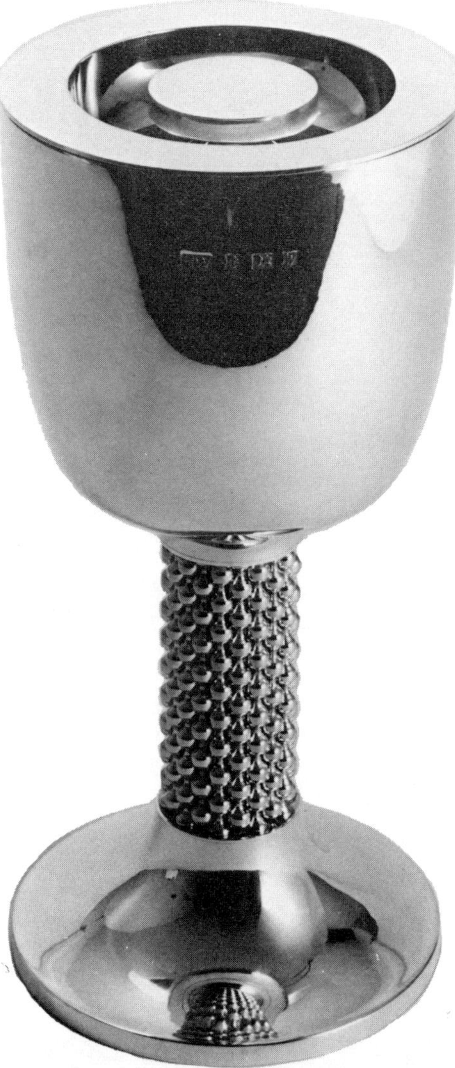

Trophy in sterling silver. Stem composed of interlocking spherical forms and, like the well of the lid, gold plated

The latest in Old Hall Tableware, a new tall slim vacuum jug of stainless steel fitted with a replaceable vacuum liner and an airtight rubber stopper so that coffee may be made before dinner and served steaming hot even after several courses

13

Sheet Metalwork—Tools and Processes

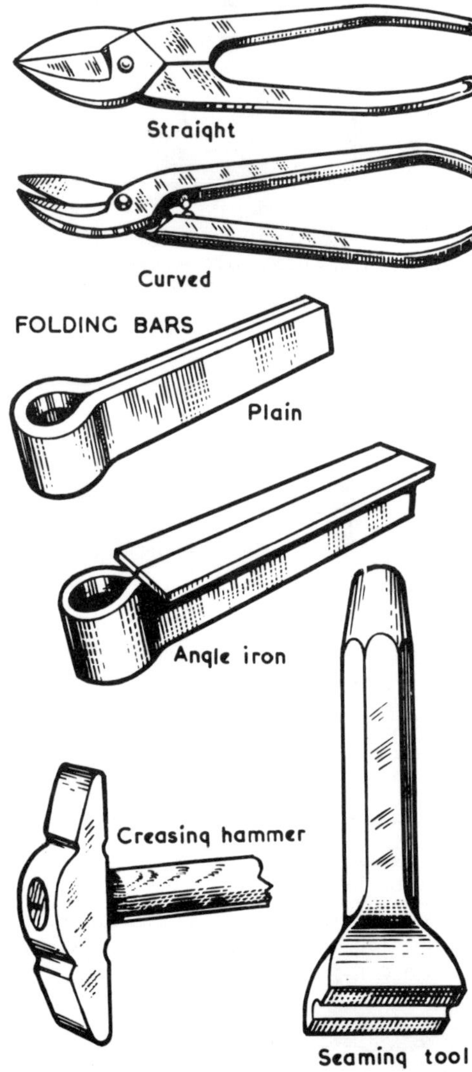

Sheet metalwork includes bending, pressing and stamping metal to shape, e.g. sheet iron car bodies, aluminium house frames, galvanised iron tanks and tinplate cans; and the joining of the parts together. Sheet metalwork in school generally involves the use of tinplate. The work is set out accurately (developments) and the metal is cut out with tinsnips and bent to shape in folding bars held in the vice or over special stakes with polished surfaces, by hand or with a mallet. A hammer cannot be used because it marks tinplate. Straight tinsnips are suitable for most jobs including external curves: bent or curved snips are used for internal curves. Work is joined by soft soldering or riveting. Shapes can be flat or curved and the latter include cylindrical and conical work. Trays, baking tins and boxes are the basic flat exercises; measures, scoops and pastry cutters are well known cylindrical examples, while the funnel is a typical conical job. Developments are essential. They can be prepared on paper in the drawing office and stuck on the metal. Simple developments such as those for flat work, rectangular trays and boxes, can be drawn direct on the metal, with pencil or a copper scriber. For flat boxes, the sides usually fold up from a flat bottom; a rectangle of metal bent round forms a cylinder and a bottom can be fitted, to make a vessel; conical articles are made by folding up sectors of circles. A semi-circular piece of metal forms a cone, the elevation of which is an equilateral triangle.

Stakes. The **Horse** holds a variety of **Heads** which have innumerable uses as special stakes:

Half-moon Stake for throwing up edges on curved work;
Hatchet Stake for a straight sharp bend;
Creasing Iron for heavier flat work, for working beads and hollows;
Round Bottom or **Canister Stake** for flat bottoms of cylindrical work;
Bick Iron for small flat work and narrow cylindrical and conical work;
Extinguisher Stake for light work, especially when the length of the bick iron is inconvenient;
Tinman's Anvil for truing flat work (top face is highly polished);
Funnel Stake for conical work.

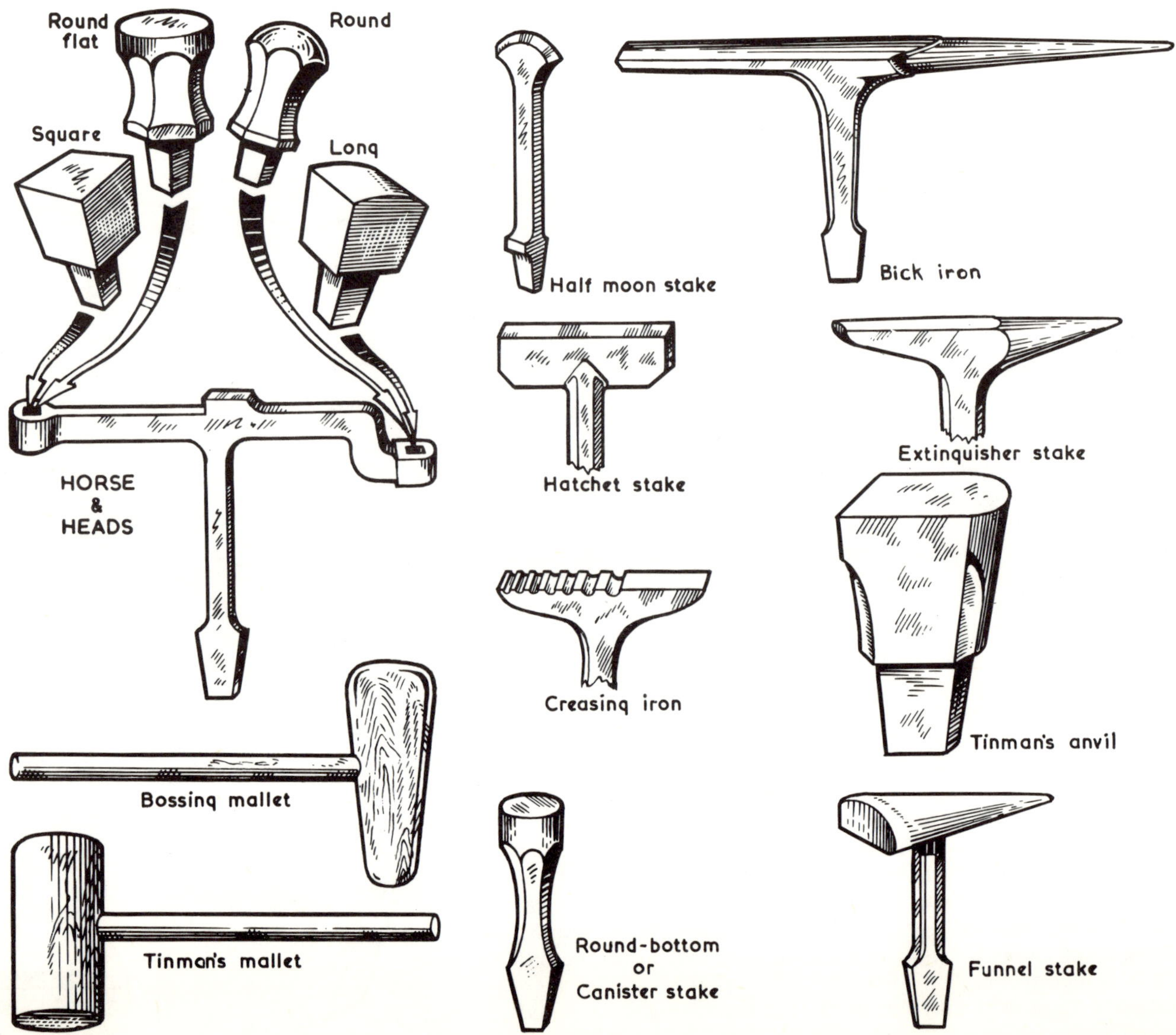
Round
flat
Round
Square
Long
HORSE
&
HEADS
Half moon stake
Bick iron
Hatchet stake
Extinguisher stake
Creasing iron
Tinman's anvil
Bossing mallet
Tinman's mallet
Round-bottom
or
Canister stake
Funnel stake

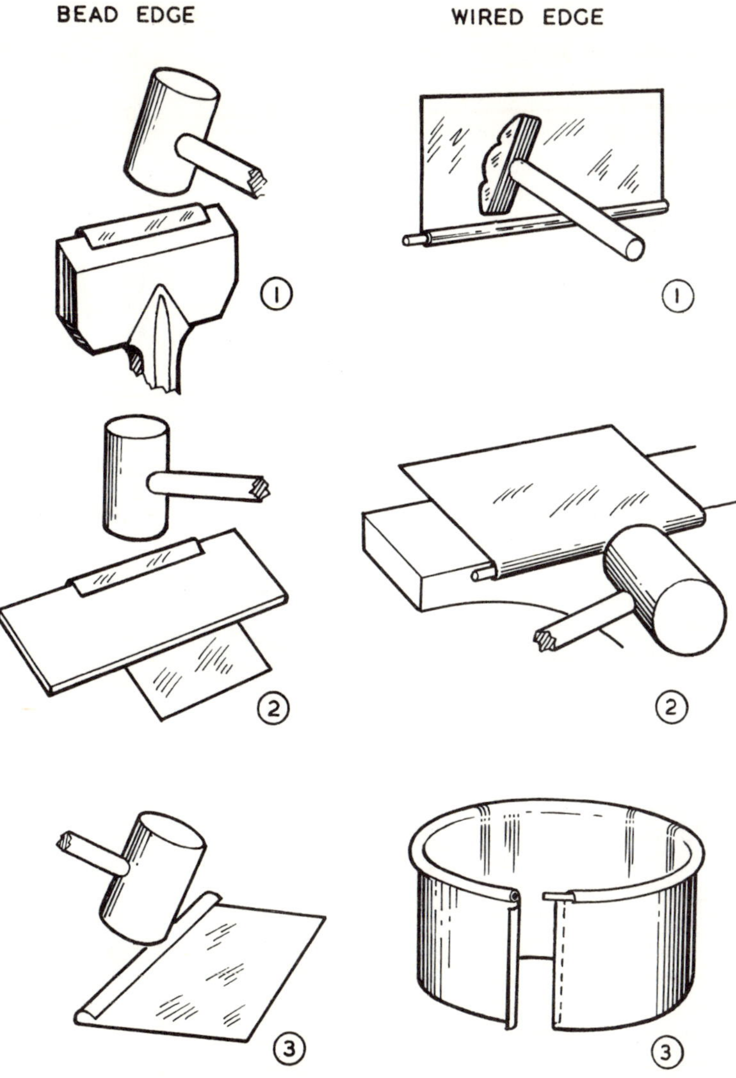

Safe Edges

Sheet metal has dangerous sharp edges and bending over the edge, a **bead edge,** or wrapping it around a wire, a **wired edge,** are common safety practices. In each case the first step is to bend the edge over a hatchet stake. To avoid a flattened bent-back edge a thin strip of metal is inserted in the bend and the edge is folded down evenly over this strip so that it can be tucked in to form a bead. When wiring the edge the wire is inserted and the edge tucked in around the wire with a creasing hammer (sometimes called a tucking or a peening hammer), as a mallet cannot be used in this case. To avoid hammer marks the edge can sometimes be tucked in with small hardwood wedges which are tapped with a hammer, but this is a two-handed job. The illustrations show a straight bead edge and a wired edge on a cylinder.

Seams

Cylindrical and conical work is joined by seaming. Two common seams are the simple lap seam and the **grooved seam.** The latter is a strong watertight joint especially if it is soldered. It is made by bending over opposite edges, one up and the other down (1), shaping the rectangular piece cylindrical (2) and hooking the two edges together to form the seam, which is malleted close (3) trued up with a seaming tool (4) and soldered. The bottom can be a plain disc fitted and soldered in position, or the bottom edge of the cylinder can be turned in and the disc rested upon this flat circular lap.

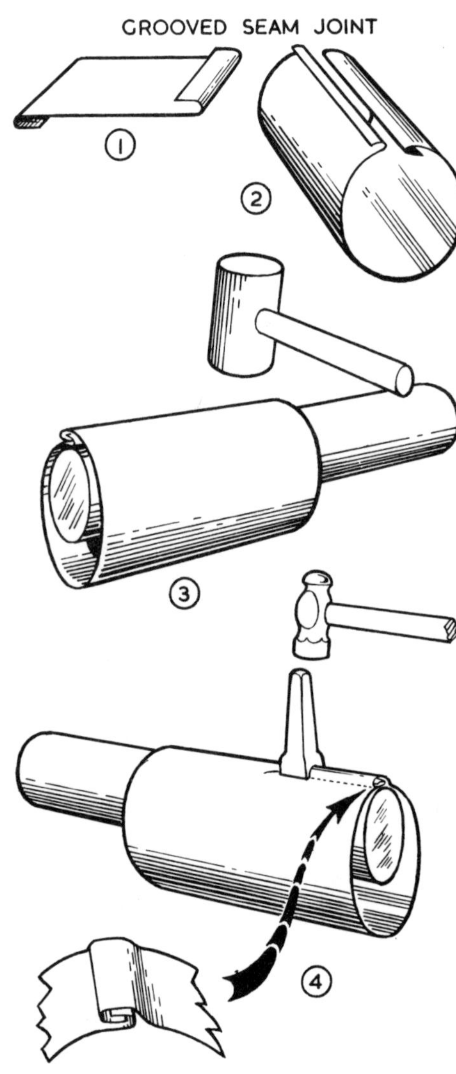

Alternatively, the edge of the disc can be turned up and the cylinder fitted inside the lap and soft soldered. The strongest and surest watertight seam for the bottom of a circular vessel is the circular over-folded seam or the **knocked-up bottom.** The bottom circle is cut larger than the cylinder circle allowing twice the width of the seam all round. Half of this, the width of the seam, is bent up all round on a half-moon stake (1) and the bottom is trued, from the outside on a flat top round stake and from the inside on a tinman's anvil. A lap, the width of the seam, is bent outwards with a bossing mallet (2), and this lap is placed flat inside the bottom (3) and secured by tapping the vertical bottom lap inwards and down upon the bent-out lap of the cylinder (4). This is trued by placing the seam upside down over the edge of the anvil or extinguisher stake and malleting carefully. The seam in this form is called a circular folded seam, or a panned down bottom. If, however, it is made neater by placing the vessel over the end of a cylindrical bar and knocking over the seam with a mallet (5), it becomes a knocked-up bottom. Finally the seam should be soft soldered.

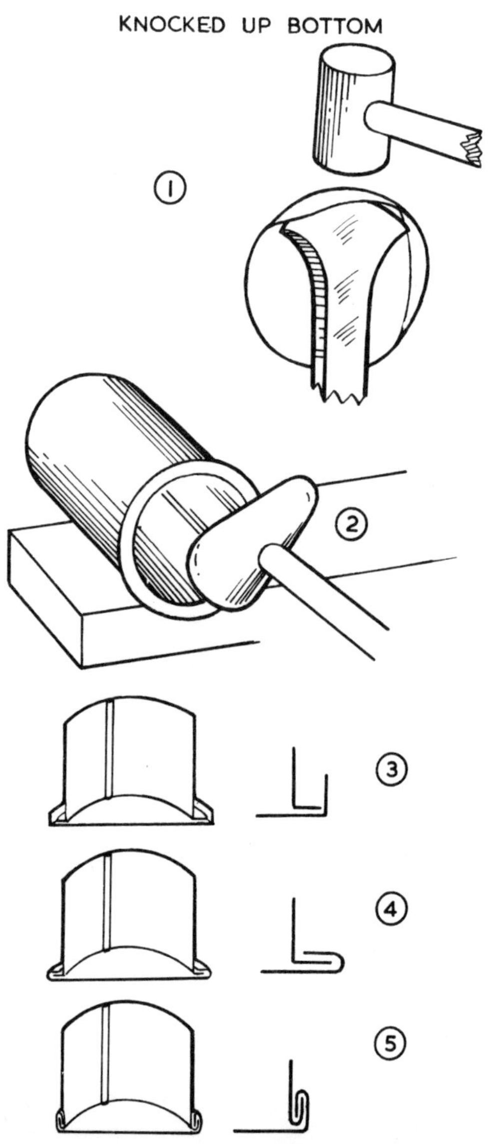

14

Sheet Metalwork—Soft Soldering

Soft Soldering is a simple way of joining metals, but it is not a strong method and it does not withstand high temperatures. It is used considerably in electrical work, especially in telephone and radio work, and on tinplate. A low melting point alloy, usually of tin and lead, is melted by a heated copper bit, wrongly called a soldering iron, or a blowpipe. With the aid of a flux it will adhere to the clean surface of some metals—especially copper, brass, lead and tinplate. The melting point depends largely on the proportions of tin and lead. Tinman's fine solder consists of two parts tin and one part lead and its melting point is 185° C. Ordinary solder, equal parts, melts around 200° C, and plumber's solder, two parts lead to one of tin, melts at between 200 and 225° C. A little antimony, up to 3%, is often added to save tin. It reduces the melting point and increases the tensile strength, and is cheaper than tin. Bismuth and cadmium are mixed with tin and lead for very low melting point solders, e.g. wood's metal (M.P. 70° C). A flux is necessary to help the solder flow evenly. It also prevents oxidation and in the case of an active flux it helps to clean the metal. Active fluxes are acid fluxes, usually based upon killed spirits, e.g. Baker's Fluid, and they cause corrosion unless the joint is washed and wiped. They should never be used on electrical work. Killed spirits is made by pouring some hydrochloric acid in a beaker and slowly adding small pieces of zinc until all effervescence ceases. Non-corrosive fluxes such as Fluxite are usually based on resin. Cored solder, which is used so much in electrical work, has a core of resin flux inside a tube of tinman's solder.

Soldering irons vary in weight between 100 g and 1 kg, and are of two main kinds, hatchet and straight irons. They are usually heated in gas soldering stoves or furnaces, but they lose heat as soon as they are taken from the stove and

SOLDERING IRONS

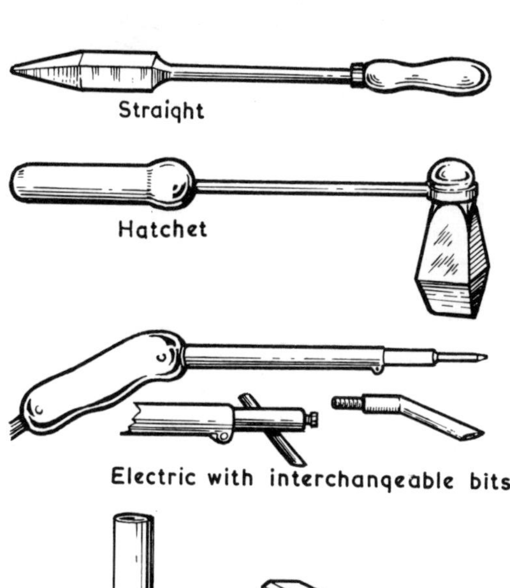

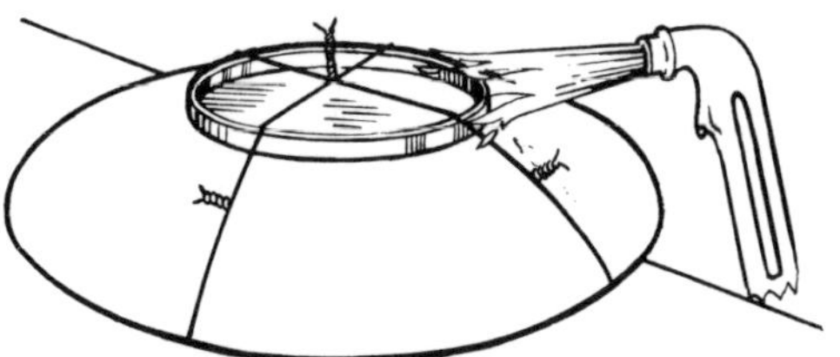

they lose heat quickly in use. Electric soldering irons are very popular today because they can be supplied with heat all the time. The two main varieties of electric soldering irons are the straight or heavy iron with a fixed bit, and the lighter types with interchangeable bits which are particularly useful on inaccessible electrical work.

Tinning. The copper bit must be tinned before use. Tinning consists of heating the bit (a green flame indicates sufficient heat for a gas heated iron), cleaning it with an emery stick or file, coating it with flux and rubbing the bit in solder until the end is tinned.

Soft Soldering. Some excess solder clings to the bit which can be applied to the joint after it has been cleaned and fluxed. The copper bit must be held against the joint to heat it before the solder will run. More solder can be picked up by the bit and transferred to the joint but for a large job it may be quicker to apply the stick of solder to the bit while actually soldering. The molten solder first tins the surfaces of the metal and then runs into the small gap. The copper bit must be moved slowly along the joint: it must be hot enough to heat the joint and melt the solder and must be changed or reheated as soon as it is cool. If it is overheated, the tinning is spoilt. The metal must be cleaned with emery cloth or steel wool. Solder cannot adhere to dirty or greasy metal.

Sweating is heating and so joining together two close surfaces which have previously been tinned. A **Wiped Joint** is the plumber's joint. The solder is melted with a blowlamp and wiped around the pipe joint with a rag while the solder is pasty, not quite molten. **Blowpipe Soft Soldering** is a quick and neat way of joining two surfaces as when fixing a base to a bowl (*see* p. 83). The soft solder can be applied in stick form but it is better cut into small pellets and placed around, preferably inside, the already fluxed joint. A small blowpipe flame will melt and draw the solder along the joint quickly and easily. Britannia metal, commonly called pewter, is soldered with a mouth blowpipe and a low melting point solder (100° C) composed of two parts tin and one each of lead and bismuth.

Tinplate is mild steel coated with tin; (*a*) "coke tinplate" by "hot dipping", i.e. dipping in molten tin and passing the steel sheets through rollers which gives a tin layer one thousandth of a millimetre, and (*b*) by electroplating, as for four-fifths of the world's tinplate. This gives a thinner layer—possibly a hundredth of a millimetre, so is slightly cheaper. Tinplate combines the strength of mild steel with the corrosion resistance, solderability and good appearance of tin. It is sold in sheets of several standard sizes, e.g. 700 mm × 500 mm; the thickness of the plate varies between 0.20 and 0.80 mm and it is graded according to weight. Useful grades for the school workshop are IC (0.3 mm), IX (0.375 mm), 2X (0.425 mm) and 3X (0.475 mm).

Plate 13. **Sculpture by Yvonne Poulton**

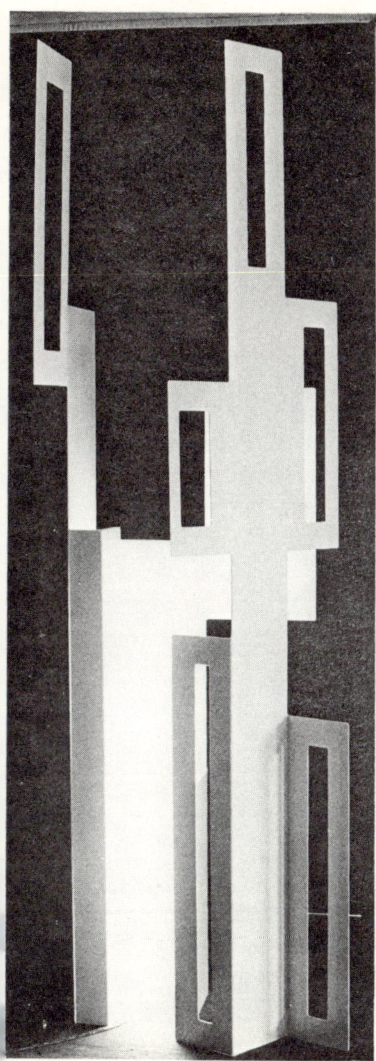

Outdoor metal sculptures in stainless steel

Plate 14. **Forged Sculptures by Students**

"Fish" forged from scrap; the waste centre piece between four cut out circles. Tutor, Paul Bridge

"Droopy Bird" forged from sheet iron. Tutor, Robert Rignall

"The Cock". Welding wire welded on to plate which has been cut and filed to shape. Tutor, Robert Rignall

Assignments

Many articles some of which are suggested on p. 86 can be made in school from commercial tins. Blocking tins can be used for wheels, tobacco tins for burners to heat steam boilers (*see* p. 78) and larger tins are used for the turbines, the watering can, the engine boiler and the toy roller which is part filled with sand before the lid is soldered on. The windmill is driven by a jet of water on simple vanes which can be inside or outside the main body. The spade is of sheet iron and the socket is formed by folding the end around the wooden handle. One tool box is of sheet iron riveted and the other is of 3X tinplate soft soldered and strengthened by bending the edges at right angles. The candlesticks are designed as Christmas table decorations and like the toys are painted gay colours. They are made of tinned iron wire and conical candle holders soldered together. The label is cartridge paper held on to tinplate by folding over the edges and is offered as an extremely elementary but useful exercise. The pots on the plant stand are made of tinplate, painted red, and are for cactus plants. The wire stand is painted white.

Yvonne Poulton's sculpture, Plate 13, suggests interesting design briefs for indoor sculptures. Pupils can fold, cut out and stand up paper shapes until they are satisfied and then transfer the idea to metal. If desired extra pieces can be soldered or riveted in position and the final sculpture polished or painted.

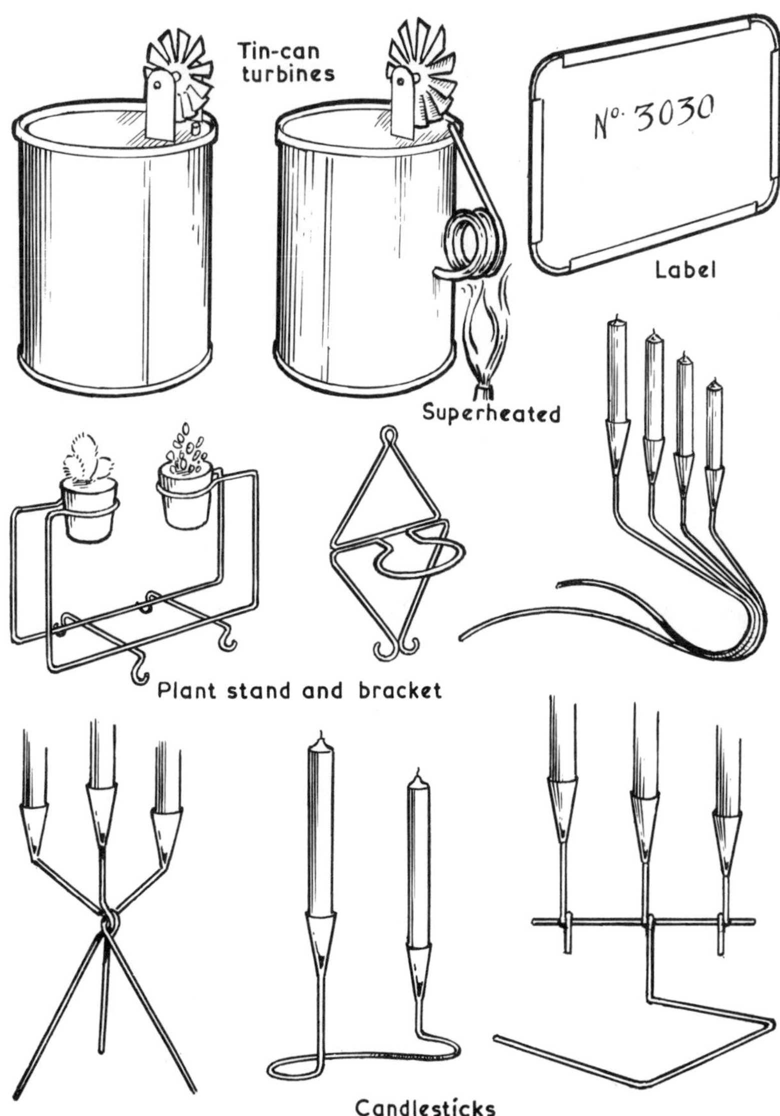

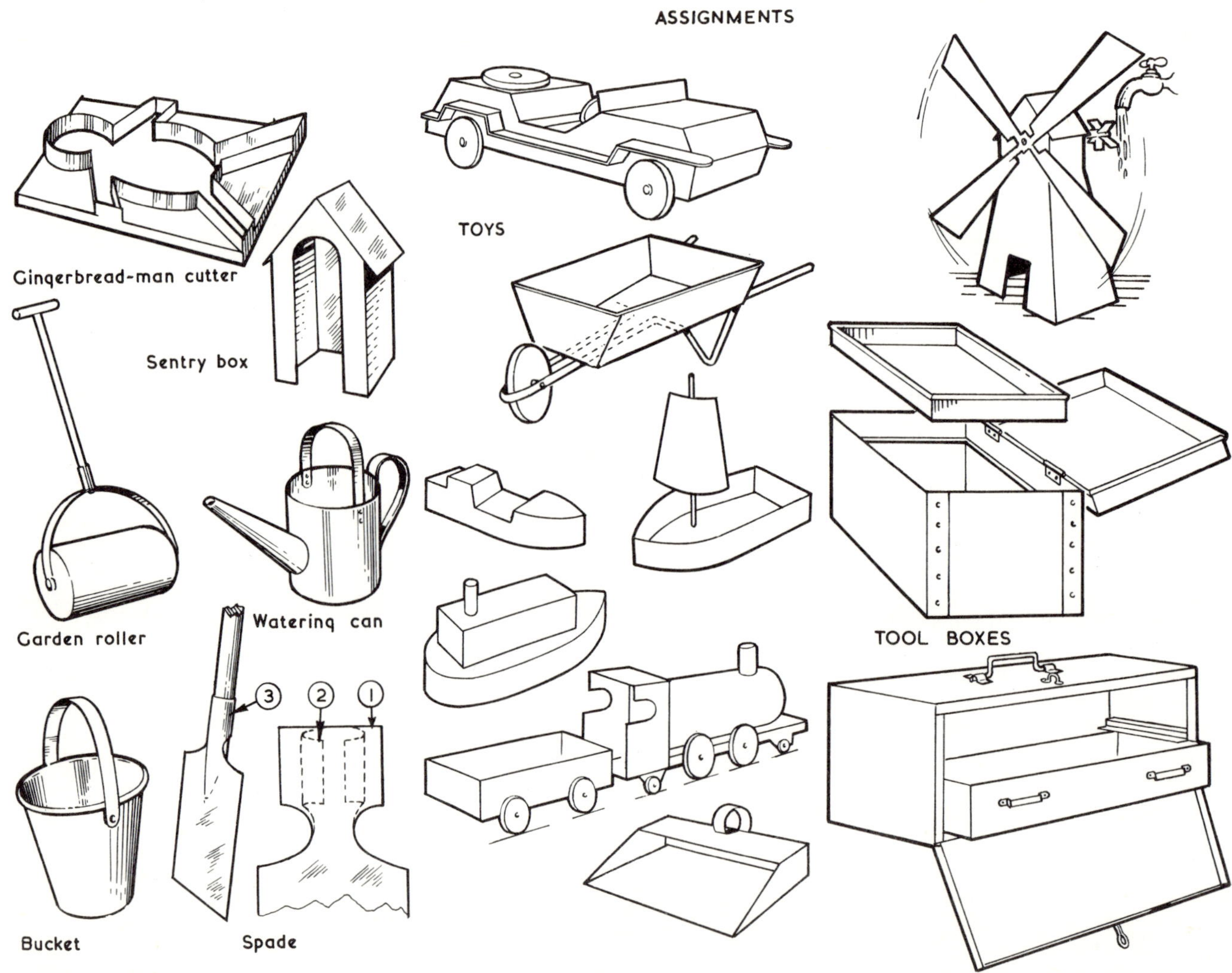
ASSIGNMENTS
Gingerbread-man cutter
TOYS
Sentry box
Garden roller
Watering can
TOOL BOXES
3
2
1
Bucket
Spade

Plate 15. **Silver Coffee Set by Alex Styles**

Made by Garrards for the town of Caernarvon on the occasion of the Investiture of the Prince of Wales. It was presented to him at the time

15

Beaten Metalwork—Hollowing, Seaming and Raising

Sheet metal can be pressed, spun or beaten to shape. Pressing is an important industrial process in which metal, e.g. motor car bodies, stainless steel sinks and aluminium boats, is pressed to shape between male and female steel dies of similar shape in very large machines.

Spinning consists of revolving a disc of thin metal in a lathe and pressing it steadily to shape with a long heavy blunt metal bar over a prepared wood or metal former which revolves with the disc. This is an interesting process but it is largely repetitive and can be very dangerous for beginners.

Beaten metalwork involves hammering sheet metal to form hollow shapes, plates, trays, dishes, jugs, basins, etc. Any sheet metal can be formed this way; stainless steel is very difficult to work but is fashionable at present; pewter used to be popular and gold and silver have always been favoured, but copper, brass, gilding metal and nickel silver are used in schools. Copper 0.80 to 1.25 mm thick is suitable for beginners but gilding metal produces the best results, especially as it can be polished to an attractive golden colour. Brass is a little harder, as is nickel silver, which is particularly suitable for domestic articles. Beaten metalwork is not precision work: a variation of one-eighth of an inch in the height or width of a hammered vessel may not matter, but it enables one to experience the flow of cold malleable metal under the influence of the hammer, and to produce pleasing shapes.

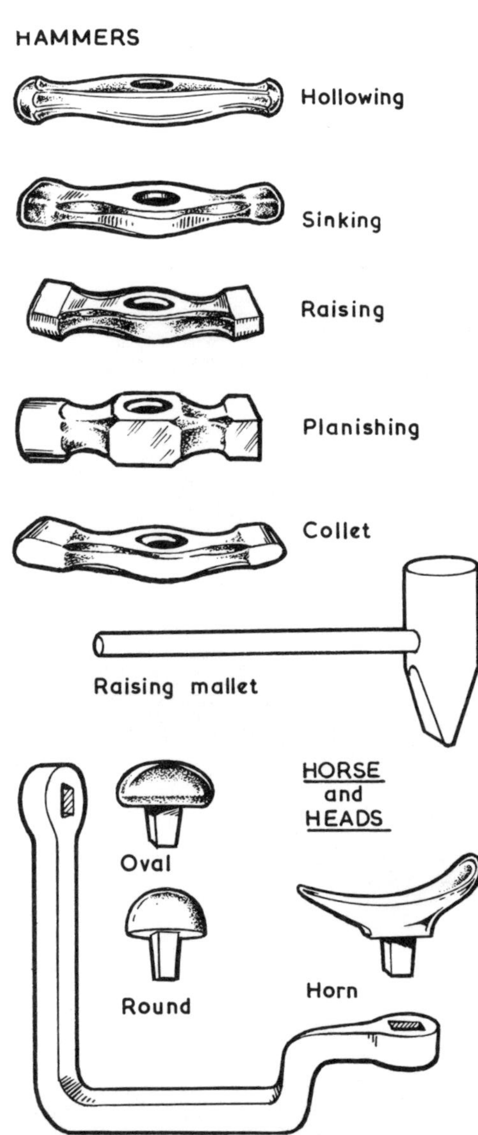

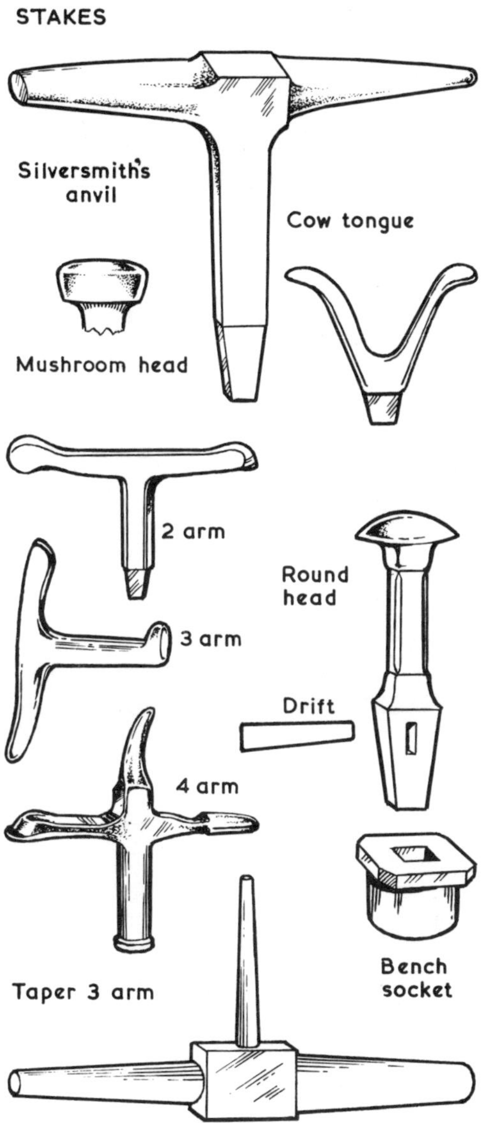

Annealing, Pickling, Cleaning. Metal can be shaped most successfully when it is soft and clean. Cold rolled sheet metal should be used as it has a better surface than hot rolled. It is supplied hard, half-hard or annealed. To ensure that the metal is soft, it is advisable to begin by annealing. Copper, gilding metal, brass and nickel silver can be annealed similarly, by heating to a dull red heat, preferably on a revolving brazing hearth with a gas blowpipe and allowing to cool, if possible on the heated coke. Copper may be quenched but quenching causes distortion; it may cause surface cracks in copper-zinc alloys and it hardens nickel silver. Heating causes oxides to form on the surfaces of the metal which are removed by pickling—dipping into an acid bath. Various mixtures of sulphuric, hydrochloric and nitric acids are used, especially for bright dips which clean immediately, but for the school workshop dilute sulphuric acid —one part acid added to eight to ten of water—is excellent and it need not be heated. Silversmiths prefer a warm bath, as it acts quickly but it gives off more fumes. Metal should be dipped cool. If hot, the acid will spurt and may cause serious harm. It will certainly burn the worker's clothing. After pickling for a few minutes the metal is washed, scrubbed with pumice powder, dried and polished with a rag. If dirty metal is beaten, small particles of oxide or other foreign matter, possibly iron filings, may be transferred to the hammer or the stake and this may damage their faces as well as the surface of the sheet metal. Damp causes rust on hammers and stakes and this can be disastrous. The working faces of stakes and hammers can be cleaned and resurfaced with emery cloth or on a revolving mop dressed with emery. The edge of a stitched mop, *see* p. 96, is coated with glue and rubbed on to and into the desired grade of emery powder. Most metals harden as they are worked and annealing is frequently necessary in beaten metalwork, especially while raising.

The fundamental processes in beaten metalwork are hollowing, seaming, raising and mounting. The latter is the assembling of parts made by the first three methods. All parts are to be planished before mounting and the usual method of joining is silver soldering.

Hollowing is a simple process, suitable for beginners and enabling them to make simple bowls, trays, spoons, etc., without much difficulty. Shallow dishes of all shapes can be hollowed. Some are useful as ash trays but the usual ash tray, octagonal or square, with a rim and possibly hollows for cigarettes, is difficult to produce successfully and is not a beginner's job. First, the blank must be cut to size; this can only be estimated because hollowing stretches the metal and this has to be allowed for. A suitable approximation for the diameter of the blank for a circular bowl is to add the diameter to the depth of the finished bowl. Thus a bowl, 170 mm diameter and 50 mm deep, can be beaten from a 220 mm blank. If the metal is stretched too much, it will become thin and may split, so tall vessels must be seamed or raised. The depth of a hollowed bowl should not exceed one-third of the diameter.

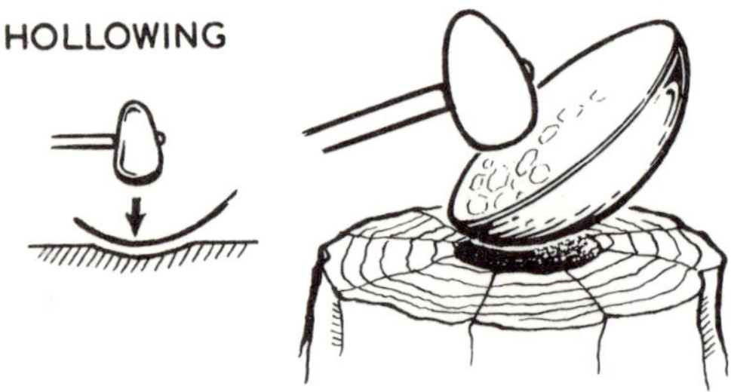

Hollowing is hammering, or malleting sheet metal into a hollow, often cut in the end of a tree trunk, although a wooden block resting on the bench or held in the vice is a satisfactory alternative. Sometimes a sandbag is used or,

for small work, a lead block, but sandbags split if carelessly used and the size and shape of the hollow vary with the power and position of the blows. After the blank has been cut, filed true, annealed, pickled and cleaned, it is hollowed, working in circles around the edge, and moving gradually inwards. To begin at the middle may be quicker but this tends to stretch the metal irregularly and may produce an ugly shape. The bossing or pear-shaped mallet is best for beginners and is always suitable for the larger curves of simple bowls, but hammers can be used more accurately, especially for small radii work.

Blocking and **Sinking** are similar processes used for hollowing shallow shapes, especially when a flat bottom is required. Blocking is the making of plates, ash trays and shallow bowls, and is done with a **Hollowing** or **Doming Hammer** which has hemispherical faces. Sinking refers mainly to traymaking and a **Sinking Hammer** has rectangular faces with the corners rounded (*see* p. 88).

Seaming is bending sheet metal to shape and joining the edges with a butt-jointed silver-soldered seam. This process is particularly suitable for tall vessels, usually cylindrical or conical, although square, hexagonal and octagonal seamed articles are popular. Seamed shapes can be splayed outwards over a cylindrical stake or raised inwards to make them barrel shaped. The bottom can be silver-soldered on, or preferably inserted and soldered one-sixteenth up from

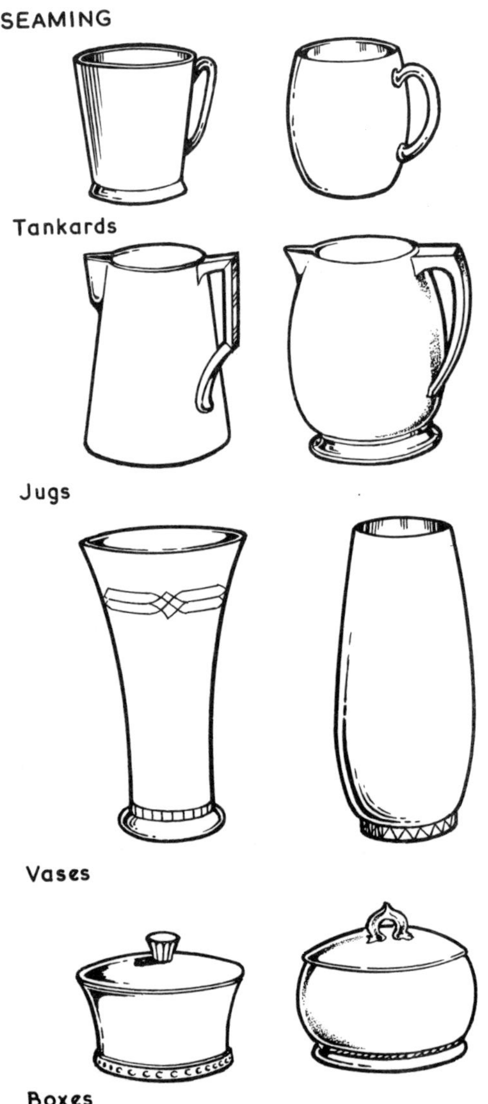

the lower edge. Another method is to raise inwards the bottom of a seamed vessel, curving the bottom and making the bottom opening smaller and smaller until it meets at a point which is sealed with a spot of silver solder. Vessels made in this way are usually mounted on circular bases. Seaming is easier than raising. Seamed work, especially flat work like the three napkin rings and the octagonal box on p. 91 can be bent to shape and polished dull, satin or matt finish.

Raising is the fundamental silversmithing process and is vital for the best craftsmanship. Any shape can be raised. The work is hammered on the outside, in circles from the middle outwards, contracting the metal on to a firm heavy stake of suitable size and shape. The work is easier if the edge of the blank is first turned inwards by hollowing. A circle must be marked on the outside for the first raising and when making a vessel with a flat base this circle indicates the base. The metal is held firmly against the end of a stake. The part struck must be just above the stake and should be forced on to it. The metal is hammered around one circle and then it is moved back, slid off the stake a little, so that the second round of hammering again takes place over the edge of the stake, and the raising continues in circles until the edge of the metal is reached. Each stage, raising from the middle to the edge or from the bottom to the top, is called a course and the process is sometimes called coursing. After each coursing the metal must be annealed. The work must be firmly held throughout so that it is not displaced by the hammer blows. If the metal is struck where it is resting on the stake, the sound of the blow will be different, solid and metallic, and the metal will be stretched. If it is allowed to ride up the stake the vibrations set up by hammering cause the base of the job to vibrate against the end of the stake and the flat base will be marked and possibly stretched and curved. Variations of shape such as turning in the top can be achieved by beginning the courses at varying distances from the bottom.

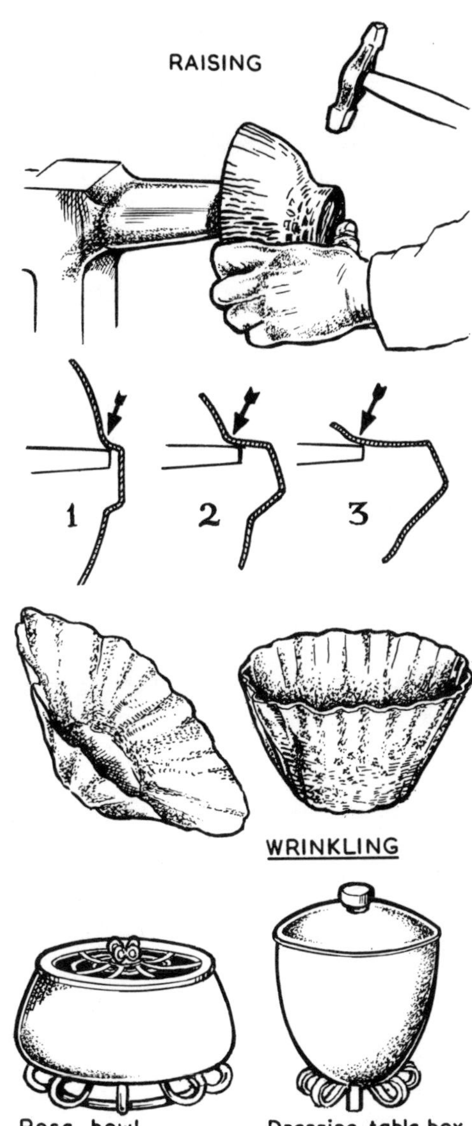

Buckling and undue creasing of the metal must be avoided and if one crease is allowed to overlap another, especially at the edge, splitting is inevitable. If splits do occur they must be silver-soldered at once.

Some craftsmen vary their method of raising by **Wrinkling** or creasing the metal radially after annealing, and before the next coursing. If this is done accurately the raising is easier and quicker but irregular wrinkling causes many problems and is difficult to correct.

A **Raising Mallet** is often used in schools by beginners; this is an ordinary tinman's mallet with one end cut wedge-shaped to form a rectangular face (*see* p. 88). This is less accurate and slower than raising with a hammer, but it does not damage the surface of the metal as a hammer does.

A **Raising Hammer** (*see* p. 88) has flat rectangular faces with its edges and corners slightly rounded. If they are left sharp, a careless blow may cut the metal.

A **Planishing Hammer** is double ended with two polished faces (p. 88). One end is always circular, slightly curved, and the other is sometimes square and flat. Such hammers vary in weight between 100 g and 2 kg, but a 200 g hammer is convenient and pleasant to use.

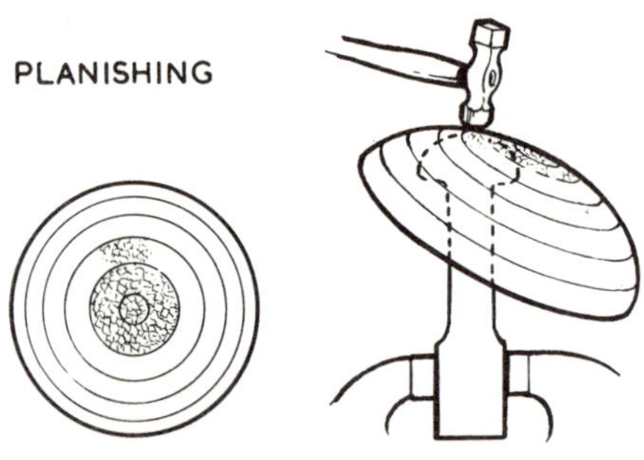

Planishing. Metal which has been hollowed, seamed or raised must be planished to true the shape of the vessel and to improve and make uniform the surface of the metal. The vessel is first malleted smooth and to shape over a suitable stake, and is then carefully hammered all over with a planishing hammer to true and improve the surface. Silversmiths and goldsmiths planish without leaving a visible mark. In the school workshop planishing hammer marks are left showing, but this is incidental, not by design. Planishing is an essential constructional process, not decoration.

Most vessels are planished from the outside with a flat or almost flat hammer on a curved stake. A flat hammer face gives good results but is difficult to use, as its sharp edges may damage the metal. The shape of the stake must be near to that of the bowl but a little more curved, never flatter. The blows must be uniform and regular, and each blow should partly cover the previous hammer marks. This is achieved on simple shapes, such as circular bowls, by drawing concentric circles in pencil, 10 mm apart, on the outside of the bowl and planishing from the middle following these lines. Each blow should be delivered the same way on the same part of the stake, the work being moved slightly after each blow, working round between the concentric circles until the whole surface has been hammered. When flat work is planished, a hammer with a slightly curved face is used on a flat stake, hammering in lines down or across the surface, or radially according to the shape of the work, but planishing in a circular or spiral direction tends to curve the surface. Raised articles often have to be planished twice, as the first planishing may not remove all the hammer marks. Hammering must be light, many light blows being much better than a few heavy ones. All parts must be planished separately before assembly. After assembly few parts of the work can be hammered as the inevitable unequal hammering and vibrations may cause distortion and spoil the surface.

The faces of all stakes and hammers must be kept in good condition, brightly polished when in use and greased when stored.

Copper Work. Copper is excellent material for early school exercises but, after heating to redness it is very soft and may be distorted by careless handling, so that it is inadvisable to complete a copper job with a silver-soldered joint. Soft soldering carried out with a blowpipe (*see* p. 83) is suitable for the final mounting of a base on a copper bowl, for then the job will remain hard. Contrary to widely held beliefs, articles with soft-soldered joints can be pickled and plated provided the joint is a good one. If soft-solder has been allowed to run outside the joint it must be removed before these operations. There should be a separate hearth for soft soldering or, at the very least, a separate large firebrick, 300 × 300 × 35 mm. The smallest spot of soft-solder present during silver soldering or brazing will, if it is in contact with the metal, spoil its surface and possibly cause a hole.

16

Beaten Metalwork—Silver Soldering; Polishing

Silver Soldering is similar to brazing. The solder is an alloy of silver, copper and zinc, and the soldering is done at a dull red heat. As in soft soldering, a flux is essential because the solder will not flow if it is allowed to oxidise. There are a number of proprietary fluxes on the market, but borax is generally suitable. Borax melts, and thus runs round and into the joint and on to the solder, so that the solder, when it melts, runs into and around the joint. As it cools, the borax solidifies glass-hard and can be removed only by pickling. There are three main grades of silver solder: easy or quick, which melts at about 715° C and consists of 67% silver, 23% copper and 10% zinc, medium (M.P. 720/765° C), 74%, 19% and 7%, and hard or enamelling (M.P. 730/800° C), 81% silver, 14% copper and 5% zinc. This high melting point is necessary, as enamelling is carried out in a furnace at red heat. The base of the coffee pot on p. 93 has three parts, a base ring, a moulding and a collet. The moulding is shaped from a disc and the middle of the disc is cut out with a piercing saw. The base ring and collet are bent round as strips and soldered with hard silver solder. The collet is then hammered to shape and the parts are assembled with medium silver solder and the completed base fixed to the coffee pot body with easy silver solder.

Hard silver solder is commonly used for seams. It is essential to use the correct solders so they must be recognised without difficulty. "Easy" is used most and can be purchased in strips and, if left plain, is recognisable. "Easy", "Medium" and "Hard" can all be bought in wire, strip or sheet form and the last two should be marked before use, "medium" by scratches and "hard" by hammer marks. When using sheet, 3 mm wide strips must be cut and marked similarly. Small pieces can be placed around the joint with the flux before heating, or the solder can be applied in strip form when the metal is red hot. Even when the correct silver solders are used, there is always a danger of the previous joints melting. If the joints become too hot the particles of solder tend to run into globules and so spoil the joint and the surface of the metal, but a coating of flux will keep the solder in its position. For intricate work, hinges and built-up handles, previous joints are protected by coating with rouge, loam or whiting mixed with water.

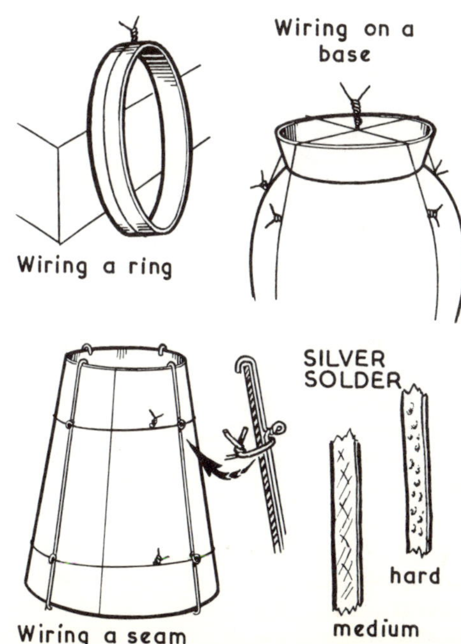

Wiring. Experienced craftsmen silver-solder joints without wiring, but this is inadvisable in the school workshop. Ring and body joints can be sprung together but expansion is inevitable and, as heating with a blowpipe cannot be uniform distortion may occur, so wiring is safer. Thin, soft iron binding wire ϕ 0.6–1.00 mm can be bound round the job and tightened by twisting. When a base is mounted on a bowl there should be extra twists in the form of loops at each side and these can be tightened or loosened at either side to adjust the position of the base until it is accurate, (*see* p. 95).

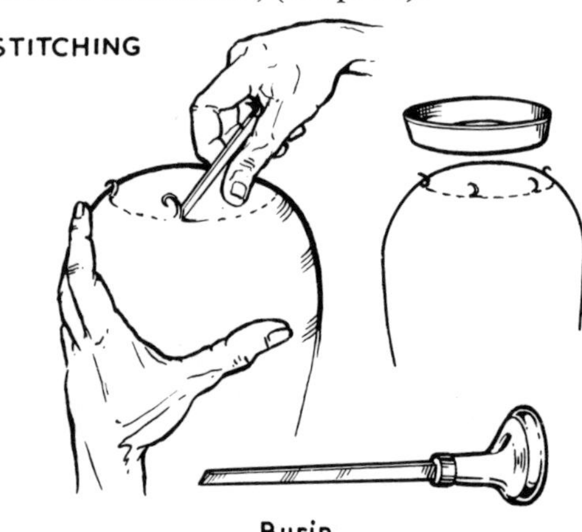

Stitching is a method of fixing by stitches, the position of a part which is to be soldered. The metal is cut under the joint when fixing a handle, or under the bowl when fixing a base, where the cuts will not be seen. An engraving tool is used which turns up a burr, and several burrs fix the position. Spouts and handle sockets are usually fixed this way.

Mounting. A job seldom consists of one piece of metal. In school it is easier and better to make and mount a base than to try to make a bowl with a flat bottom. Mounting is assembling, joining together parts which have been hollowed, seamed or raised. The ring base is the simplest mount. A strip of metal, say 6 × 3 mm is bent round, allowing a slight overlap, so that both pieces can be sawn through together to form the joint which is silver-soldered (see p. 95). The ring is planished circular and fitted and soldered to the bowl. Planishing stretches the metal and careless planishing may make the ring too large. In fitting, the exact position of the ring must be marked. A circle should be scribed on the bowl and a mark on the bowl made to correspond to a mark on the ring. Finally, this ring can be silver- or soft-soldered to the bowl. A built-up base as on the chalice or coffee pot (p. 93) consists of several parts made separately and silver-soldered together before mounting. This silver soldering in stages involves the use of the different grades of silver solder.

Polishing. Beaten metalwork is polished by holding the job against a revolving mop. Of the many kinds of mops, two are essential in schools—stitched or cutting mops for the first polishing and soft, open mops—unstitched, unbleached calico—which are for finishing. An abrasive is rubbed against the revolving mop and transferred to the work. Tripoli is the best abrasive for this work and Lustre, a proprietary polishing compound of tripoli and a fatty binding material, is suitable for schools. Emery polishing compound on a stitched mop is suitable for polishing hammers and stakes, whereas silver and gold are polished with rouge, using a swansdown mop for the final high polish.

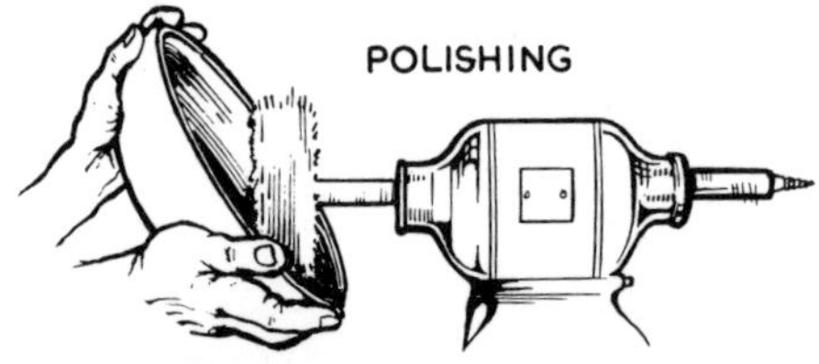

Plate 16. **Silver and Enamel Casket by Louis Osman**

Louis Osman was born in 1914 and is also an architect. He designed this casket as the gift of the British Government to Brunei at the coronation of its ruler in 1967. He also designed the crown of pure gold worn by Charles at his Investiture as Prince of Wales

17

Brazing

Spelter. Brazing derives its name from the practice of joining iron and steel with a low melting point brass, called spelter, which is often 50% copper and 50% zinc, but sometimes contains a little tin or silicon. Brazing is a form of hard soldering and, like silver soldering, is carried out at red heat but at a slightly higher temperature, and similar flux, e.g. borax, is used, although particular trade fluxes are used with special brazing materials, e.g. silicon bronze or silver brazing alloys. Spelter is available as powder, when it can be mixed with flux and water and brushed on to the joint as paste. It can be applied in small pieces cut from sheet or strip, also before heating, or in strip, rod or wire form during heating.

Brazing in the School Workshop usually takes place on a portable hearth, the heat being produced by a gas blowpipe, for which the air is supplied at pressure by means of a compressor as illustrated. The heat must be concentrated on to the job, which should be well packed in coke or with firebricks, with a firebrick set up behind so that the heat is reflected back from the firebrick on to the work and thus contained on the hearth, not dissipated in the atmosphere. The joint must be thoroughly cleaned, securely fixed together before brazing, possibly wired or clamped, and securely placed on the hearth so that it remains in position. There is always expansion and contraction when joints are heated so some movement is inevitable, and it is helpful for beginners to have the job rigidly constructed before brazing, e.g. corner joints bent square from one piece as illustrated, or by riveting and screwing,

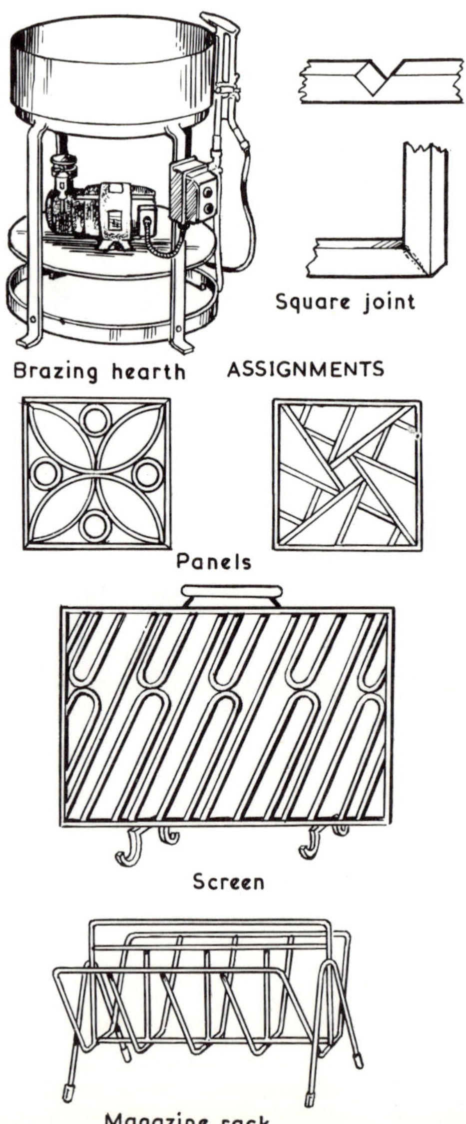

which is desirable on most of the suggested exercises. The end of one rod can be joined to the side of another by spigot riveting (*see* p. 42) or by a screw through the side into the end.

Pickling. To clean up the work after brazing it must first be pickled to remove the flux which has solidified. One part sulphuric acid diluted with eight parts water is a suitable pickle, although often a little nitric acid is added. Iron tends to dirty the pickle, so it is advisable to reserve a separate pickle bath for brazing.

Silver Brazing. Silver brazing alloys are used considerably in industry today for low temperature brazing. "Easiflo" and "Melteesi" are two of the many alloys and these are proprietary silver–copper–zinc–cadmium alloys with about 50 % silver melting around 620° C. They are often used in school instead of easy silver solder.

Assignments

Most of the brazing assignments especially those on the previous page involve the bending of mild steel or brass of consistent section, square or round, to prescribed shapes, brazing the joints and finally brazing the parts together. The drawings show the interesting possibilities of design briefs particularly the second panel which consists only of straight pieces of metal arranged and fitted inside a square.

Those on this page offer more variety. Different shaping is involved and this can be varied indefinitely, a second metal, brass or copper, is introduced for the candle holders and for the handles and some of the parts might be riveted together before brazing. Firstly a poker is shown inside the stand, but now that coal is losing favour poker and tongs are not always necessary, so a new design brief is to replace the traditional stand with an arrangement for the two pieces used to tidy the hearth.

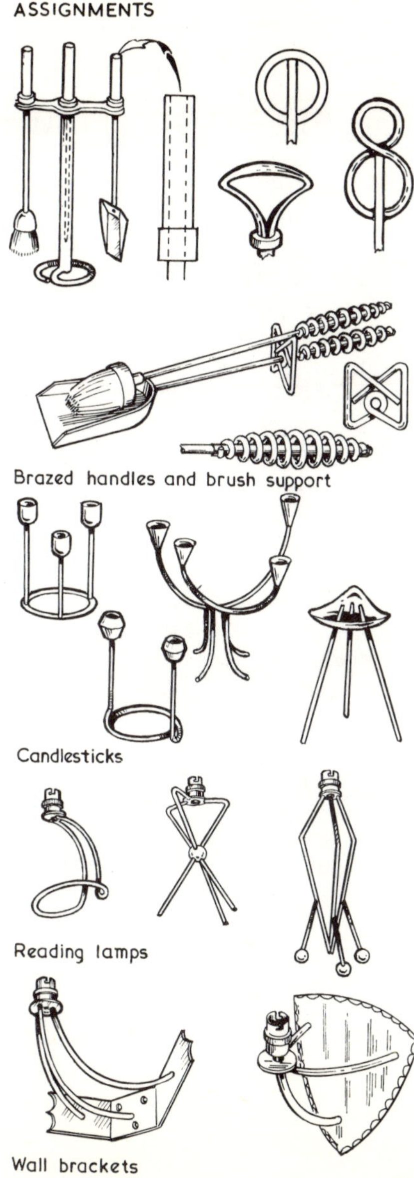

18

Forging—Tools and Processes

The Forge. Iron or steel heated to about 600° C becomes red hot; at 1,200° C it becomes white hot and between these temperatures it is plastic and can be forged, i.e. hammered to shape. The best forging metal is best quality wrought iron, but this is expensive and difficult to obtain. Other qualities of wrought iron may crack and split at the ends and are less reliable than black mild steel, which is recommended for school forging. Forging can be practised as soon as metalwork is started.

Metal is heated in a forge. Small Welsh coal or 12–20 mm washed smithy breeze gives the best forge fire but coal is dirty and coke breeze is becoming increasingly difficult to obtain so gas forges with large coke or firebricks and sometimes large square brazing hearths are used successfully for forging. Coal and coke fires can be lit with paper and wood but this causes smoke and a gas poker or blowpipe is more convenient, but gas supplied to the forge through an independent pipe is much better for starting and can be used for maintaining heat. Coal and coke cause clinker and dust both of which must be removed, as a good clean fire is essential, and there must be ample heat well spread out as in a well banked fire so that the metal can be heated evenly. The forge illustrated is for a coke fire and it can be adapted for gas. It has a water-cooled tuyere, a heavy nozzle, usually at the back of the forge for an air blast which is provided by bellows, an electric fan or compressor. The hearth is of firebrick but in a small forge it might be of cast iron, a saucer shaped plate fitted into the sheet iron bottom. The forge fire tools are the rake, shovel and the poker which has a bent pointed end for removing clinker.

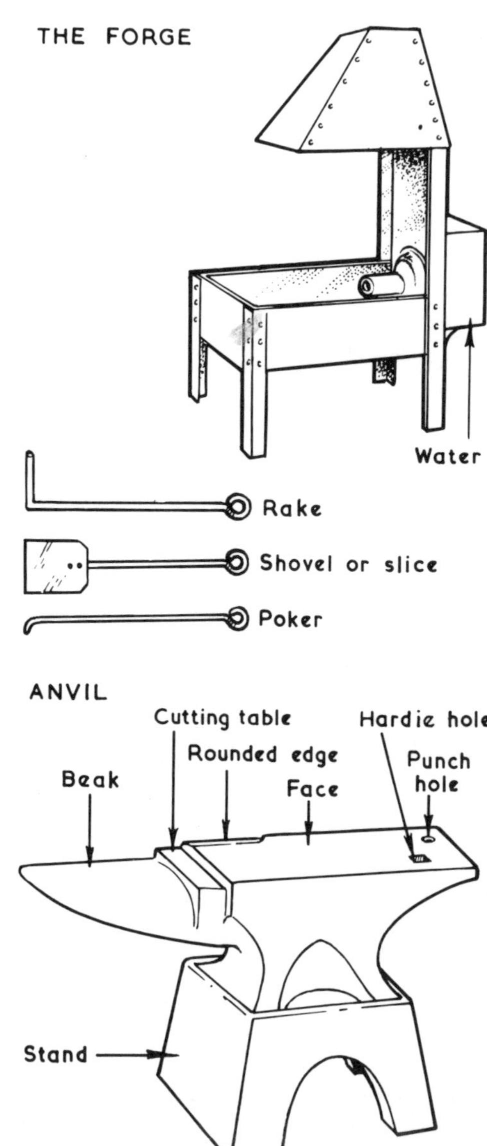

Tongs. Beginners find forging easier if the metal is long enough to be held in the hand; but short lengths must be held in tongs. There are at least a dozen pairs of tongs to a well-appointed forge. Each of the tongs shown is made in various sizes, measured and described by their length, to suit the various kinds of work. 350 and 400 mm are suitable and heavy enough for school. Open-mouth tongs for rectangular metal, close-mouth tongs for thin metal, and hollow or round-bit tongs for round or square metal, are all essential in the school workshop. Pick-up tongs are used for picking up and holding small pieces of metal which have been partly shaped; box-tongs hold heavy square or rectangular metal, e.g. 50 × 25 mm and flat-mouth tongs are for thinner metal e.g. 30 mm × 8 mm. Rivet tongs, seldom used for rivets today, are useful for holding round or square metal at right angles to the tongs, and bolt tongs are for heavy round or square metal as well as bolt-shaped forgings. Pincer tongs, for metal with a wide collar or with some shaping at the ends, are often used in schools for lifting crucibles, which are heated in the forge to melt metal for casting. Universal tongs have three holes with a groove running down the inside of each jaw and have a variety of uses. Bent or crook bit or side-mouth tongs hold flat metal which cannot be held at either end and band jaw or hook tongs are for manipulating rings, loops and bands. Scroll tongs are used in conjunction with a scrolling iron (p. 114) to make scrolls.

Anvil and Hammer. Near to the forge must be the bosh, a cast or galvanised iron rectangular tank for water. The anvil is placed on a cast iron stand or a solid block of wood. Blacksmiths used to sink part of a tree trunk into the ground and secure the anvil to it with heavy nails or bent spikes. The beak of the anvil should be to the left of the blacksmith who, if he is right-handed, stands with his left foot forward near the anvil stand, and getting well over his work as he hammers it. The hammer should be held near the end of the shaft, not close to the hammer head and it should be as heavy as can be used easily and comfortably, generally 700–800 g for a boy.

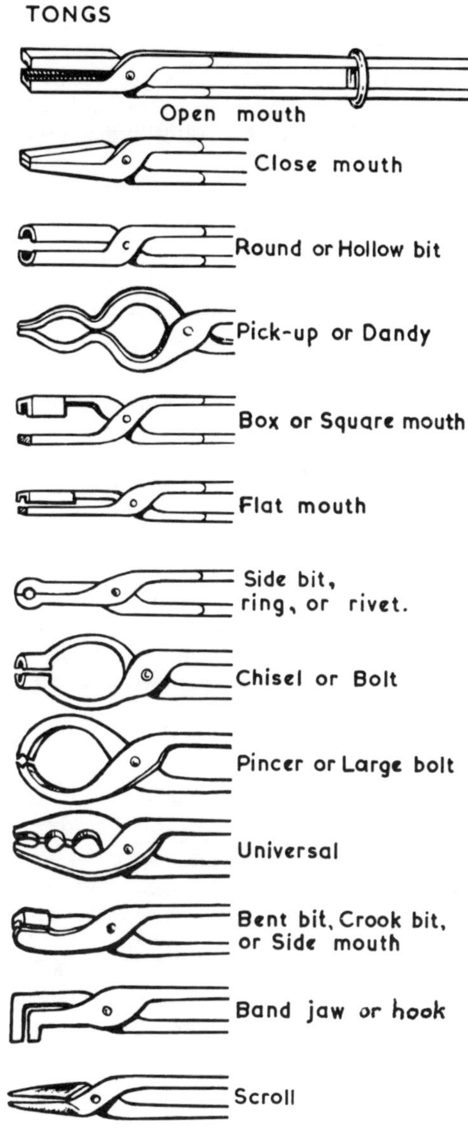

The general-purpose metalworker's hammer, the engineer's ball peen, is quite suitable for forging, but blacksmiths and some teachers prefer straight or cross-peen hammers. Boys find it easier to use a hammer with a shortened haft, so it is advisable to cut about 50 mm off a new hammer haft.

The metal must be hot and must be reheated regularly, as soon as it becomes dull red. Hammering metal which is too cool is the most serious fault in school forging. Mild steel and wrought iron can be worked at a bright orange, which is near to their melting point, but cast steel should not be heated above bright red. Cast steel burns and is spoilt before it melts. The major operations in forging are drawing down, upsetting, bending, cutting and welding.

Drawing Down involves making the metal thinner, reducing its cross-section; the first process practised could well be drawing down to a point, forging a taper. Firstly, the metal is hammered at the end on all four sides to make a short sharp taper. Then it is hammered behind the point, turning it every few blows and gradually lengthening the square taper. Metal to be drawn down is first hammered on the beak, to draw it down rapidly, and then on the face of the anvil to give it a good surface. Tapers can be flat as for a flat chisel, square as in a wall holdfast, or circular as in a centre punch. Flat tapers are drawn down by hammering on opposite sides, the edges being hammered only to keep the width parallel. Square and round tapers always begin in the same way: by forging an even square taper approximately to size. It is rounded by hammering the corners, first making it octagonal in section and eventually circular. Care must be taken to avoid piping, i.e. the forming of a hollow in the end of the taper, and splitting. These, as with most faults in forging, are caused by careless hammering or by working the metal when it is not hot right through.

DRAWING DOWN A TAPER

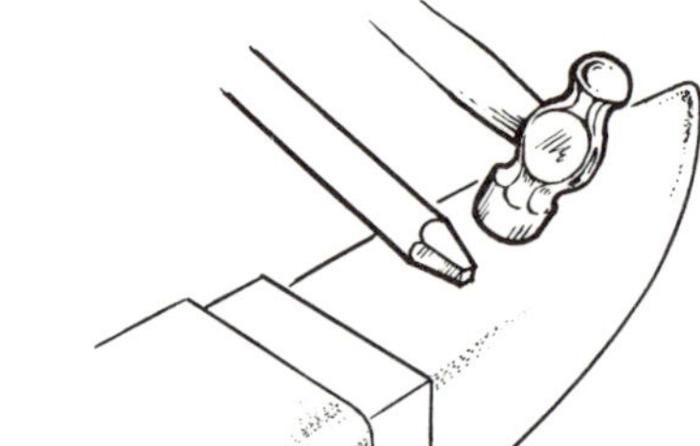

Short square point

Lengthen the square taper

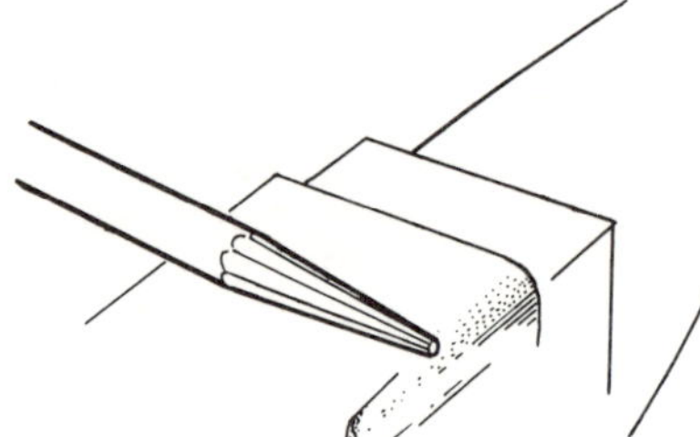

Hammer corners octagonal

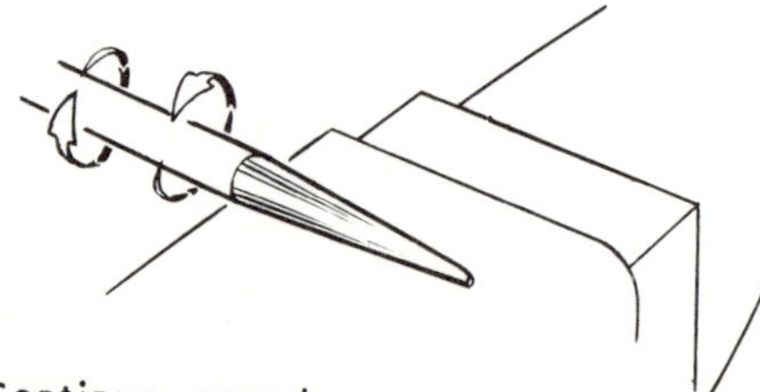

Continue – round

Upsetting or jumping up is the opposite of drawing down. It involves increasing the cross-section of part of the bar. It is a difficult and slow process and very little can be achieved in one heat. The metal must be very hot and is made shorter and thicker. As it thickens only where the metal is hottest, the bar must be heated carefully. The end of a long thick piece of metal can be upset by jumping it up and down, bouncing, on the face of the anvil. A blacksmith upsets a smaller piece by holding it in tongs horizontally across the anvil and hammering the end of the metal, but it may be more convenient to hold it in the vice or, with metal half an inch or more in thickness, to hold it upright in suitable tongs with the hot end down on the face of the anvil, and to hammer the cold end.

OTHER HAMMERS

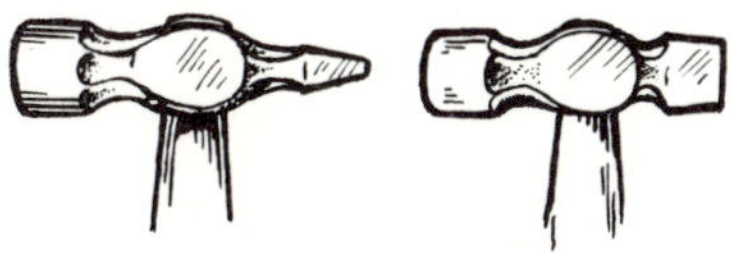

Cross peen Straight peen

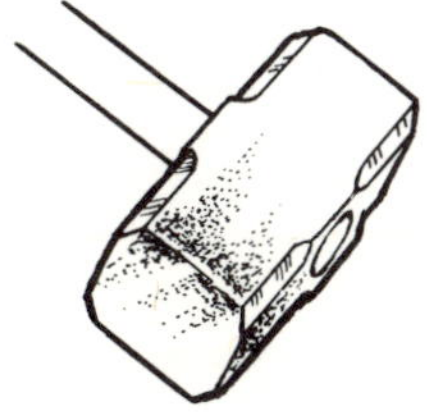

Sledge hammer

UPSETTING

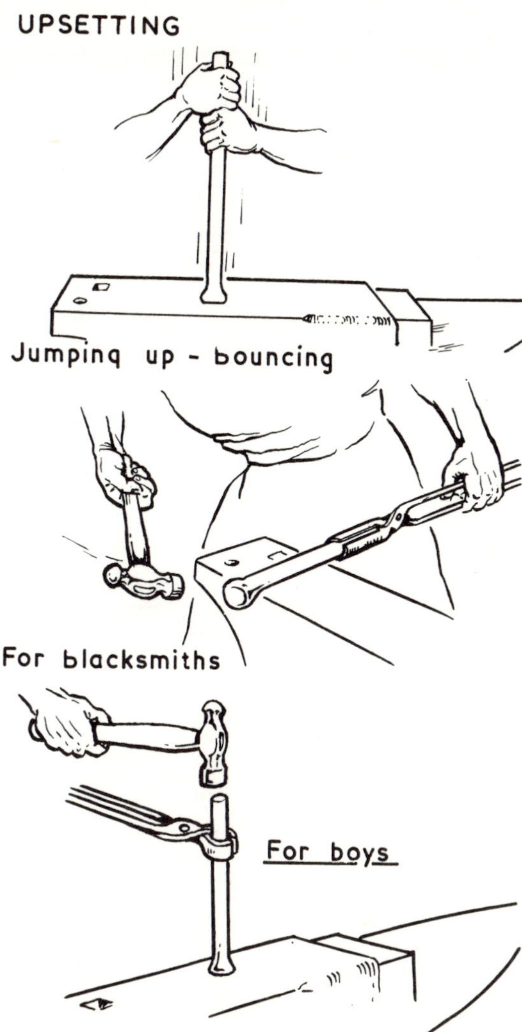

Jumping up - bouncing

For blacksmiths

For boys

Bending to shape is the most common and most varied of the fundamental forging operations. A simple right-angle bend will not produce a sharp right-angle corner. A sharp corner needs more metal and this can be produced only by upsetting before or during the bending. During this operation, only the metal at the bend should be heated. The metal away from the corner must be kept cool by quenching. It will be easier to obtain a sharp right-angle bend on light stock, say less than 12 mm square, by upsetting in the vice after simple bending over the anvil. The corner is heated and the metal is placed tightly in the vice, horizontally along the jaws with a 3 mm gap left between the side of the vice jaws and the inside of the bend. Then the corner is hammered back on to the vice. The metal is then reversed, the bend is placed in the vice and the other part of the corner hammered. Finally, the bend must be trued up on the anvil.

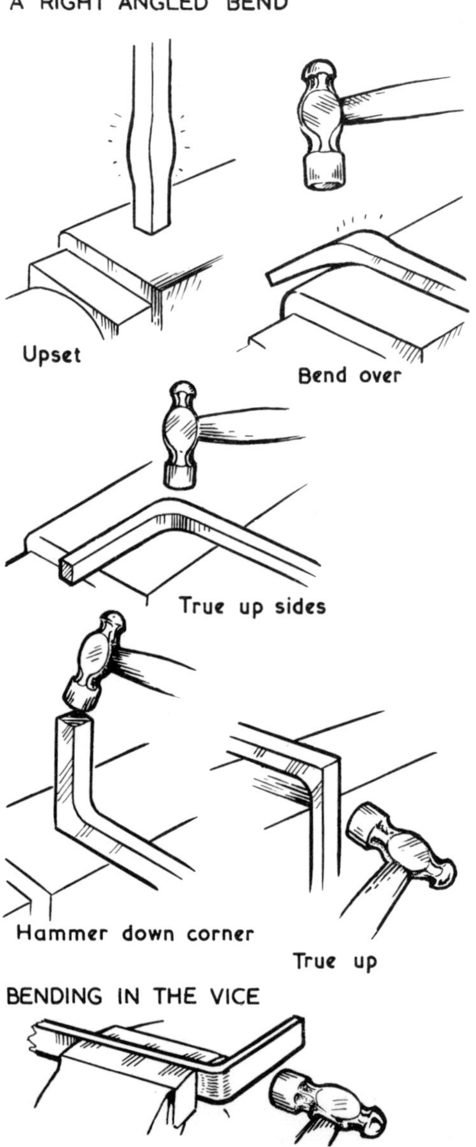

Forming an Eye is an important bending process. The length of metal needed for the eye is estimated, and is equal to the length of the central circumference, i.e. three times the mean diameter, e.g. a 40 mm external diameter eye of 8 mm metal will need 3 × 32 mm = 96 mm of metal. Sometimes this distance is marked on the metal with chalk or a centre punch dot, but it is better to draw a chalk line the estimated distance from the square end of the anvil. Then the metal, heated about this distance from the end, is placed along the anvil so that the end of the metal touches this line. If the hand holding the metal is lowered, the metal can be hammered to form a bend of about 45° in the correct place. The corner can then be hammered to a right angle over the side of the anvil in the ordinary way. To form the eye, the metal is turned over and curved back over the beak beginning at the end of the metal and working back towards the right angle. It is turned again and curved round over the beak until the end meets the corner. The eye can be finally closed and trued over the side of the anvil. Never attempt to form an eye directly by trying to bend the metal into a ring over the beak without the right angle. This will produce a lop-sided loop which only a skilled blacksmith could forge into an eye. The eye must be forged to a true circle which is centrally placed about an imaginary axis.

FORMING AN EYE

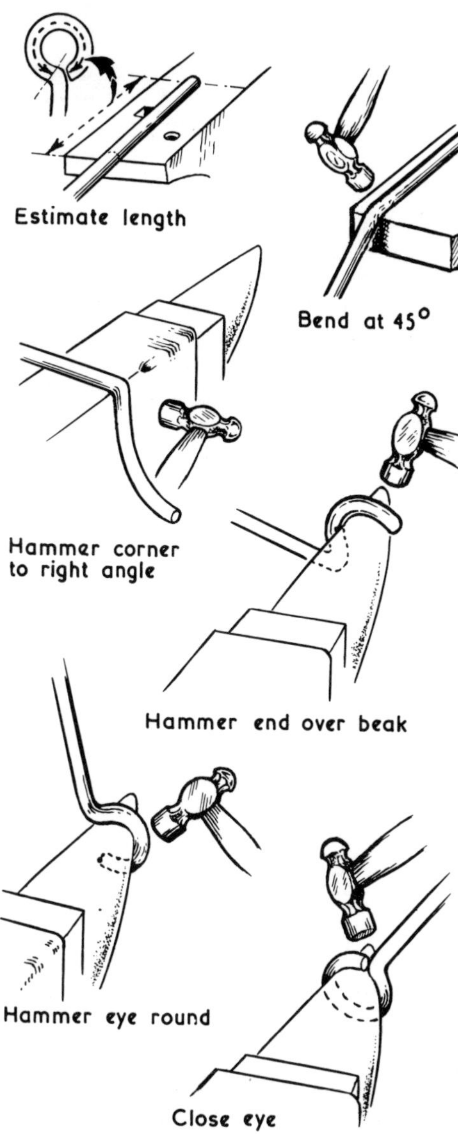

Twisting is a simple but very popular decorative treatment. The easiest way to obtain a good even twist, if the metal cannot be twisted cold, is to heat evenly that part of the metal which is to be twisted, hold it horizontally in the vice and twist with a bar of metal in which there is a central hole the same size as the cross-section of the metal. A large tap wrench serves excellently for square stock. The part to be twisted must be between the vice and the bar which is held in two hands and turned steadily. Careful heating is essential: metal made very hot for a short length will produce a short sharp twist but a good red heat along all that part of the metal to be twisted will give a long regular twist. Light stock is twisted cold and a long length can be twisted in a tube to keep it straight.

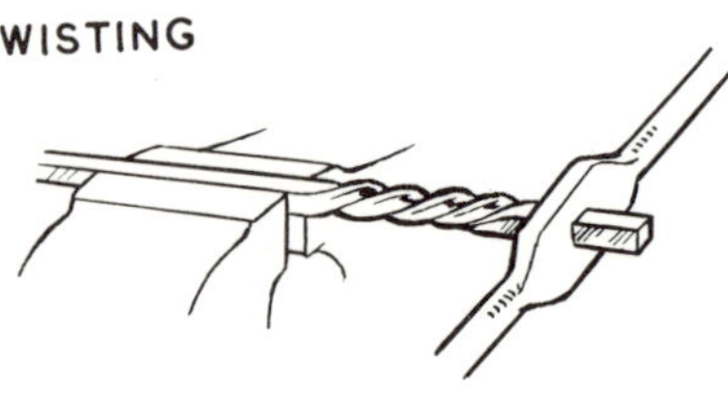

Cutting can be a single- or double-handed job. The operations described so far have been "one-man" operations, but often the smith needs an assistant, who "swings" a sledge hammer. He is called a striker. Metal up to 25 × 12 mm or 20 mm square can be cut by one boy on his own. It should be heated where it is to be cut and this part placed on the hardie and hammered to form a vee cut, "nicked", flat metal on two sides and square metal all round. Then the metal is placed on the anvil with the nicks above the far edge and the overhanging piece is struck with a hammer so that it breaks off.

Heavier metal is cut on the saddle, the cutting table, of the anvil by a set, which is struck with a sledge hammer, a double-handed operation. A hot set is used to cut hot metal. It has a sharper cutting edge than a cold set, which is used to cut cold metal on the anvil. The edge of a hot set must be kept cool, if necessary by dipping in water, but a good set usually has enough metal in its body to absorb the heat at the edge. On no account must a set be used on top of a hardie; this would be inaccurate as a cutting operation and extremely dangerous.

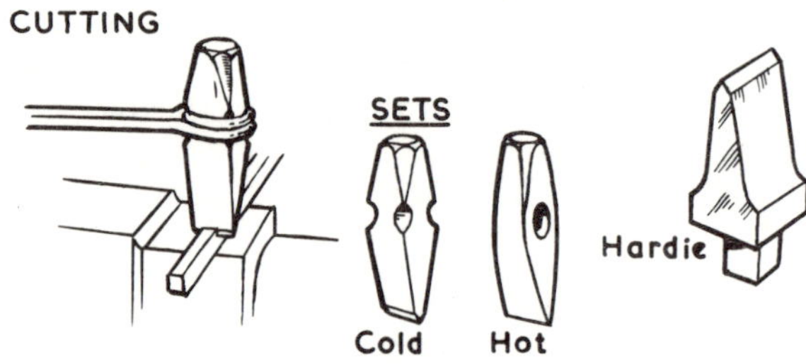

Swaging usually needs a striker. Top and bottom swages, 12–40 mm hollows, are used to true up round metal and to change square metal so that its cross-section is circular. The bottom swage fits into the hardie hole; the metal held in one hand, rests in its hollow while the top swage, held in the other hand, is placed above the metal. This top tool is struck with a sledge hammer, the metal being turned between blows. When rounding light stock, the bottom swage may be used alone. The metal is rested in the hollow and hammered circular. **A swage block** when resting on its edge is used for swaging to forge larger sections round or square. It rests on a cast iron stand like an anvil stand and can be used with or without top tools. When it is horizontal its greatest use is for bending or punching.

Fullering is a similar operation which produces round grooves, 12–40 mm wide according to the size of the fullers, usually across the metal, but in some cases along its length. It is useful in forming shoulders when part of the metal has to be made thinner. After fullering the metal can be more easily hammered up to the shoulder. When it is shouldered on one side only, the top fuller is used alone. If the bottom fuller is used alone, it is difficult to keep the metal straight and true. When reducing the thickness of metal it is quicker to make a series of hollows on both sides of the bar with top and bottom fullers and flatten afterwards.

Flattening is usually a double-handed operation; the flatter is held on the metal and hit with a sledge hammer. It is for finishing metal which has been thinned or "spread", made wider as well as thinner.

Setting in forging refers to the use of a set hammer, which is used with a sledge hammer to true up the corners of shoulders.

Punching is the making of round or square holes in hot metal by driving a punch through. Blacksmiths prefer punching to drilling, as no metal is removed and more metal is left each side of the hole. Punching is begun on the saddle of the anvil but when going through the metal the punch must be above the punch hole. A sledge hammer is used and after punching one side a dark mark shows on the underside of the hot metal; this is a cool spot caused by the end of the punch, which serves to indicate the position on the reverse side. One of the disadvantages of punching is the tendency of the metal to split, so that for large holes the metal should be upset. Punching should begin with a small hole and it is easier for students if this hole is drilled. Punches taper only slightly. Those that taper considerably may be a special shape, e.g. oval, rectangular or square, or simply round, and they are called **Drifts.** These are used with a hand hammer and a thick glove should be worn. A drift is often used to true up a punched hole.

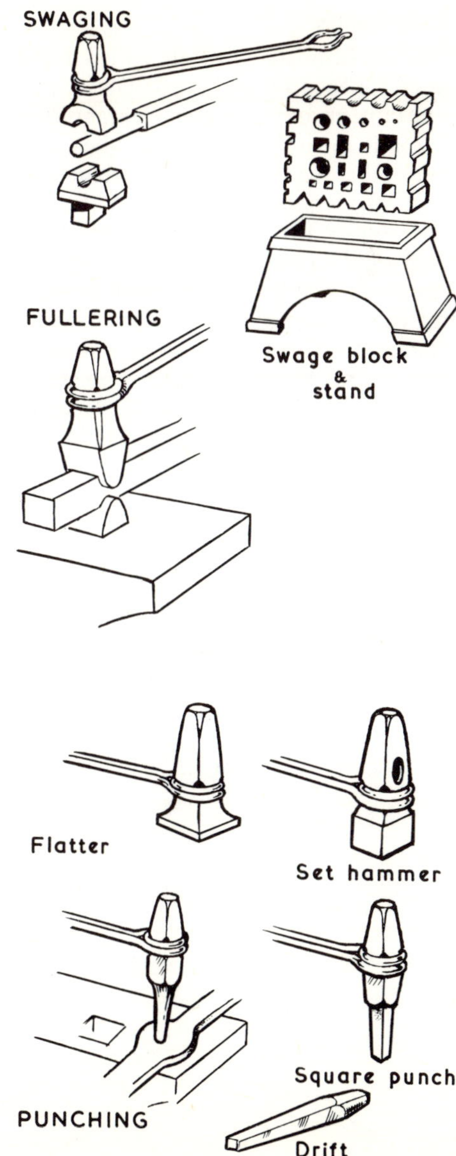

Assignments

Low carbon steel, often called mild steel, is the easiest metal for forging and is excellent for the early exercises. The pipe clip, garden line peg, cleat, holdfast and cabin hook are all made entirely by forging, the clip from 8 mm diameter metal, the peg tapered and flattened from 10 mm round, the cleat, drawn down each end, fullered and shaped from 12 × 6 mm metal, and the cabin hook from 6 mm square mild steel rounded at each end and twisted in the middle. The wall holdfast is forged from 10 mm square metal but the hole must be drilled. These, as with most of the elementary forging exercises, should be left from the hammer, i.e. hammered, not filed, to shape and left with a hammered finish. Exercises like the hasp and staple, hoe, trowel, shovel, eye bolt and line winder combine forging with bench work.

FORGING ASSIGNMENTS

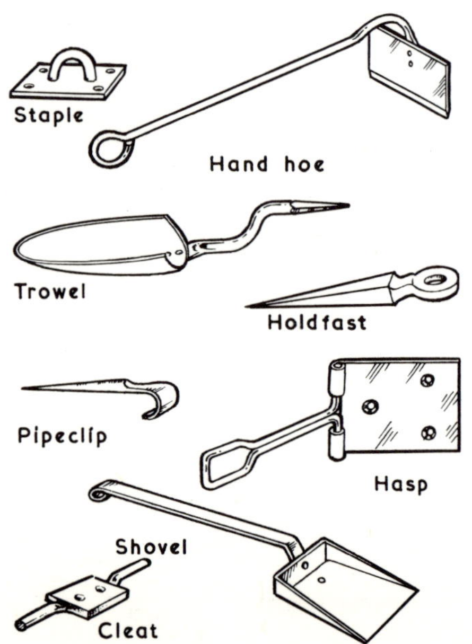

ASSIGNMENTS IN MILD STEEL

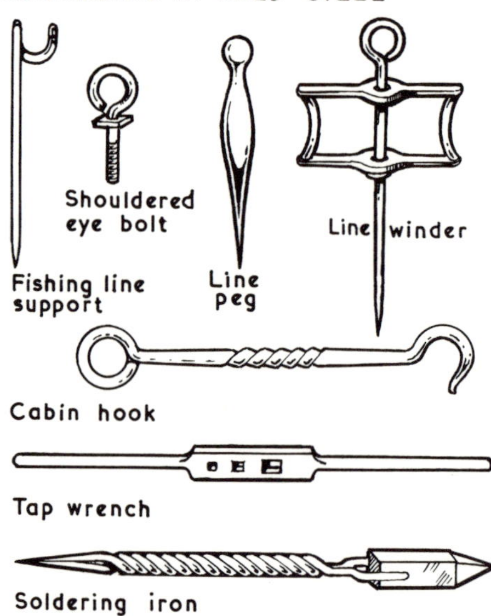

The eye bolt is screwed and has a shoulder brazed on and can be used with the cabin hook instead of the more usual staple. A forged tap wrench is most suitable for large taps, 15 mm and above, and it involves excellent practice in drawing down and swaging, square punching and case hardening. The metal should be at least twice the width of the widest hole. The drawing down needs careful hammering as there is a tendency for the corners to fold away from the narrow side on to the wide side and to form fine hollows along these sides which show as distinct lines on the finished handles; the middle is case hardened.

The fishing line support has the metal folded back on to the stem and welded (*see* p. 113) before the end is curved; the soldering iron has 5 mm mild steel rod passed through a hole in the copper bit twisted tightly and the two ends welded and forged to make a square tang.

Designing Fire Irons

Hearth Furniture may be somewhat out of date but good pokers, shovels, brushes, tongs and toasting forks look attractive and are still popular. Provided they are not attempted too soon they present an enjoyable task and excellent scope for design. Those illustrated have three parts, working end, stem and handle and the parts must go well together. When designing a poker the three parts are a bit to go in the fire, a handle to hold and a rein to give length so that the hand is not burnt. To forge a good bit, the end of the metal should be upset, and if the handle is to be upset as well, both ends must be upset before any shaping is begun. Very good pokers can be forged this way, using, say, 16 mm. round stock and drawing down the middle. A good poker cannot be produced by just forming an eye, forging a point and twisting the middle of 8 mm square metal.

Forged toasting forks can be very attractive and fascinating, but are difficult to make. In one case two 3 mm round prongs are wired each side of a 6 × 4 mm stem and the end brazed or welded. The prongs can then be bent back and forged to their correct shape. The other fork is forged from 19 × 5 mm metal; the end is split with a cold chisel to form three prongs. These split ends are bent out, forged round, and bent back to their finished position. This fork is more difficult because the middle is drawn down to 5 mm square and twisted.

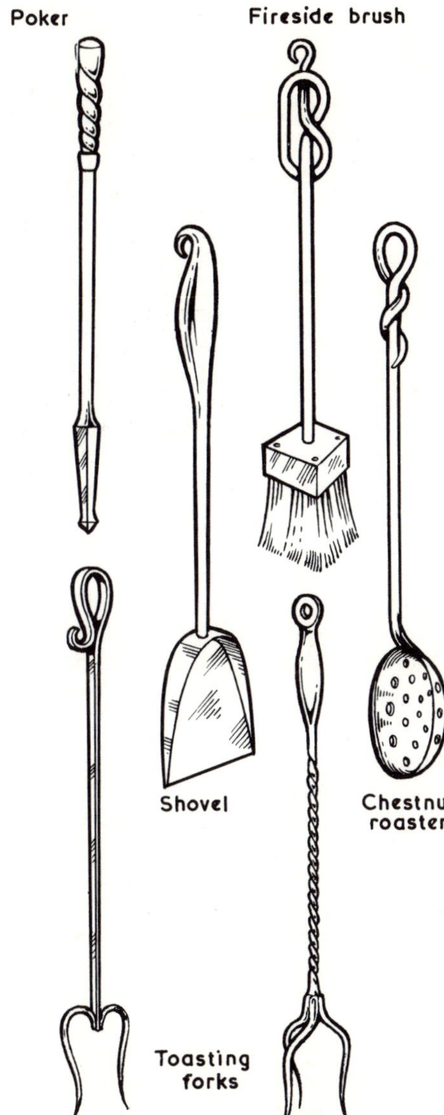

19

Forging—Toolmaking and Heat Treatment—Welding

Toolmaking can be introduced after the first elementary exercises. It is precision work involving greater accuracy, the forging of cast steel and hardening and tempering. Plain carbon steel with about 0·9% carbon is the cast steel generally used in schools and if this metal is made red hot and quenched, i.e. cooled suddenly, it becomes dead hard and much more brittle. This makes it unsuitable for most purposes except possibly scribers, scrapers and files. The hardness and brittleness can be decreased a little and the metal made much tougher if it is tempered, i.e. reheated a little and again quenched. Only the working part, cutting edge, of the tool is hardened and tempered. The rest of the tool can be softer as is the case with a cold chisel the body of which should not be dead hard but soft and tough enough to absorb the hammer blows without breaking the chisel or jarring the hand.

Hardening involves heating the edge or point of a tool to red heat and quenching by dipping it vertically and moving it vertically up and down in the water. If it is left to cool in one position, there is a sudden change in temperature where the air and water meet, and this may cause a crack at the water line. If the heated tool is quenched too quickly by being dropped completely into water, probably on its side, the too sudden change of temperature and of size tends to cause distortion, cracks and even breaks—possibly all three. Good sound hardening needs care as the metal often cracks when quenched, although sometimes the cracks are fine hair cracks and very difficult to see. Water is the usual quenching liquid, but it is the most severe and should not be very cold. Water, brine (a saturated salt solution), and oil are all used for quenching and they give varying degrees of hardness in that order. Oil cooling, being the least sudden, causes the least distortion but water and brine quenching make the metal harder. Clean rainwater at room temperature (15° C) is the best quenching water for hardening.

Tempering follows hardening. The hardened part of the tool is polished and heated carefully, possibly in a bunsen flame. As the metal is slowly heated, colours appear on the brightened surface. This colouring is a film of oxide and varies from pale straw, very hard, to dark blue, hard and tough and suitable for springs. The tool is heated behind the point and the colours are watched as they move towards the point. As soon as the desired colour reaches the point the tool is quenched. Some examples, beginning with the hardest tools are: light straw for lathe tools, 220° C; straw, hammer faces, 230° C; dark straw, drills, 240° C; brown, taps, 250° C; dark brown, punches, 260° C; light purple, cold chisels, 280° C; dark purple, screwdrivers, 300° C; dark blue, springs, 315° C. Some tools, e.g. a dowel plate, are hardened and tempered throughout.

Hardening and tempering can be done in one operation; by heating the point of the tool to redness, quenching only the point and so leaving enough heat in the body of the tool for tempering. The end of the tool is polished while it is still hot with an emery stick, or rubbed with a piece of old emery wheel to produce scratches, which are watched in order to see the tempering colours as the heat from the unquenched portion travels down towards the quenched and hardened point or edge.

Plate 17. **Gates and Lanterns, Vigelandsporten**

Gustav Vigeland, 1869–1943, a Norwegian sculptor whose wrought ironwork is prominent in many parts of Oslo. He employed two or three smiths, mastersmith Alfred Mikkelsen, and his studio is now the Vigeland Museum

Plate 18. **Details of Wrought Iron Gates by Gustav Vigeland**

Detail of main entrance gate, Vigeland Sculpture Park 1927

"Young Women with Vines" Gate inside the Sculpture Park near Monolit, 1935

Case Hardening gives a hard outside skin to medium and low carbon steel. The steel article is heated in contact with materials containing carbon, coke, charcoal, bones, etc., to about 950° C. The steel is packed amongst the carbon which must be in a steel box, preferably sealed, and when heated in a furnace for about five hours and quenched, a hard shell between one and two millimetres thick can be obtained. An easier method is to heat the article and rub it in prussiate of potash (potassium ferro-cyanide), but this gives off poisonous fumes and in school it is preferable to use one of the commercially prepared case-hardening compounds such as Kasenit. This gives a very shallow hard skin, seldom greater than a quarter of a millimetre and several dippings are necessary before the article is finally quenched.

Annealing and Normalising are two other important heat treatments. Annealing makes plain carbon steel as soft as possible. The steel is heated to redness and left in the furnace or amongst the hot coke until it is cool. Normalising restores the normal working properties and for this the metal may be cooled in air.

Assignments

Tools were probably the earliest assignments in history and the earliest metal tools were hammered to shape probably with stone hammers. All the tools shown here are of cast steel, the only suitable material for forged tools in the school workshop. The working ends are forged to shape, filed and, if necessary, ground to an exact cutting edge but the metal bar may be left in its standard form for the body of the tool. The tool end should be polished with emery cloth so that it looks good and will show the tempering colours which will be given for each tool. The scriber of 4 mm square silver steel (1·1% carbon) is left hard, as can be the two small scrapers used for scraping soft solder from beaten metalwork. One scraper is made of 8 mm octagonal steel and the other, with a tang filed one end so that it will fit into a file handle, is from 5 mm silver steel. A flat metal chisel is a popular forging exercise in school and 12 mm hexagonal steel is a suitable material but in practice the size of the chisel, tempered dark purple, will depend on its use. The centre punch, brown, is 8 mm octagonal steel and the loop handled screwdriver, 10 mm round, is tempered blue.

TOOLMAKING ASSIGNMENTS

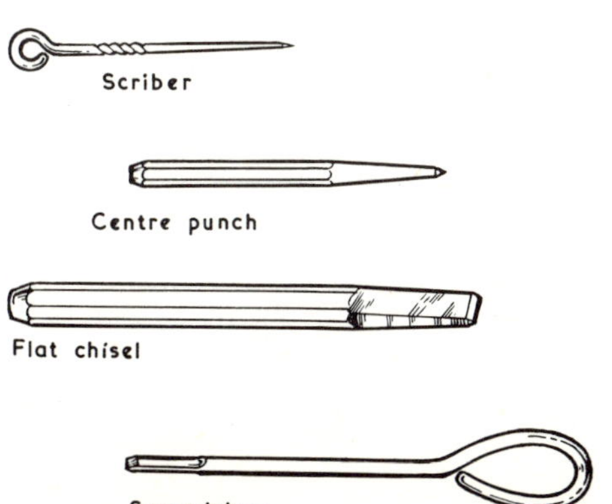

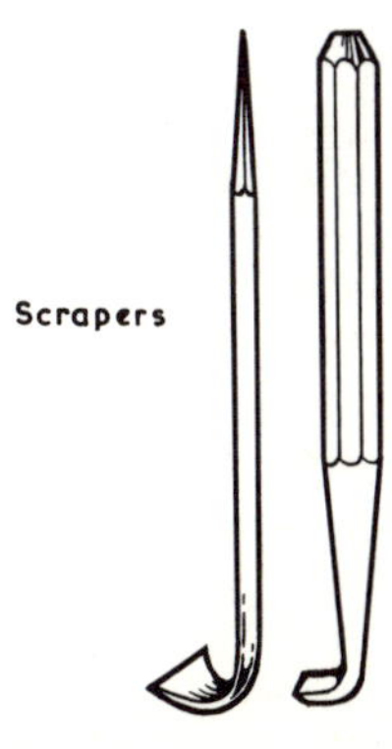

A case opener is a double ended tool, lever end dark purple and tack lifter dark brown. Its size, 200–500 mm long and material section will depend on its use. Scrapers (*see* p. 32) vary in size but a three square scraper might be made from 16 mm round steel. The brace screwdriver can be of 10 mm round steel drawn down in the middle and tapered one end to fit a No. 8 wood screw and the other end a square taper to fit a woodworker's brace.

The plugging chisel, the centre bit and the bolster all need upsetting. After upsetting the thickened ends are hammered flat but this must be done very carefully as hammer blows stretch the metal in all directions and sometimes lengthening is necessary as in the chisel and sometimes the metal has to be widened as in the bolster. The thickness must be controlled by hammering the flattened surface equally except at the very end which should be left until the final truing up. For the chisel the width must be controlled by hammering back the sides but the bolster end which will require much upsetting will have to be hammered back at the end while increasing the width. After upsetting the middle of the centre bit will be drawn down but the greatest difficulty will be filing the end to shape as it must be absolutely accurate. The bit should be tempered harder than the chisel and the chisel a little harder than the bolster and the colours should be between dark brown and purple. The Phillips screwdriver is drawn down from round or square steel, the tang for the handle being a flat taper, the middle drawn down round and the "Phillips" end filed to shape and tempered brown to purple. It needs a wooden handle which should be turned on a woodturning lathe. The striking or marking knife, brown, can be made from flat or square steel. It has a bevel on one side and is sharpened on one side only.

In forging, metal is easily overheated and it should not be hammered when it is below red heat. In all

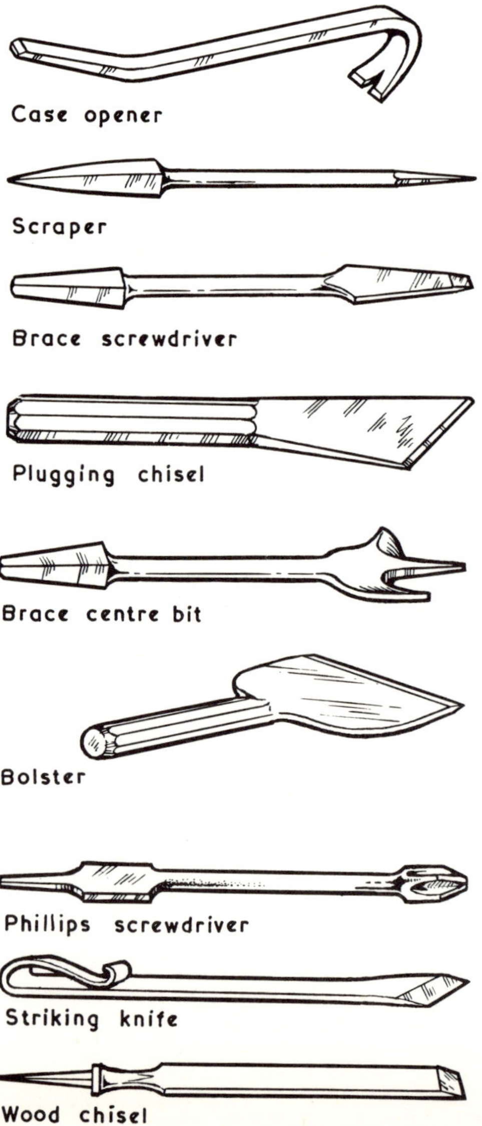

toolmaking wrong heating or forging at the wrong temperature may cause faults which, unnoticed at the time, may later cause distortion and cracks especially during heat treatment. This applies particularly when making woodworkers' chisels which have to be hammered flat, parallel and smooth along their length and tempered light purple most of the way up, not just at the end. It might be easier to use thinner metal the same section as the blade but this would present problems because of the thickness at the tang end. An excellent assignment, though difficult, is a hammer head especially if one of those used in beaten metalwork (*see* p. 88) is made and used. The forging is an interesting exercise and the eye should be punched although it is helpful if a small hole is drilled first and filed oval. Fullering helps to obtain a good shape but the hardening and tempering need especial care owing to the unequal sections which increase the likelihood of distortion and cracking. The faces must be hard, medium straw, but the eye should be blue or not hardened at all.

Welding

Welding is the original method of joining iron and can be used successfully on low carbon steel. The blacksmith does this by heating his metal in the forge fire, placing two pieces of metal, one on top of the other and hammering them together, but this needs good judgment and considerable skill. Both pieces of metal must be at welding heat, i.e. the metal white hot and beginning to give off sparks, and they must be placed accurately and hammered very quickly, and in the right place. If the weld is to be successful, the metal must stick after the first hammer blow. This can be done in the school workshop but the most successful way of welding in the forge is to work on one piece of metal only, as in the fishing line support and the soldering iron (*see* p. 108). Several modern methods of welding have outdated smith's welding, and the best known of these are oxy-acetylene and electric welding. Both give much more heat than the forge, and the heat can be localised and the process carried out on any part of a large job that cannot be placed in a fire, and in any place, as when welding plates in the making of ships. Oxy-acetylene, sometimes referred to as torch welding, is easier with thin metal which has to be welded by hand, but electric welding is quicker on heavy jobs and is utilised considerably in machine welding. Both methods use intense flames and the welder must wear goggles or work behind a coloured screen. One very great advantage of these modern methods is that other metals, e.g. cast iron and aluminium, can be welded.

20

Forging—Decorative Smithing

Decorative ironwork is eminently suitable for schools. It can be seen in churches and in town and country houses, as gates, screens and as railings. It offers freedom of shape, problems of design and a wide variety of work. It is possible to obtain pleasing results from designs which consist largely of the making and assembling of different kinds of scrolls, mainly S- and C-scrolls as shown in the single and double candlesticks. Wrought iron or mild steel, 12 × 5 mm, is used considerably for simple decorative work in schools but thinner metal should not be forged as it can be bent cold.

Forging Scrolls. First the end of the metal, the inside of the scroll, must be prepared. It is spread (fish-tailed), and curled on a scroll block which fits in the hardie hole. When several similar scrolls are required, the metal is heated and bent round a scroll iron, a master scroll which is higher in the middle so that the metal can be pulled or bent round it. A chalk line is drawn on the scroll iron to indicate the end of the bending—particularly necessary when making similar

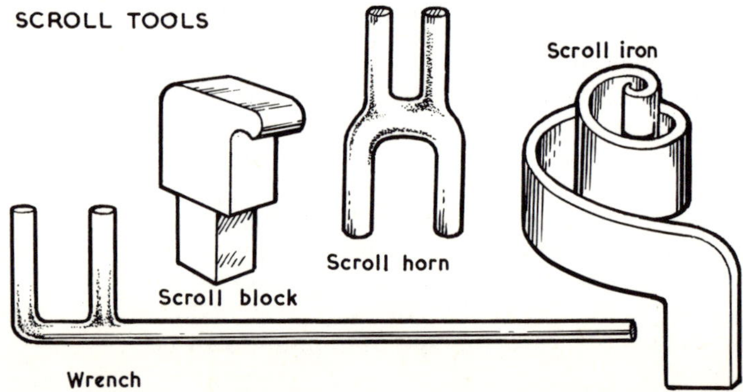

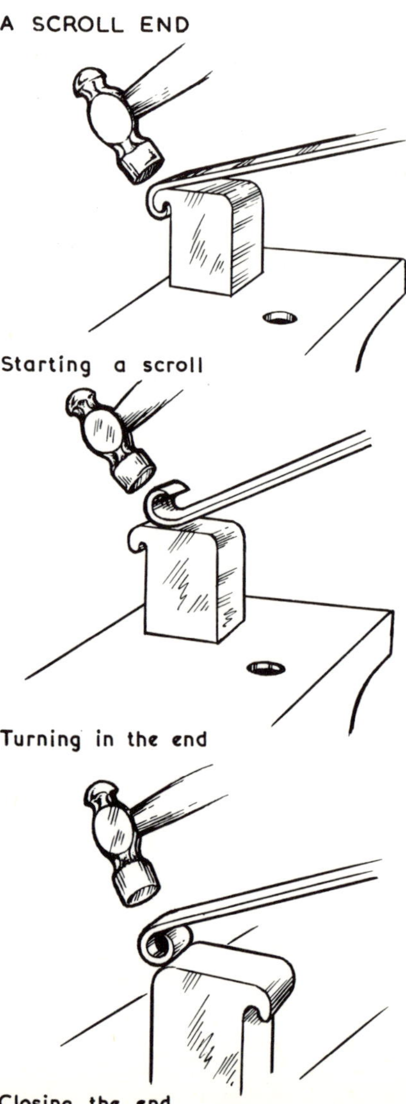

SCROLLING

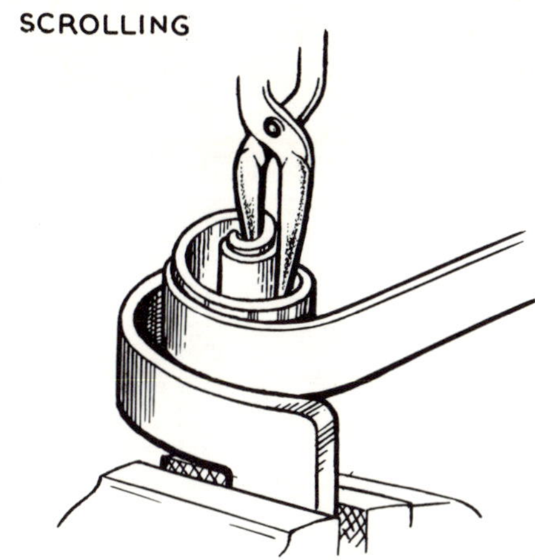
Forming a scroll with scrolling iron

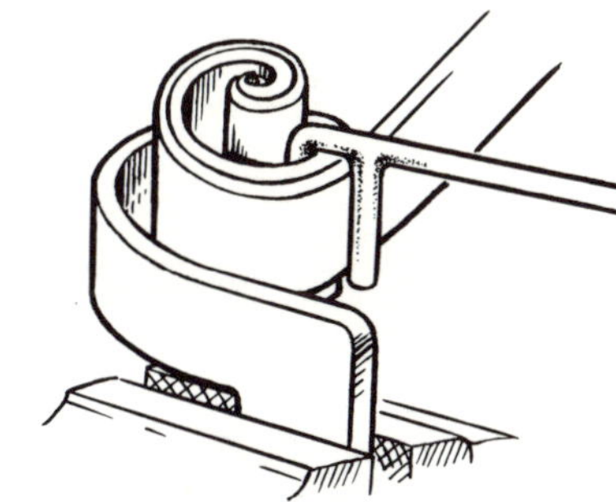
Truing scroll with wrench

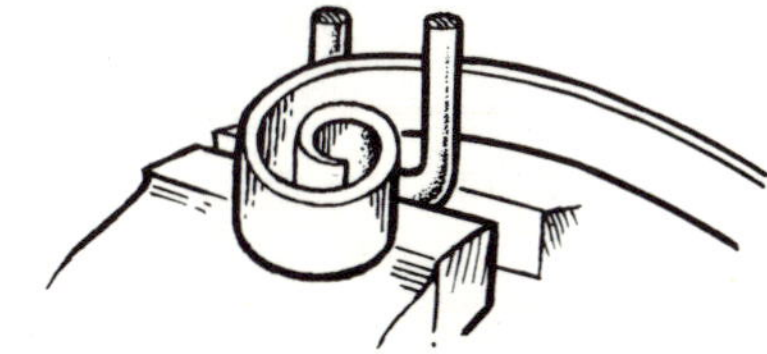
Forming a scroll with scroll horn

scrolls; the prepared end is tucked inside the scroll iron and held with conical pointed scroll tongs (p. 101) and the metal is pulled round the scroll to the chalk line. The inside of the new scroll is now hammered down, level with the outside. The wrench is used to correct the curvature of a scroll or to bend it close to the scroll iron if it has been bent carelessly. A single scroll, e.g. a scroll iron, is made with the help of scroll horns and a wrench. The iron is heated, placed between the horns which are held in the vice, pulled round to form the scroll and moved backwards and forwards as necessary to obtain an accurate form. It is trued up with the wrench while still in the scroll horn.

Assignments

Most of these assignments are based on scrollwork and the making involves the assembly of scrolls. A blacksmith usually welds his scroll in position but this may be very difficult in school. Brazing, riveting and screwing are sound methods of joining scrollwork and are probably more suitable for school workshops. The screwing can be enhanced by decorative bolt heads and nuts, e.g. spherical nuts. A knocker must be heavy and one end of the thick metal must be drawn down before the scroll is made. The thin end of the scroll forms the inside of the knuckle the other part being brazed through the backplate. The trivet is formed by riveting two scrolls together. Three scrolls could be used and then only three legs would be riveted underneath. Of the candlesticks shown, one is 6 mm square

FORGING ASSIGNMENTS

ASSIGNMENTS

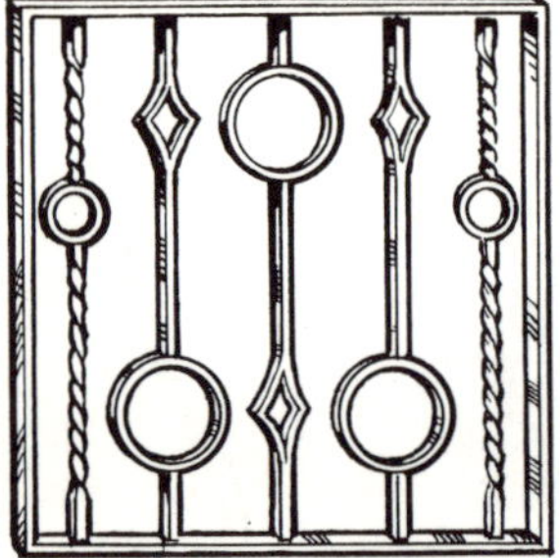

GRILLES

Fireguard

metal bent circular to form a base and upwards for the stem, another is an S-scroll riveted to a small base and the third has a similar scroll fixed on to a metal tray. One of the double candle-sticks is composed of C-scrolls. The grease trays and candle holders may be of iron, brass, copper or gilding metal. The panels can be used singly as grilles: two, three or four could be arranged together to form a larger grille, a screen or a gate. The fire screen should have fine mesh expanded aluminium, colour anodised, screwed behind it to serve as a decorative spark guard. Electric light fittings can be simple, as are the candle sticks, but the examples shown increase the range of the work. The table lamp has two large nuts fixed on to a tube and three scrolls screwed to the nuts. The two lamp bracket consists of two S-scrolls riveted to two horizontal strips which are fixed to a vertical wall plate. The pendant light has three complicated scrolls screwed to two large nuts. Simple S-scrolls are riveted inside the main curves. Two brackets are shown, one for a hanging lamp or a bell which could be adapted for a gong or a sign and the other, a much better form for outside lights, has the lamp fixed rigidly above a square tube which protects the wiring. The top of the lamp must be removable in order to fit the bulb. When the bracket is to be fitted to the corner of a house, the main upright member could be of angle iron.

LAMPS

Plate 19. **Coventry Cathedral**

Coventry Cathedral, destroyed by German bombs in the Second World War, was rebuilt in 1956, architect Sir Basil Spence

Crown of Thorns. Designed by Sir Basil Spence and made by the Royal Engineers in wrought iron

St. Michael and the Devil. One of Sir Jacob Epstein's last works, it is sculptured in bronze, is 7·5 m high and weighs 5 tonnes

Plate 20. **Churchwork**

Font by Robert Welch in cast iron and cast aluminium with a bowl of translucent dark blue perspex. Made for the Episcopal Church at Rutgers, New Jersey, U.S.A. It is 1.5 m tall and weighs 74 kg

Llandaff Cathedral, Cardiff. Epstein Majestas and organ case

Llandaff Cathedral was seriously damaged by a German land mine in January 1941 and was rebuilt 1949–1958. The Majestas cast at the Morris Singer Works, Lambeth is in unpolished aluminium. The organ case is supported on a parabolic arch and both are of reinforced concrete. Sir Jacob Epstein worked in close harmony with the architect, Mr. George Pace of York

21

Casting

A hard rigid substance which could be melted and poured so as to form a desired shape was to be an important element in the development of human civilisation. Metals are produced by melting and a great many of the metal articles around us, at home, in school, at work or in the street, are made by casting, i.e. pouring molten metal, into a specially prepared hollow, a mould. In industry the casting workshop is called a foundry and the best-known foundry metal is cast iron, but copper alloys, brass and gunmetal, and aluminium alloys are used considerably and can be cast in school.

The Pattern. Castings may be solid or hollow, and are made with the aid of a pattern which is used to produce a shaped cavity, usually in sand, into which the metal is poured. The pattern can be exactly like the desired article or it can be divided into sections. If the casting is to be hollow special adjustments are necessary and extra parts may be added to the patterns.

The Mould. The simplest patterns are for solid castings which are flat on one face and can be made in a plain wooden box, or in one-half of a two-part moulding box of wood or metal. This method would produce an **Open Mould,** but it is better to use both halves of the box. The pattern is placed on a smooth board, plain side down and the "drag", the bottom half of the box, is placed over it. Sand is pressed tightly around the pattern and rammed down until this half of the box is full. The sand which is packed close to the pattern, about an inch all round, should be riddled, but the rest can be shovelled in. The sand is "strickled", that is, levelled off by drawing a strip of wood across the top. Another board is placed on top and the complete unit, both boards with half of the box complete with pattern and sand between them, is turned over. The original board, now uppermost, is removed and the surface of the sand is dusted over with parting powder, a fine dry sand which will not stick, e.g. sea sand or one of the prepared powders recognised in industry, and the other half of the box is placed above, excess parting sand being blown off with bellows. The two halves of the box are now in their correct position, the drag below and the cope above. Gate sticks or runner sticks, sometimes called sprues, are next placed in position and the cope is filled with sand, rammed and strickled. Gate sticks are circular sticks, slightly conical, 20 to 30 mm diameter, and long enough to stand above the top of the cope, so that they can be removed easily. They serve as patterns for the vertical holes, gates, through which the metal is poured. All moulds need at least one gate stick to form the runner, but others are generally used for risers, which are essential for large castings or if the metal has to make a long run, as when several articles are cast in the same mould as shown on p. 119. Risers aid the escape of steam and gases, relieve the pressure on the mould and provide an extra reservoir of metal to allow for liquid contraction, and allow slag and other impurities to float on top of the metal clear of the casting. They are helpful in school because the metal can be seen rising in the riser as the mould fills. The bottom of the gate stick is pushed in the sand at the side of the pattern to provide a hollow for the metal, a pool, which helps the metal to flow smoothly into the mould cavity. If possible, a riser stick should be placed above the highest part of the pattern. When the sticks have been removed the cope is lifted off and the sand, if well rammed and of the correct moisture, will

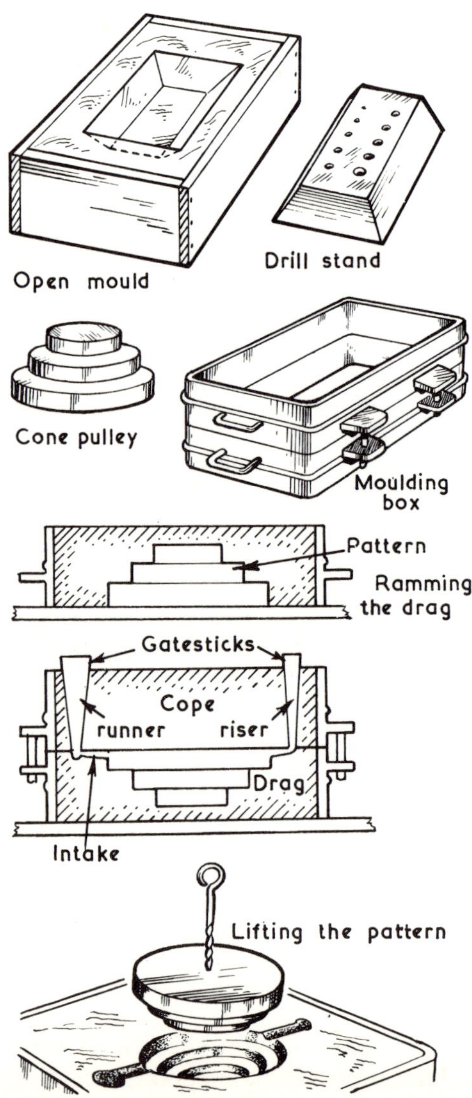

remain in position when the cope is moved. The parting sand prevents the two halves of the mould from sticking together, which would spoil the mould.

Moulding Sand. Sand is the most common and convenient, and the best moulding material. More or less porous, it enables air, steam and gases to escape through it; it is very refractory, so that the hot metal does not melt or bake it, and it retains its shape when heated and adheres when compressed. Different kinds of sand are suitable for different metals, but Mansfield red sand is used for copper alloys and aluminium alloys and is favoured in schools. Hensall sand, to which coal dust is added, is best for iron and steel. The best moulding sand is obtained from the beds of rivers in the neighbourhood of slate or granite, or in the coal districts, and is called greensand because it is damp. Today, however, in large foundries sand is bonded mechanically to produce a standard mixture. The moisture content should be between 5% and 7%, but is best judged in school by squeezing a handful. When the hand is opened carefully, the sand should keep its shape without sticking to the hand and it should break up easily when dropped. Sand that is too moist is dangerous, as the metal may spurt and the excess steam given off spoils the casting. Sand which is too dry tends to crumble and will not keep its shape.

Removing the Pattern. To take this from the mould the sand at the edges of the pattern should first be moistened slightly with a soft brush to prevent the sides of the mould crumbling. A gimlet or screw hook is screwed into a previously prepared hole in the pattern but a metal plate with a tapped hole is let into the back of a pattern, which is used frequently. The pattern is tapped sharply, rapped, in several directions, to loosen it, and is then lifted out carefully, steadily and vertically. If any part of the mould crumbles, it is usually remade entirely, but slight faults can be corrected with **moulder's tools**. These can be made as school exercises.

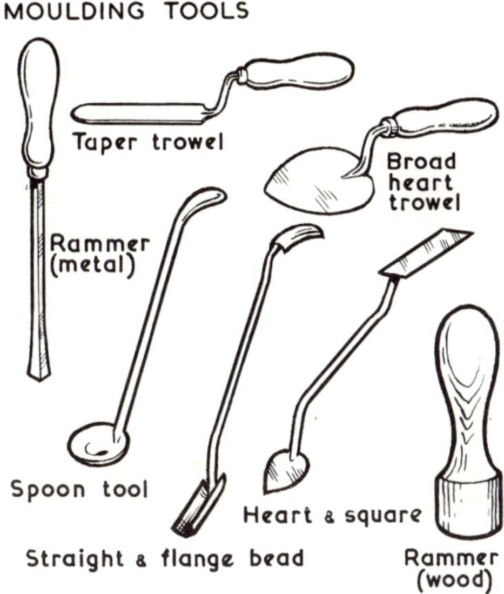

Completing the Mould Gates and Vents. A channel, called an ingate, must be cut in the face of the drag between the runner pool and the mould cavity. When several articles are cast in the same box as shown opposite a channel must be cut between each cavity and to the bottom of the riser if it is outside a mould cavity. A pouring gate or feeder head, shaped like a funnel, is cut out at the top of the runner. The cope is replaced above the drag and there must not be any loose sand in the shaped cavity or between the two faces. Cast iron moulding boxes have corresponding fittings, pins on one half and holes in the other, and often they are set one on one side and two on the other, so that the cope cannot be replaced the wrong way. Similar precautions should be considered when making wooden boxes. Complicated or large castings may need vents so that gases may escape more easily. Vents are narrow holes made by pushing pointed wire through the cope to touch or almost touch the pattern. During pouring there are high gas pressures inside the mould which might even lift the cope, so it is advisable to clamp the two halves together or place weights on top.

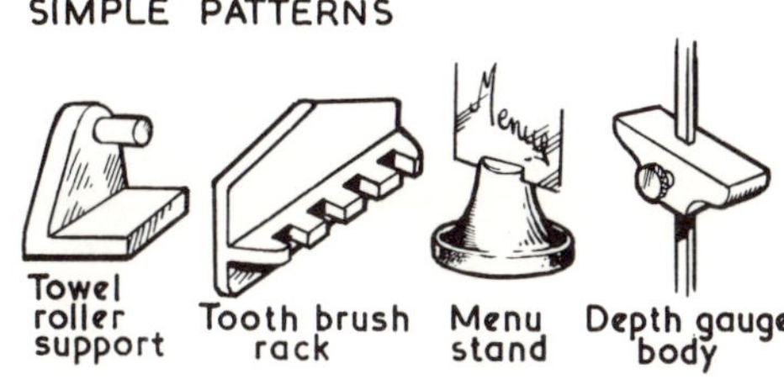

Four articles in one moulding box

Articles as cast

Melting the Metal. The mould is now ready for pouring. Lead can be melted in an iron ladle but iron and steel are melted in a cupola, which is like a small blast furnace. Brass and aluminium alloys are melted in plumbago crucibles, preferably in a furnace, although they can be heated in a forge. The crucible is warmed, then charged with small pieces of solid metal and more metal is added as that melts. Thin scrap must be used carefully as it tends to cause excessive oxidation. When casting aluminium alloys degassing helps to prevent porous castings. A small degassing tablet is pushed to the bottom of the melt just before pouring, using a perforated inverted hollow and leaving it there until all bubbling ceases. Chlorine gas is liberated which combines with the hydrogen in the molten metal to give off hydrochloric acid gas. Metal is best poured about 100° C above its melting point, often called its freezing point in industry today.

Pouring is dangerous and great care must be exercised. It should always be done with the crucible in a shank ring, not in tongs. The shank can be controlled easily by two people, one supporting and steadying, while the other controls and turns the shank and so tips the crucible. A small crucible can be poured while in a single-handed shank, but with tongs the pouring position is difficult, awkward and dangerous. The box should be placed in a large metal tray, say 750 mm square and 150 mm deep with a layer of sand in the bottom, so that if the metal is poured badly it will not spatter or run on the shop floor. This tray should be conveniently near to the furnace, which should be installed at ground level, and it is advisable to spread sand on the floor over which the crucible is carried. One should never stand between the furnace and the tray. The sides of the tray serve as a rest or steady for the shank containing the crucible of molten metal and they will prevent people from getting too

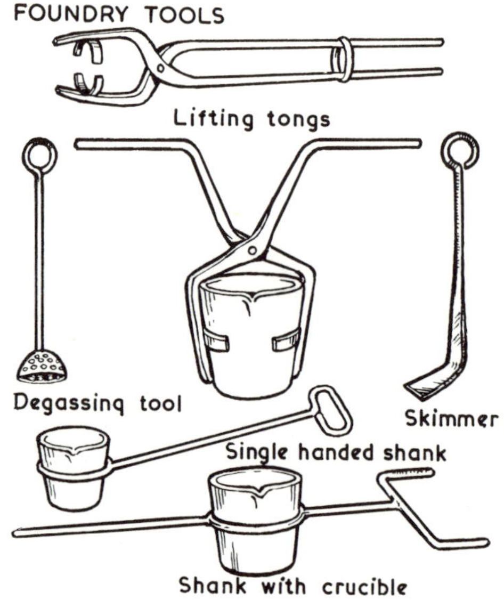

close to the moulding box. The crucible is removed from the furnace or fire with tongs, which must be of the correct shape and size, and placed in the shank ring where the dross, a film of oxide, dirt and slag floating on top of the metal, is skimmed off with a heated skimmer. The crucible must be held close to the pouring gate and poured so that the metal enters the mould cleanly in one smooth, steady and continuous stream. If poured too quickly there may be blow-holes in the casting, due to the steam bubbles being unable to get away or turbulence in the molten metal caused by metal splashing within the mould. If poured too slowly, the metal in the mould may become pasty and begin to solidify. This prevents metal flowing further into the mould cavity and is called a misrun. While pouring, care must be taken to keep back from the lip of the crucible any dross left after skimming. Pourers should not lean over the flask in case the metal spurts upward, as may happen if the metal is poured too quickly or if the sand is too moist. Gloves should always be worn while attending the furnace or when pouring. Any tools which come in contact with the melt must be first warmed to ensure that they are absolutely dry. Molten metal remaining in the crucible after pouring should be poured into small ingot moulds, but if metal is left in the crucible it must be tilted on its side inside the tray. Metal left in the bottom may, as it expands on reheating, crack the crucible if it is left upright.

ASSIGNMENTS

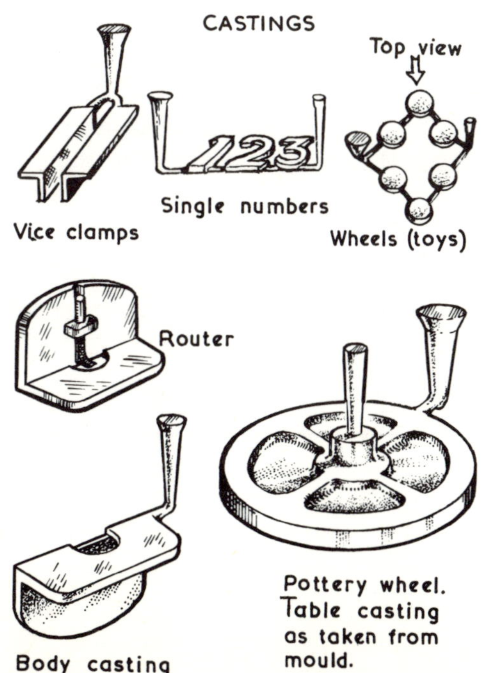

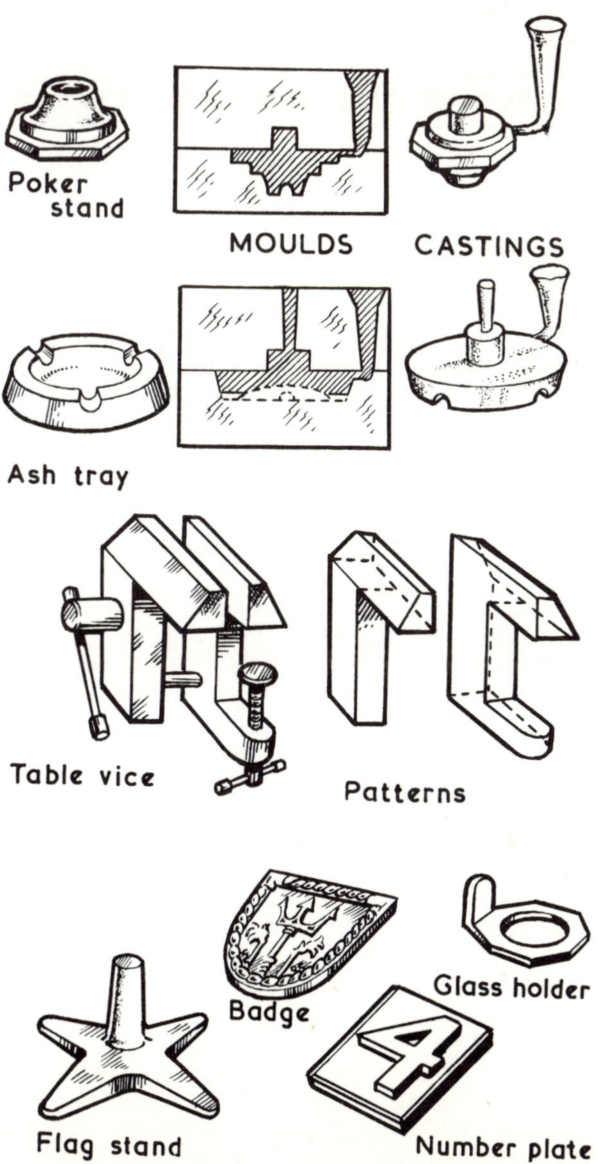

Metal for the School Foundry

Brass and Bronze can be used for foundry work in school but **aluminium alloys,** preferably **L.M.4** or **L.M.6,** purchased in notched ingots, are most suitable. Both are strong, hard, resistant to corrosion and to hot tearing—the tendency to cool and shrink unequally, so setting up stresses which cause small cracks (tears) in the casting. L.M.4 machines better and has a wider melting range (520–620° C) than L.M.6 (565–575° C), which is more fluid and is much better for anodising. Brass is cast around 1000° C and aluminium bronze, which is 90% copper and 10% aluminium, and gunmetal (88% copper, 10% tin, 2% zinc), both referred to as bronze, are cast at about 1200° C.

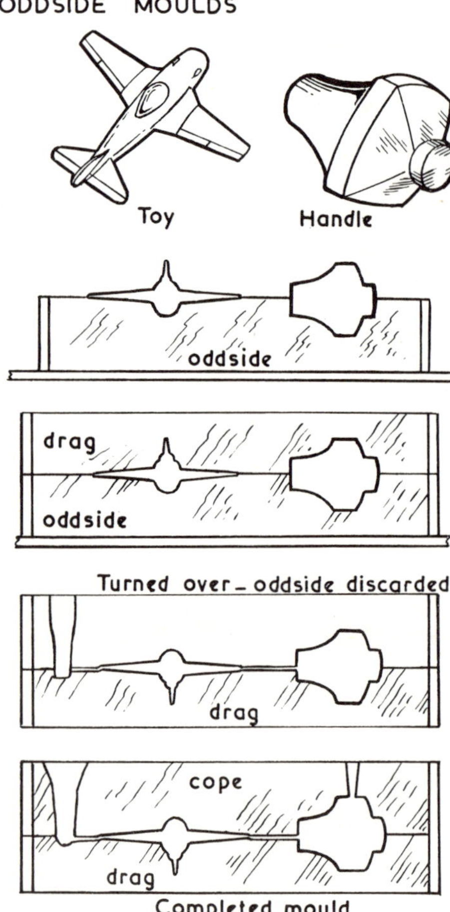

Oddside Moulding is used for one-piece patterns which do not have a plain face and when both the cope and the drag have to be shaped around them as on cylindrical work. The top part of the box is placed face upwards on a board, filled with sand, rammed and strickled off. Then sand is scooped away with a trowel so that the pattern can be pressed in to the required depth, usually half-way. This is the oddside, which is used as a temporary support for the drag and is afterwards remade. The surface of the sand and the pattern are dusted with parting sand and the drag is placed over the oddside and made in the usual way. Both halves are then turned over together and the oddside removed, and the sand knocked out leaving the pattern in the drag. The face of the drag is dusted, the top half of the box is put back in position and the cope is completed. Gate sticks can be used to form the runners and risers, or they can be cut with a metal tube sharpened at the end on the inside. The way in which the pattern is arranged in the mould, and how the metal is poured, is most important.

Split Patterns do not require an oddside. The pattern is made in two parts, equal halves if possible, dowelled together. The lamp base (5) on p. 131 and the rudder strap shown on p. 126 are cast from split patterns. That part of the pattern without the dowels is laid flat on a board and half of the flask, moulding box, is placed over it, and the bottom half of the mould is made. Then it is turned over the other part of the pattern fixed in position, and the surface dusted with parting powder. The other half of the box is placed in position and the mould completed as before. The two halves of the flask are now separated, and the two parts of the pattern are taken out separately.

SPLIT PATTERNS

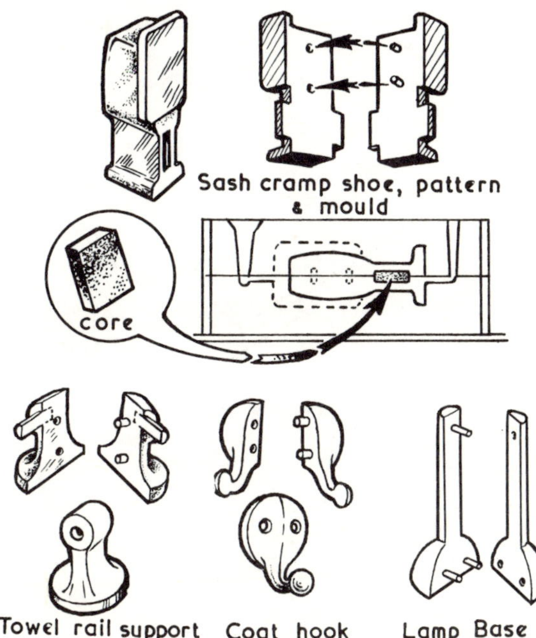

Patterns can be made of wood, metal or of plastic materials. Wood patterns are easiest to make, especially in school. Smooth grained wood which will not shrink or warp much is desirable, and yellow pine and Honduras mahogany are most suitable, but are expensive and difficult to obtain. Good clean white pine is often used today. Metals shrink on melting, so patterns are made slightly larger than the desired article: 5 mm in 300 mm or one sixtieth is the allowance for aluminium. So that patterns may be easily taken out of the sand, they are made very smooth and varnished or polished. All sharp internal corners are avoided, radiused, and vertical sides are sloped a little so that the sand is not disturbed. This slope is called "draft" and is between 3° and 5°. Allowances are also made on patterns for machining.

ASSIGNMENTS FOR ODDSIDE OR SPLIT PATTERNS

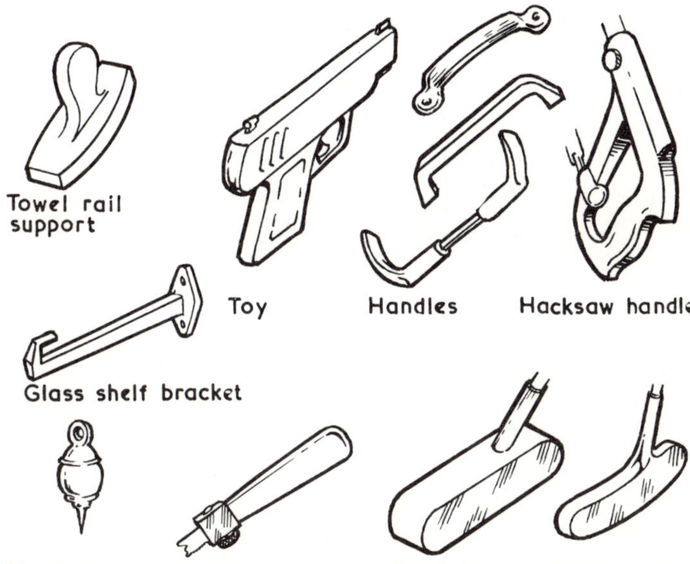

Either method can be used for the articles illustrated above because they are all symmetrical about a centre plane. The aluminium golf putter is larger than the bronze putter because their weights should be the same.

Board or Plate Patterns are patterns fixed to a board. Usually they consist of two half or part patterns, each fixed to opposite sides of a board; 12 mm resin-bonded plywood serves excellently, or a metal plate for metal patterns. The parts of the pattern must be accurately placed so that they correspond exactly, and the board or plate must have location holes so that it will fit accurately between the two halves of the box. The board is supported across a box and the pins on the flask fit down through the holes in the board. When this part of the mould is complete, it is turned over with the board, and the other half of the box having holes fits over the board and the pins. Both the cope and the drag are made similarly against the board as for simple patterns. The small cylindrical hollows shown on the boards are for the bottom of the runner sprues. Underneath them are hemispheres of wood or plastic material to form hollows for the pools of metal. Board patterns are difficult to make but the mould making is easier especially in school. The coat hook shown has a rubber pad to act as a door stop. Alternatively the end could be cast with a hemispherical hollow in which a small rubber ball could be glued. Most of the examples illustrated in this chapter could be cast by this method. The choice of method depends on the practice favoured by the moulder.

Cores are essential for most castings. Solid castings would as a rule, be too heavy and wasteful. Hollow castings are usually made by resting a baked sand core in the mould and pouring the metal around it. The simplest core is a cylinder, often made in a core making machine, designed to make a hole through a casting as in the pulley or part-way through, as in the face plate, shown opposite.

Core Prints. Moulds for hollow castings must include extra hollows in which the core can rest. The pattern has additions, usually made solid with the pattern and called core prints, to provide hollows. Most of the articles illustrated need two core prints added to the pattern as for the cramp shoe and the enlarger stand, but the faceplate pattern needs only one which must be carefully worked out so that the core will not fall into the main cavity of the mould.

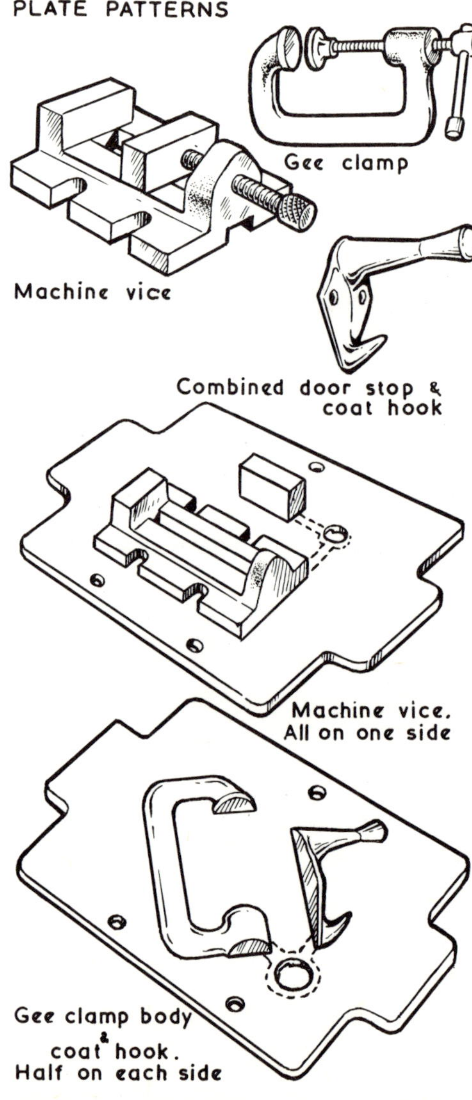

Core Boxes. Cores usually need core boxes, as shown for the rudder strap overleaf, in which the sand is pressed to the necessary shape before it is hardened. The boxes are made in two parts so that the sand core can be lifted out.

Hardening Sand Cores. Cores are made of river or beach sand bonded together with one of the many synthetic binders used in industry called core oils, but linseed oil can be used in the school workshop. They can be baked in furnaces but CO_2 hardening is often preferred in industrial foundries, because it saves time. Sodium silicate (water glass) is mixed with the sand and carbon dioxide gas is passed through the core, hardening it in a few seconds or minutes, depending on its size. A simple furnace suitable for baking cores in school can be built up by supporting and surrounding a sheet iron shelf with firebricks. The core is heated with bunsen burners for about half an hour. After casting, the core is broken up so that it can be removed easily.

Casting Bells

Large bells (there is one in Moscow weighing over a hundred tonnes) are cast in bell metal—78% copper, 22% tin—mouth downwards but it may be easier to cast small bells mouth upwards as shown. Patterns for large bells were of clay, built over specially prepared cores, and separated from the core and the outside mould by wax. The whole is baked and then the clay pattern can be taken out in pieces before casting. The core determines the thickness of the metal. The core of the rudder strap fills the gap between the two strips of metal.

Cast Iron is very important industrially but it is cast at about 1400° C, a temperature which is very difficult to obtain in the school furnace.

Steel Castings are poured at 1700° C and need special heat treatment afterwards, usually annealing.

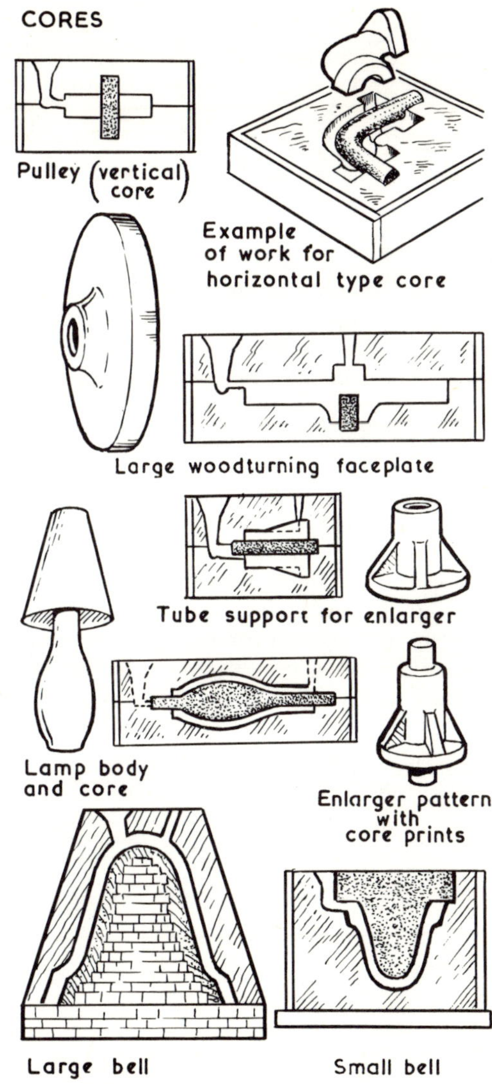

Malleable Castings are made from white cast iron and also need heat treatment usually annealing to make them tougher and stronger but they are not as strong as steel.

Chilled Castings are usually of grey cast iron made in moulds in which parts are of metal which cool—"chill"—parts of the iron casting more quickly and make these surfaces harder (*see* p. 168).

Cire Perdue Casting—sometimes called the lost wax process—consists of making the pattern, which is really a core, slightly smaller than the required article, covering it with wax and making the mould over the wax. Then the whole is heated and the wax runs out leaving room for the molten metal (*see* p. 180).

Die Casting is casting in accurately prepared moulds, called dies, usually made of steel and in two parts which separate for the casting to be removed. Pressure die casting involves forcing the molten metal into the dies under pressure. These dies are extremely accurate and very expensive, and the process, which is often fully automatic, is used only when very large quantities are required. It gives exceptionally fine definition and is used considerably today, e.g. to make domestic equipment, toys in zinc and plastic materials, zinc alloy components of motor cars (carburettors, door handles, etc.) and machine parts.

CASTING A RUDDER STRAP

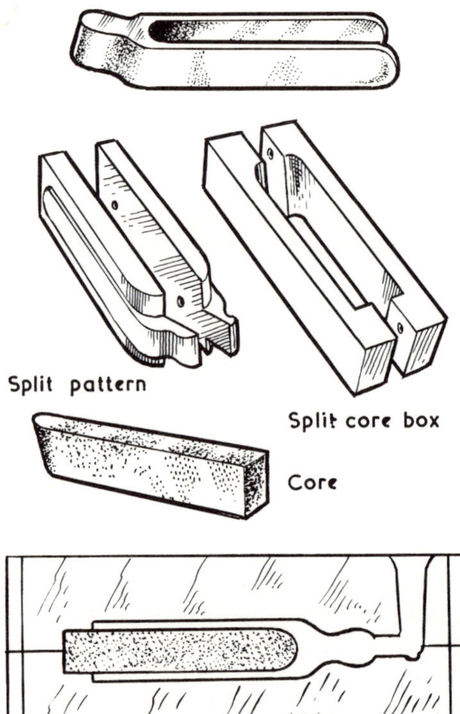

Section through moulding box

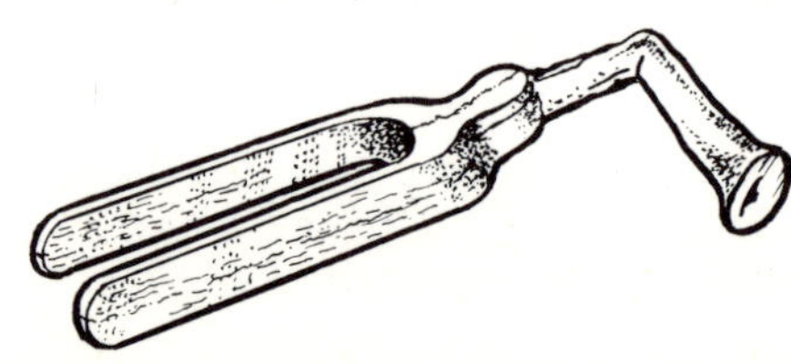

Strap as cast

Plate 21. **Cast Iron Tableware by Robert Welch**

Tablelighter, nut-cracker and fruit bowl of cast iron finished black matt vitreous enamel. Pepper-mill in cast aluminium with a wooden knob available in black, orange and blue enamel. Designed for Old Hall Tableware Ltd.

Plate 22. **Cast Sculptures—Students' Work**

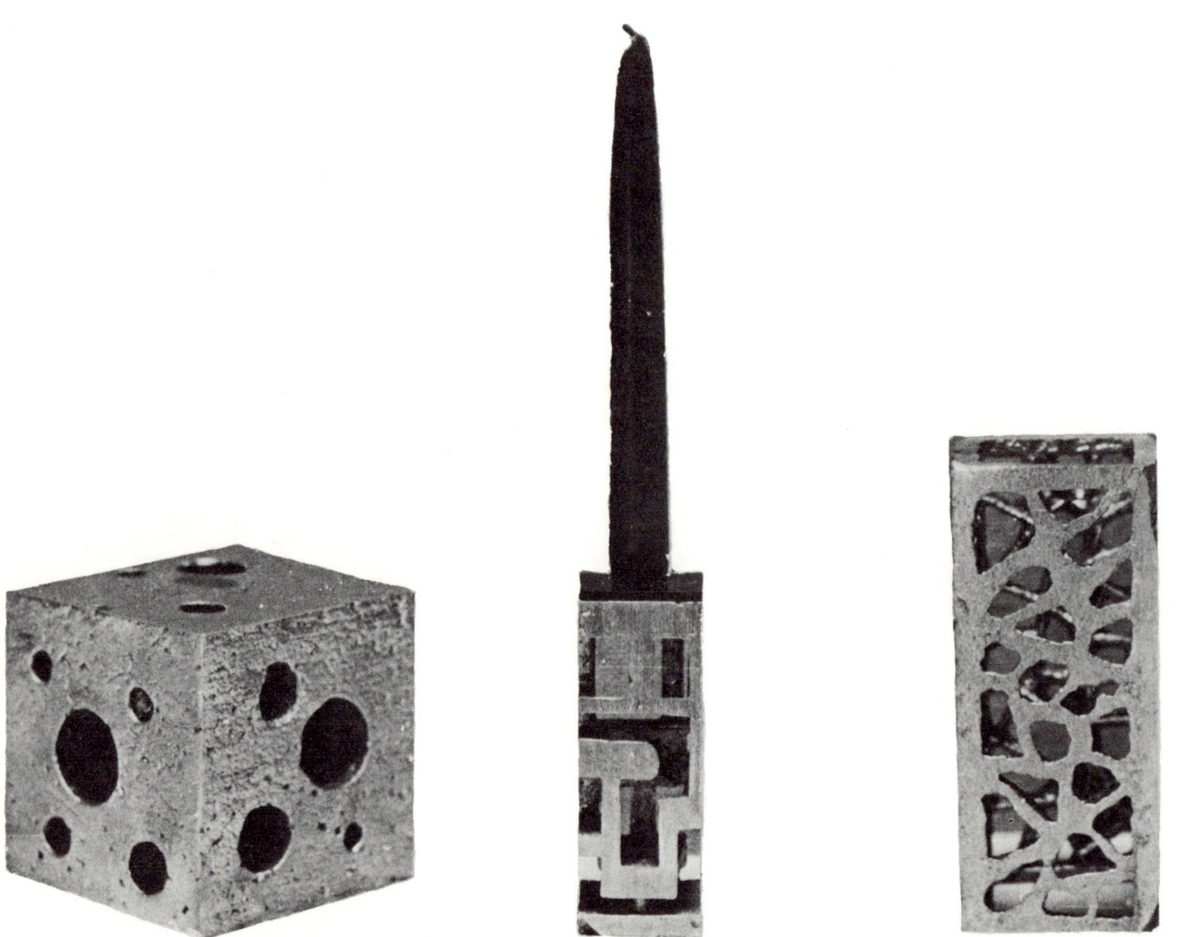

Students' Work at the City of Leeds and Carnegie College
Three examples in aluminium alloy (LM4) sand castings using polystyrene patterns. Tutor, Robert Rignall

22

Design: Problems and Assignments

Assignments with Tubing

This topic might be considered as part of the assignments on brazing, but designing frameworks is an essential part of design study and it can be very interesting. Tubular frameworks are excellent for many domestic articles and may have particular value in the school workshop because oddments of tube can often be purchased very cheaply; often they are given away as scrap. There is no limit to the design possibilities with tube—ladders, steps, stairs, swings, trolleys and carts on two, three, and four wheels, and ladder-furniture, which is dependent on square tube, including height-adjustable book-cases, cupboards, desks, and sideboards. Tube offers plenty of scope for design briefs and apart from the ideas suggested above alternative designs can be prepared for all the illustrations given; some might be adjustable or collapsible in order that they can be taken apart—knock-down fittings—or special group projects might be undertaken (e.g., garden-furniture: tent, hammock and awning frames; folding stools; chairs and tables; arches; fencing; etc.). Round tube is by far the cheapest, but square, rectangular and oval tube can be obtained and some furniture looks very fine and is very strong when these alternative tube-sections are used. Building up frameworks by using two or more basic framework patterns of simple shape—as in the stool, table and climbing-frame constructions shown—offers further design-exercises. Tubes of different diameters can be used together, as in the central-column table shown, or when arranging for one tube to slide into another as might be desirable in the whirligig clothes-drier.

Joining Tube

All the suggestions can be brazed or welded together, but as rigidity is an essential problem in these designs some parts may be riveted, bolted or screwed together before brazing or welding. This can be especially helpful to young people who are not experienced in brazing and welding. End-to-end jointing, as when completing the closed frames for the trolleys or the circles for the hose-reel, can be achieved by fitting a tight plug inside the two ends which meet together. The final joint must always be cleaned and brazed or welded. Steel tube can be joined end-to-side, as follows.

(1) Make, fit, and braze mild-steel plugs into the ends which are to be joined.
(2) File the plugged ends to fit round the sides of the other piece—the other half of the joint.
(3) Drill and tap the end plugs for suitable size screws.
(4) Drill clearance-holes in the sides, and screw through the sides into the ends.
(5) Tighten the joint, and braze or weld together. The joints can, of course, be made by simply filing the ends of one piece to fit round the other, followed by brazing or welding, but some form of clamping is then necessary when brazing or welding.

DESIGNING FRAMEWORKS WITH TUBES

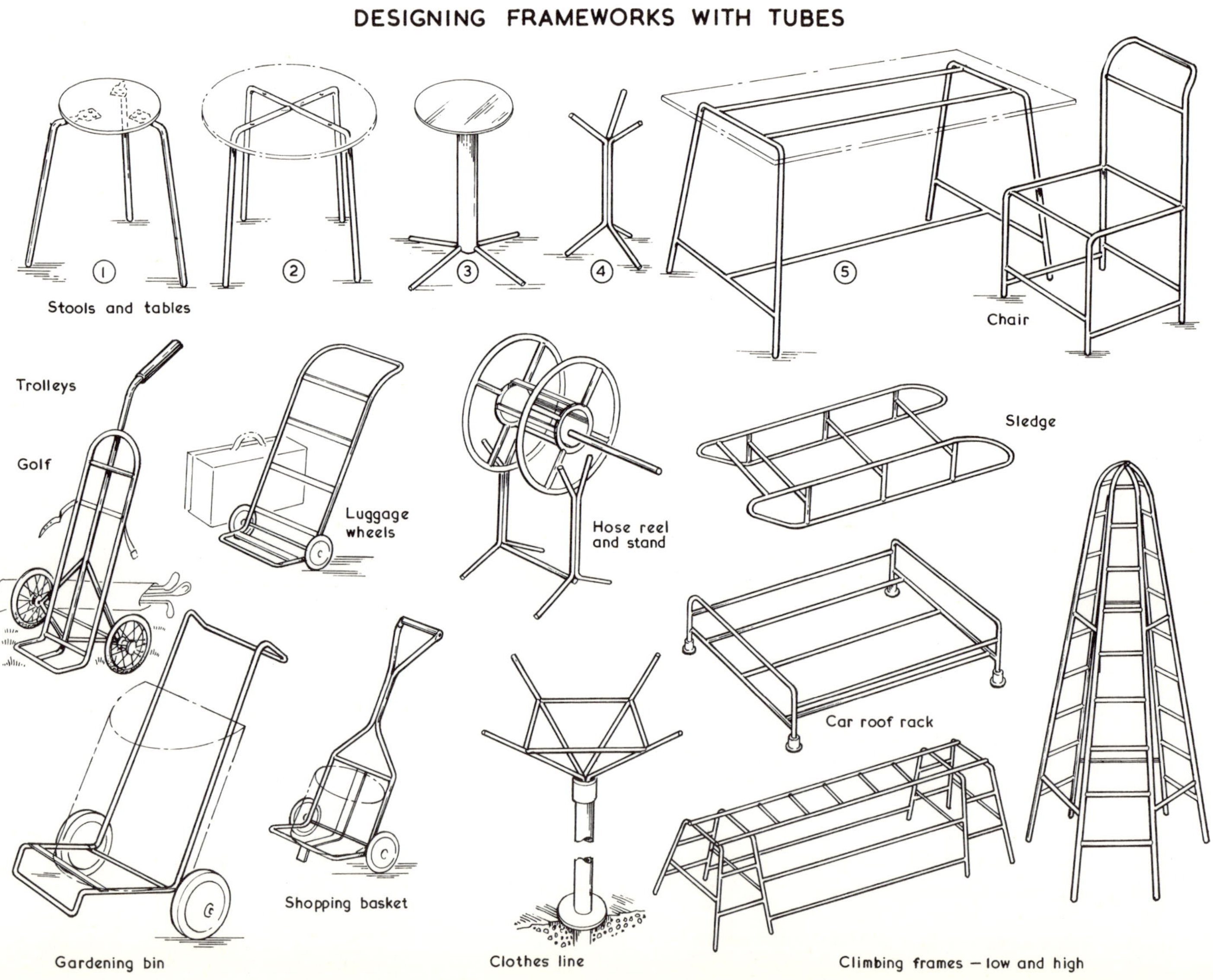

Stools and Tables

(1) The tube at the top of each leg must be flattened or have an extra piece fitted and brazed so that the ends can be screwed to the top. Alternatively, the ends can be riveted and/or welded or brazed to a flat plate which can be screwed to the top.

(2) Two frames crossing, cross-halved, or flattened and brazed or welded (possibly riveted first).

(3) Stout centre-tube with a base of lighter tube or, preferably, 30 mm × 5 mm bar tapered at each end for the base. This framework, because of the heavier materials, should be welded. If the base is to be of flat metal, it can have two pieces horizontally cross-halved and fitted into the column—in which case small feet might be necessary to lift the framework from the floor. Alternatively, the base could have three side legs instead of four and the top construction can be varied.

(4) Three lengths of tube, all bent to the same shape and welded together. The ends should be flattened for screwing the top and wood or rubber feet are necessary.

(5) A strong structure for a rectangular table. Compare this with those on p. 133.

Chairs

There are many ways of making tubular chairs and only the obvious is suggested. The fixing of a seat, canvas in this case, is another problem.

Trolleys

These must always be light, easy to manoeuvre and comfortable to handle, and they must stand easily. *Golf*—narrow design with straps fitted for the golf bag. *Luggage wheels*—a strong standard shape for wheeling heavy cases and trunks. *Shopping*—designed to take and fit a large oval basket so that the basket can be removed and replaced easily, or a large cardboard case like those used for packing bottles. Sometimes arrangements are made for hanging the basket. *Gardening*—made to take a large light bin, rectangular or semi-circular in shape, which is made of plywood or hardboard, both of which can be bent to shape after steaming. The bin can be bolted to the framework which is rigid and may not need cross-members; it needs a hinged lid, preferably sloping, and can be used for clearing up leaves, moving plants or small bushes, or for carrying equipment. Small wheels from old prams or pushchairs, or even wheels from large toys, might be sought from parents in order to make cheap trolleys.

Hose-reel and stand—it is difficult to bend tube into small circles, so strip is easier for the inner circles, but tube is stronger and can be used for the outer wheels and the spokes. The stand is made as table (4), but with four bent shapes welded together in pairs and joined by cross-ties. Special attention must be given to the top tie to make it detachable so that the reel can be used independently.

Sledge—must have a strong framework, and extra ties must always be considered. Long wooden strips are fixed to the framework for the children to lie on and the cross-bar in front is for holding on.

Car roof rack—the first thing is to measure the roof of the car and decide upon the position for the uprights. Then the end-frameworks can be bent to size and the cross-members cut to length and fitted for assembly.

Climbing frame—low frame for crawling above and below, over and under, with a ladder. It consists of four identical frames jointed to make two end-stools with connecting rails and cross-pieces. It can be adapted to be used as a pivot for a large seesaw. High frame for climbing and swinging. Made from three tall ladder frameworks, bent at the top, and fixed so that they can be separated for storing. The cross-ties which hold the frameworks together are screwed or bolted in position.

Whirligig clothes-drier—a stout central-tube is essential as this has to take the weight of all the clothes and fit into a hole in the concrete. It could be adjustable for height by having an inside tube, and extra cross-ties might be convenient, although holes and a nylon cord will be better for small clothes. It might be better if it were made of aluminium-alloy tube, so that it would be lighter and made to fold up like an umbrella. The design also suggests an idea for making a large sunshade awning.

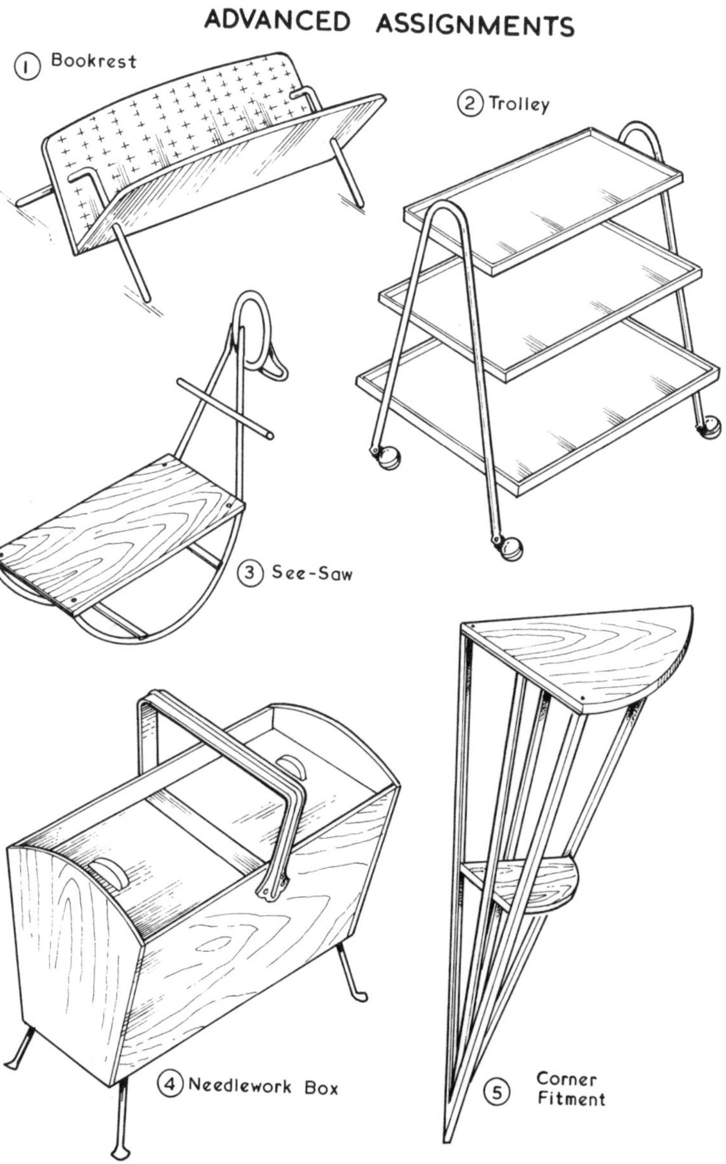

ASSIGNMENTS USING OTHER MATERIALS WITH METAL

The essential design problem concerns the material and several alternative materials always should be considered. The problem is more interesting, of course, if two or more materials can be used together. Students should be encouraged to consider this, and simple furniture offers excellent opportunities.

(1) **Book-rest.** The dimensions will depend on the size and number of the books. In this simple job, 6 mm mild-steel or brass can be used for the two ends (which also serve as feet); 5 mm plywood is not attractive, but is strong and can be excellent when painted or covered and is useful for the shelf and the back. The book-rest shown is covered with Fablon which is easier to keep clean than wood and looks extremely pleasing.

(2) **Trolley** and (3) **seesaw**, made from mild-steel tube (*see* p. 127) and wood. The trolley shelves have plastic laminate glued on the wood.

(4) **Needlework box** of solid wood with brass-tube legs soldered on to turned brass feet with a decorated, brass-strip handle.

(5) **Corner fitting.** This has a metal framework and shelves of plate glass or coloured Formica glued on to plywood. Wooden shelves can be fitted easily, but glass will need to be supported in frames, carefully made of angle metal. Mild-steel or brass angle is also used at the corners with strip in between, brazed together at the bottom, but screwed or riveted and then brazed to the two-shelf frameworks.

The ideas offered by several materials offer a fascinating variety of ideas when designing and making table lamps and occasional tables.

Table Lamps

The first four give subdued light, often preferred when watching television. The light is shielded by screens of coloured plastic ribbon or raffia wound on to metal frames. The other lamps are made of wood and metal with shades of metal (Nos. 6 and 7) or oiled paper or plastic sheet fixed on to metal frames (5 and 6). Three lamps (Nos. 5, 6 and 7) involve useful turning exercises, 5 and 7 having turned wood bodies and No. 5 has a base of cast aluminium, (*see* pp. 122 and 123). Brass tube is used for Nos. 6, 7 and 8. Brass feet might be added to 6 and 8 so that they will stand firmly as the flex will be threaded up through the brass tube. These shapes are only suggestions which should be varied, but in every lamp the wiring must be considered as an integral part of the design.

Occasional Tables

Tables are traditionally of wood but those shown here have metal legs and underframings and use plastics, tiles and glass for the tops. They could have tubular legs as suggested on pp. 128 and 135 but on this sheet only No. 9 uses tube.

(1) 10 mm round mild steel legs fitted and brazed into metal plates which are screwed on to a plywood top. The edges of the plywood are painted to match the feet which are wooden balls.

(2) 12 mm legs and a riveted and brazed framework screwed to a top of chipboard faced and edged with Formica.

(3) 10 mm legs riveted and brazed to plates which are screwed to a plywood top as shown. The top is edged with solid wood wide enough to allow for the fitting of ceramic tiles which might be made in the school pottery studio.

(4) Legs and top edging of 15 × 15 × 3 mm angle iron with 15 × 5 mm strip rails. The top is made up of linoleum printed in the art studio and glued to plywood or chipboard.

(5) 10 mm mild steel rods screwed and brazed to a central tube. The top of the tube is fitted with a flange and the ends of the rods are flattened so that all can be screwed to a decorated wood top, painted, veneered or covered with patterned plastic sheeting.

(6) 12 mm rods intertwined and screwed to a commercial table top.

(7) Mild steel strip 18 × 6 mm bent jointed and brazed to form a continuous framework. D.I.Y. shops sell attractive table tops and decorated Formica, sometimes patterned and cut circular but these are obtainable only in limited sizes so it may occasionally be desirable first to choose and buy or make the top and design the legs and framework to suit the top.

(8) 10 mm square mild steel leg frames with bracing and, possibly, rails of brass strip. The top is of small square tiles built up on edged plywood.

(9) Legs and underframing of 12 mm square tubing with 10 × 10 × 3 mm angle for the top edging, all jointed and brazed or welded together. The top is of plate glass and it rests in the angle metal frame.

The desirability of using various materials and of introducing colour into metalwork make small tables excellent design briefs, especially with classes which have practised forging, brazing and welding. A decoratively forged framework can be designed for a square, rectangular, circular or semi-circular table, the top of which might be of coloured material, or white opaque glass or armour plate glass, plain or smoky.

OCCASIONAL TABLES

Plate 23. **Embassy Tableware by David Mellor**

Silver teapot and cutlery. Part of a range designed for use in British Embassies

Plate 24. **Stainless Steel Tableware by Robert Welch**

"Alveston" tea-set with a satin finish designed by Robert Welch and like the "Alveston" cutlery selected for presentation to the Russian Head of State. It is made by Old Hall Tableware Ltd.

23

Design and Materials—Structures and Strengths

Material Problems

In assignments, one of the fundamental problems is the choice of material. The strength of the material is an important consideration, often a vital one, in all design. This book is concerned mainly with metals which are essential materials and there are a great many of them—but we cannot consider metals exclusively, nor should we try to work with metals alone.

Basic materials as found in the earth, sea and air are called elements and there are more than a hundred elements; but most materials are obtained by mixing elements and one of the main reasons for mixing is to make the material stronger. If a material lacked strength completely it would disintegrate, so every material has sufficient strength to hold it together and to help it withstand its particular surroundings and conditions (e.g., temperature, external wind and rain or internal moisture), all of which may be changing all the time. If the strength of a material can be found, so also can its weaknesses, and it might be possible to correct these in order to improve the material and increase its usefulness. A knowledge of materials enables us to use them correctly and good design depends on a sound understanding of materials.

Man has always tried to strengthen materials available to him and find new ones which possess better qualities. Since the Bronze Age, when tin was added to copper to harden and strengthen it, the metallic elements have been mixed to make better metals, and it is now such common practice to strengthen iron by adding carbon that there are more than a hundred different steels and pure iron is never used when strength is necessary. Technologists are producing many new synthetic plastics, using mainly coal and oil, and these new materials have four great advantages: (1) they combine lightness with strength; (2) they are corrosion and rot proof; (3) they can be easily moulded into complex shapes and (4) they are inexpensive. Nevertheless, these plastics are being further improved by adding traditional materials (e.g., carbon, glass, asbestos, linen, silk, cotton, and powdered metal). Fibre-glass (glass fibres impregnated with polyester resin) is strong enough for chairs, boats, and even cars. Similarly, paper sheet is made harder and stronger by treating it with thermosetting resin and then subjecting it to intense heat and pressure to convert it to plastic laminates (Formica). These have become universally used for table tops and working surfaces in hotels, restaurants, kitchens, and so on.

Concrete is now used in vast quantities and this introduces new design problems. Cement, a manufactured material, was used in a rough form by the Romans, but afterwards forgotten, until 1824, when it was rediscovered and called Portland cement because it was thought to resemble Portland stone. It is mixed with the traditional materials, sand and stone, in selected proportions to produce concrete of the required strength for the job in hand. When the concrete is to be used for large construction work in building, it is reinforced by embedding in the mixture steel bars, coils of wire, zig-zag strips and wire mesh arranged in certain positions so that when the concrete sets hard it will be strengthened in the right way and in the right places. There are innumerable methods of reinforcing, and the reinforcement must be worked out according to the requirements of each job, in order to make each concrete constructional part strong enough to take its place in the overall design. The strength of reinforced concrete can be calculated accurately before it is made and the designer can estimate the the necessary strength of each of his constructional members. The organised combination of concrete and steel has produced some fascinating architectural developments, such as the use of large unbroken surfaces, flat and curved, horizontal and vertical, and we now have buildings erected on pillars with long landscape windows and flat roofs supporting roof gardens.

Designing structures

Even strong materials have to be selected and arranged correctly, if they are to give maximum strength and this constructional aspect is the responsibility of the engineer or designer. When a bridge gives way, or a block of flats collapses, or the surface of a motorway breaks up it may be the materials which lack strength, but it is more likely to be due to faults in the design or in the construction. Strength can be assured by using very stout material, but this may be unnecessarily extravagant in material, heavy in construction and possibly ugly in appearance; this is bad design.

Consider the small tables shown on p. 133 and the sizes of the metal legs. They could be of 20 millimetres square metal, solid or tube, but this would be unduly heavy and wasteful of material. Engineers can calculate accurately the size of the material necessary for the stress involved and calculations might well prove that 5 millimetre diameter metal legs are strong enough to support the table-top and all that might go on it, but such legs would look thin and might not make rigid tables. The illustrations suggest how the legs might be braced to form strong and rigid frameworks, but such bracing might be considered too complicated for a simple table and too expensive to produce. For the vertical legs for an occasional table 15 millimetres square or 18 millimetres round, metal tube would give ample strength and be economical in material, and give a pleasing appearance.

Strength is just one of the designer's problems. Obviously, when setting out drawings for bridges, buildings, motorways, ships, cars, etc., the designer has many more complex calculations to work out, together with estimates which have to be prepared before a final decision can be made.

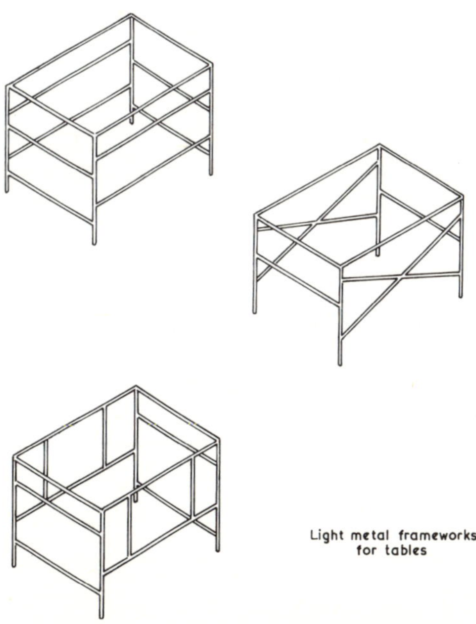

Light metal frameworks for tables

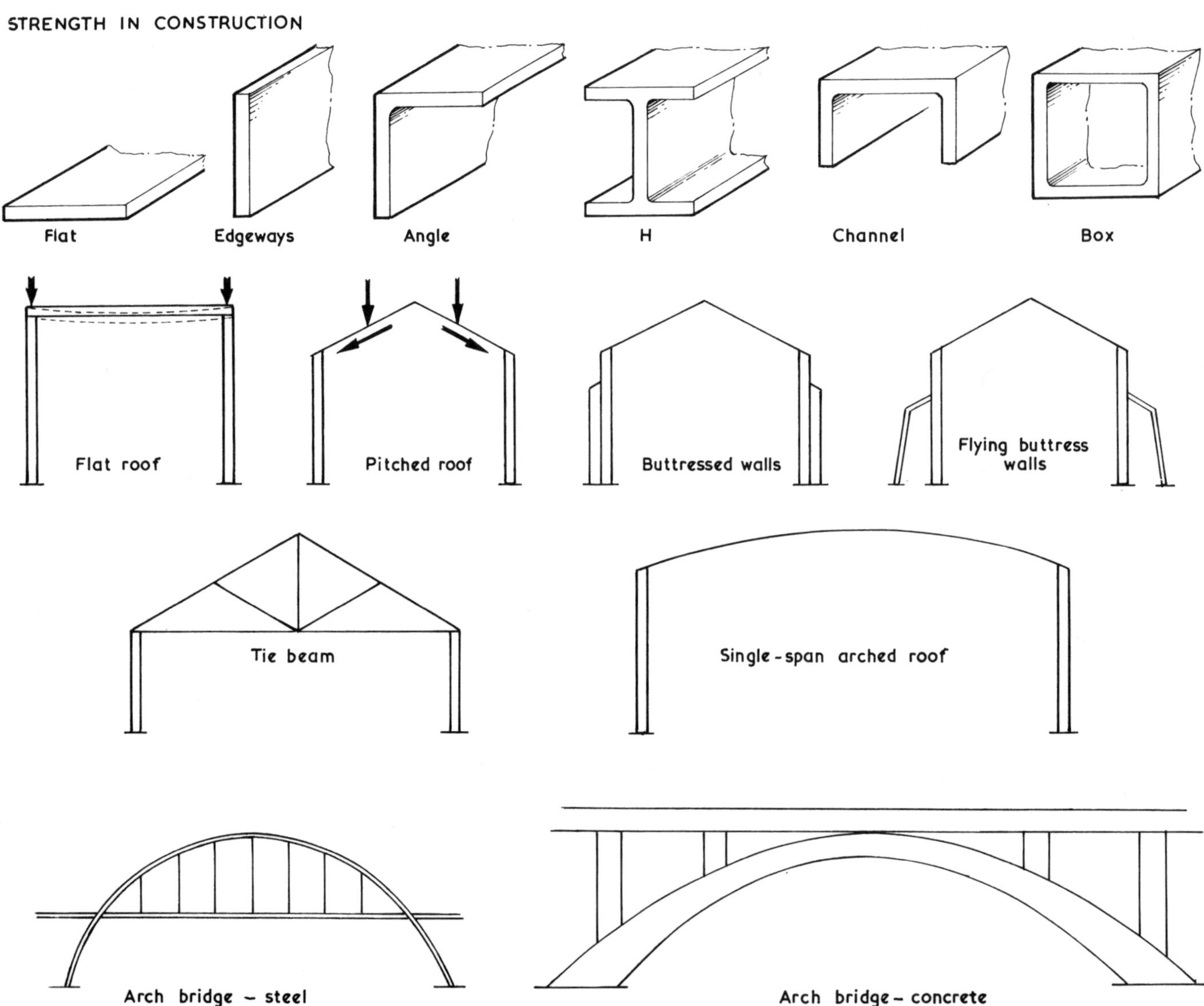
Flat
Edgeways
Angle
H
Channel
Box
Flat roof
Pitched roof
Buttressed walls
Flying buttress walls
Tie beam
Single-span arched roof
Arch bridge – steel
Arch bridge – concrete

Metal Sections

Take a strip of paper and notice how flimsy it is, but fold it at right-angles along its length and see how its rigidity and strength increases. In the same way angle iron is much stronger than strip. Consider the problem of building a bridge and take account of the strength of a rigid strip of wood or metal. It would support more weight if it were used edgeways, but while it is flatways there is room to put more on it. Because of this, strips were put together to form the H-section, the channel-section and the box. These sections are used for steel girders in building and the aim is to achieve the maximum strength with the minimum material.

Buildings

Early buildings were simple with flat roofs and all weight directed downwards but the roofs sagged in the middle and rain and snow tended to accumulate. This led to pitched roofs, two sloping surfaces meeting at a ridge so that rain and snow fell off. But these roofs were heavier and tended to push the walls outwards. To counter this, walls were strengthened with buttresses and some special buildings like cathedrals had ingenious and elaborate flying buttresses which joined the walls only at the top—like struts. Tie beams were introduced and these led to interesting roof structures to keep the walls and the sloping rafters, which rested on the walls, in place. These structures, however, though strong added weight and took up space whereas the aim in roof construction is to combine strength, span, lightness and space. This is best achieved by using a modern material, like steel, in the form of a simple curved span—as is found in aircraft hangars and on bridges.

The construction of bridges is a good design and engineering study and the diagrams opposite show the two different ways in which different materials are used, steel being much stronger in tension than in compression and concrete, like cast iron being stronger in compression. This is particularly interesting now that our motorways set so many over-and-under problems. Reinforced concrete combines the strength of steel and concrete and this is illustrated by the design of the motorway bridge shown here, a construction which combines the old-fashioned beam bridge (named after the early bridges where a plank of wood was placed across a stream) and an arch bridge. The Forth Bridge, a nineteenth-century, all-steel cantilever bridge, is described on p. 154, and other bridges which should be studied are suspension bridges and cantilever bridges in reinforced concrete.

Concrete arch bridge over motorway

The Common Stresses

Strengths of materials are affected by internal and external stresses. Internal stresses are often the effect of faults in the material (e.g., badly mixed concrete, knots in timber, bad rolling, or wrong heat-treatment for steel), but it is the three simple external stresses—tenacity, compression and shear—which are always considered in estimating the strength of a material.

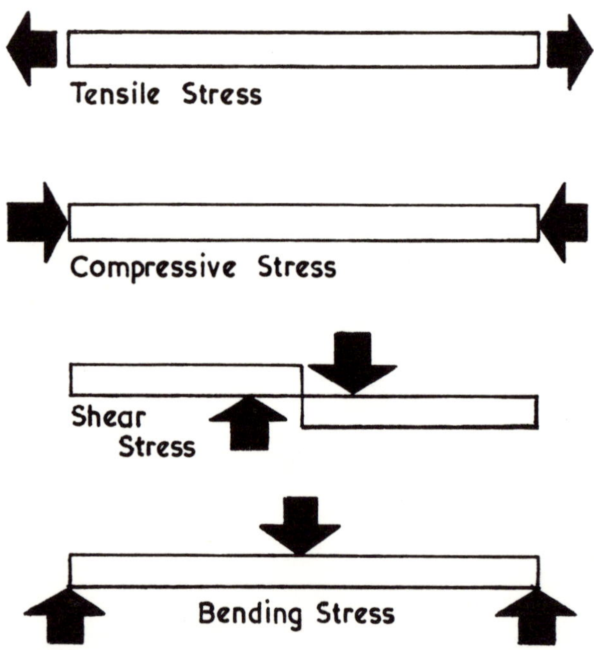

Tenacity, or tensile strength is the power of a material to withstand fracture when being stretched, when components are subjected to forces acting away from each other (e.g., the "tug-o'-war" stress when a chain is lifting a load). Eventually, the stretched component may break, but it will first become longer and its diameter will be reduced. This is possibly the most important mechanical property and with some special high-tensile steels it may exceed 1500 N/mm² (100 tons per square inch)—see p. 150.

Compression is the opposite of tension. The failure to withstand pressure when a component is subjected to forces acting towards each other with a squeezing or crushing action which may result in distortion. This is illustrated in a column taking a load—as in the supports of a bridge, or a vertical pillar holding up any part of a building, or in rolling or hammering—when before fracture occurs there will be a reduction in the dimension between the forces and an increase in other directions; the height of a column, in other words, will decrease while its breadth and width are increased, before it fractures.

Shear is a resistance to the action of two parallel forces acting in opposite directions. It is the resistance to the stress caused by the tendency of two parallel planes to slide over each other, and can be likened to the action of a pair of shears or scissors.

STRESS DIAGRAM

Bending stress is another often-mentioned stress, but actually it is a combination of the above three simple stresses. This is shown up in the illustration, where the weight of a train causes a bridge to sag or bend. The lower side (away from the load) is stretched—*tension*—which causes the other side (inside), which is in contact with the load, to contract—*compression*—and there will be *shearing* action when the load is just inside the columns. The amount of bending is known as *deflection*.

When studying the strengths of materials, "live loads" and "dead loads" must be considered. The dead load is the external force which exists all the time, or is applied steadily, while live loads are loads which are applied suddenly. For example, the weight of a bridge is a dead load, but the weight of a train passing over it is a live load.

To summarise, in metalwork the strength of a metal is the internal resistance of that metal offered to externally applied forces.

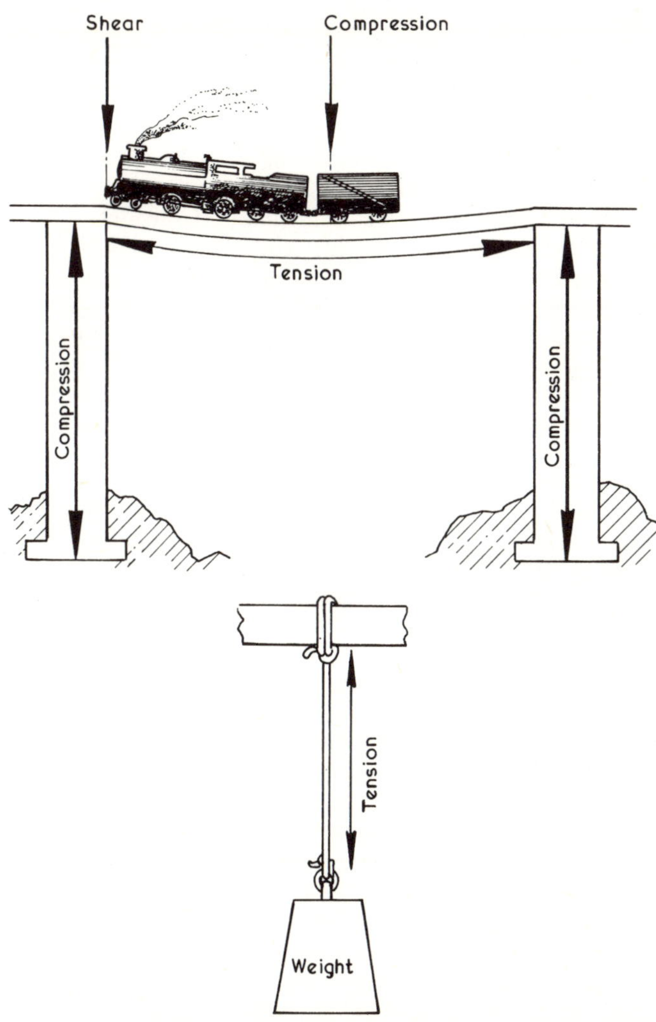

24

Materials—the Common Metals and Alloys

Look around your workshop and your home and list the different materials which are around us. How many of these materials are metal? Consider a modern motor car in which twenty metals may be involved. Metals of many kinds and in some form enter into every aspect of our life. Of the elements in the earth, air and sea 50% is oxygen, 25% silicon and about 14% metals of which about half is aluminium. Chemists tell us that there are 70 metals today but few of us could name more than ten. Some of the rarer metals are little more than novelties but some will become extremely important and titanium, uranium and germanium (used in transistors) are already well known. Accepted distinctions among metals are "metals" and "alloys" (pure metals and metals mixed with other metals), "ferrous" and "non ferrous" metals, "base" metals, "precious" metals and "rare" metals, including rare earth metals. Iron is the only ferrous metal but the term is used to include all the alloys which have iron as their main constituent. Gold, silver and platinum are the accepted precious metals and of the base metals there are seven that are used very frequently: iron, aluminium, copper, zinc, lead, tin and nickel; of these tin and nickel are by far the most expensive. Alloys are becoming increasingly important: there are already hundreds of different steel alloys and nearly as many light metal alloys; brass is the most popular of the many copper alloys. Iron and steel, the ferrous metals, still form the most important group of metals.

Iron and Steel

Iron and Steel are the materials most frequently used in the school workshop, in machines, for tools and as a basic material for metalwork. Next to aluminium iron is the most prolific metal, 5% of the earth's crust, and like most metals it is obtained from ore, rock or stone in lump or powdered form containing sufficient metal to make its extraction worthwhile.

Iron Ore. Haematite is the principal high grade iron ore often containing 60% iron and there are extensive supplies in many parts of the world but transport is expensive. There is plenty of iron in Britain but most of it is low grade carbonate, 20–33% iron and vast quantities are found in Lincolnshire and Northamptonshire just below the surface where it can be easily mined: the top soil is removed before mining and replaced so as not to spoil the appearance and fertility of the country.

Iron and steel are basic commodities so there is much world trade in iron ore and scrap iron and steel. The world's production of ore is more than 750 million tonnes which with the aid of between three and four million tonnes of scrap iron and steel produced nearly 500 million tonnes of pig iron and 600 million tonnes of steel. USA produced 90 million tonnes of ore and imported 20 million tonnes of high grade ore to make 130 million tonnes of steel. USSR produced about 190 million tonnes of ore for approximately 125 million tonnes of steel while Japan, now an important industrial nation and the third largest steel producer has increased its production from seven to nearly 120 million tons in twenty years in spite of the fact that Japan has very

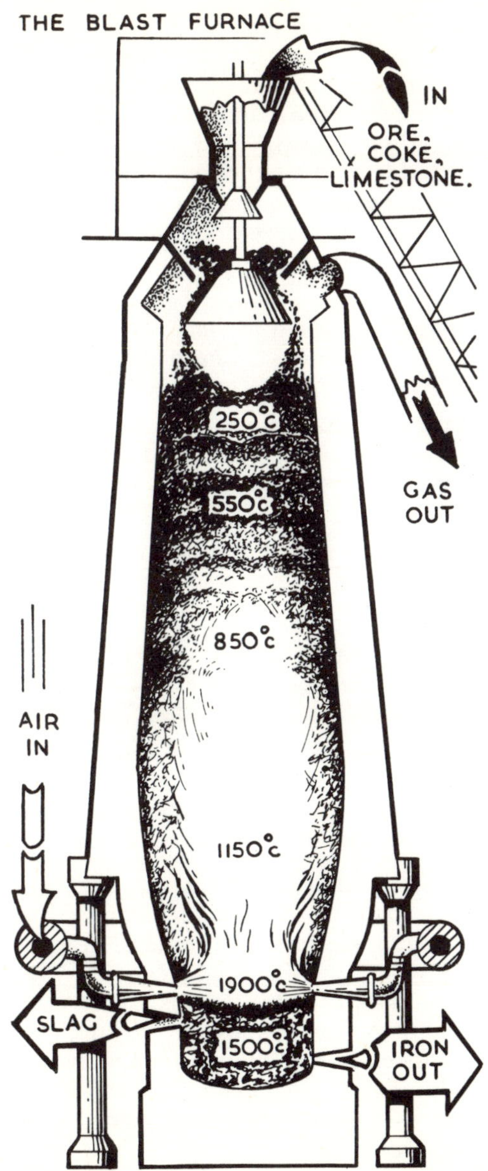

little iron ore. In 1972 Japan imported 96% of its ore—more than 50 million tonnes—mostly from Australia which has recently developed vast resources. In 1970—Britain's best year—the United Kingdom produced 12 million tonnes of ore and imported about the same amount which with some 20 million tonnes of scrap produced 28 million tonnes of steel. The amount of scrap used in steel production depends on the quality of the scrap, the quality of the steel required and the method of production.

Charging the Furnace. Iron ore is transported to the iron works, broken into lumps less than six inches across, or sintered, placed into skips, conveyed to the top of the blast furnace and, with skips of coke and limestone which acts as a flux, tipped into the bell hopper. Coke is a cleaner fuel than coal and less likely to be crushed into dust. Dust will prevent the heated gases ascending inside the furnace. It might even clog the furnace and prevent its burning. When the ore is fine and mixed with ore dust it is **sintered,** i.e. it is crushed, mixed with fine coke and heated to form a solid mass which can be easily broken into briquettes which are tipped into the blast furnace. More than half the iron ore used is sintered. There are two bell hoppers. The top hopper is opened first and closed when the charge is inside. Then the other hopper is opened so that the charge can enter the furnace without its being open at the top and without wasting hot gases. Blast furnaces were once left open and the glow in the sky could be seen for miles around, but this does not happen today.

The blast furnace is a tall cylindrical steel casing sometimes 30 metres in height and 12 metres in diameter at its widest part, lined with refractory material, usually alumina firebricks. The widest part is the belly. Above it is the stack and below it the bosh in which the smelting takes place and which, being the hottest part of the furnace, is water cooled. A hot blast of air, blown into the furnace through tuyeres at a pressure of 300 N/mm^2 (20 tons/square inch) increases the heat and, incidentally saves fuel. Three or four hot blast stoves as shown in the illustration opposite are filled with open chequer brickwork heated by the waste gases from the blast furnace. Two stoves are being heated while one or two discharge the hot blast. Stoves are switched over about every half hour so that the hot blast can be maintained. The lighting of a blast furnace is an elaborate procedure. Wooden scaffolding is erected inside, coke is added and the hot blast introduced gradually and, only when it is well alight, is the charge added. The charge consists of iron bearing material (ore, sinter and scrap) coke and lime roughly in the proportions of 10:4:1 but this must vary with the quality of the ore and the pig iron required. The furnace is kept burning steadily and continuously for years, usually until the lining burns out, and it is kept full, being charged every ten to fifteen minutes, in some cases automatically. Iron runs out through a tapping hole, the iron notch, which is plugged with clay. The iron runs through channels in the sand floor into large ladles, to be made into steel while still molten, or into a series of small moulds in a pig casting machine to be used cold. Slag is run off much more frequently, sometimes continuously.

Cast Iron has been superseded by steel when strength is the main consideration but it is still very important and about one quarter of all British iron is made into castings for machines, radiators, baths, pipes, stoves, etc. Selected pig iron and scrap are mixed and melted in cupolas, like small blast furnaces, to form the quality of cast iron required. Cast iron contains between 1.5% and 4.5% carbon and is harder and more brittle than steel: it cannot be bent or forged to shape although recently alloy irons have been developed for special purposes and these are much stronger. The carbon can be free or combined with the iron, when it is called cementite or iron carbide.

Grey Cast Iron is fluid when molten, is tough, but can be machined as it is not very hard and, as most of the carbon is in the form of graphite flakes, the fracture appears grey.

White Cast Iron is less fluid, harder and less brittle and the carbon is as cementite. The break shows a crystalline fracture.

Chilled Iron Castings are of grey iron, made by quickly cooling parts of the casting by making parts of the mould with iron.

Malleable Castings are of white iron annealed so that the strength, toughness and elasticity of the castings are improved.

Wrought Iron is almost pure iron and was the iron used in ancient times. It is made in a puddling furnace and it resists corrosion far more than plain carbon steel but is little used today.

Steel. We live in an alloy age and steel (iron with 0.05% to 1.5% carbon) is the most important alloy. This is plain carbon steel and is produced in great quantities. Alloy steels are special steel which include small amounts of other metals. Early steel was made in cementation furnaces by heating best Swedish iron with carbon and this was improved by Huntsman, a Yorkshire clockmaker in the crucible process but electric furnaces have superseded both these processes (*see* p. 144).

Acid and **Basic** are the two fundamental processes in steelmaking. At first only the best iron ore was used to make iron and steel, and furnaces were lined with siliceous refractory material. This is the **Acid Process** which is excellent when using ore or pig iron which contains little sulphur and phosphorus, two harmful impurities which are usually found in iron ore. The blast furnace removes 95% of the sulphur but none of the phosphorus during smelting but the acid process in steelmaking does not reduce either. Later, as the demand for steel increased, low grade ores containing more phosphorus had to be used and lime was added to encourage the sulphur and phosphorus to combine with the slag. Unfortunately lime reacts with silica and destroys the siliceous lining so dolomite bricks had to be used. This is known as a basic lining and produced the **Basic Process** (*see* p. 156) which produces most of the world's steel today. It takes a little longer but is cheaper because inferior ores can be used to make the pig iron. In any case there just is not enough low phosphorus iron ore.

THE BESSEMER CONVERTER

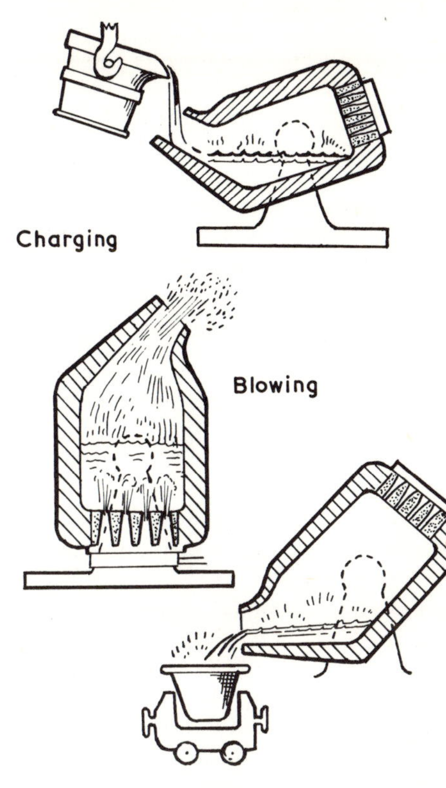

Bessemer Steel, introduced in 1856 by Sir Henry Bessemer, was probably the greatest and most sensational development in steel making. Steel was produced at high temperatures, quickly and in great quantities at a quarter its former price, just when it was needed for the new steel age for steamships and railways and machinery. Bessemer steel is a low carbon steel produced cheaply by blowing air through molten pig iron. The cold air increases the temperature as it burns out impurities and carbon, manganese and silicon in the form of spiegeleisen (ferro-manganese) and ferro-silicon are added. Twenty-five tonnes of steel can be made in twenty minutes but the process was not so well developed in Britain as it was abroad. The open hearth process was preferred in this country and by 1950 the number of Bessemer plants was reduced to three or four.

Open Hearth Steel has been made in great quantities and is reliable but the process takes ten hours or more and is now being replaced by the electric arc. L.D.—A.C. and Kaldo processes. Many varieties of steel can be made in the open hearth regenerative furnace which may hold up to 300 tonnes of metal. The charge, solid or molten pig iron and scrap with some lime for flux and a little iron ore to get rid of the excess carbon, rests on the hearth and is heated by gas or oil flames which pass above it. There are regenerators on either side beneath the hearth which are heated by the gases on their way to the chimney and so preheat the air and sometimes the fuel; they are used alternatively and the direction of the heating is reversed approximately every twenty minutes. Customers stipulated the exact composition of the steel required, spoon samples were taken and analysed by chemists, and the composition corrected before the final tapping.

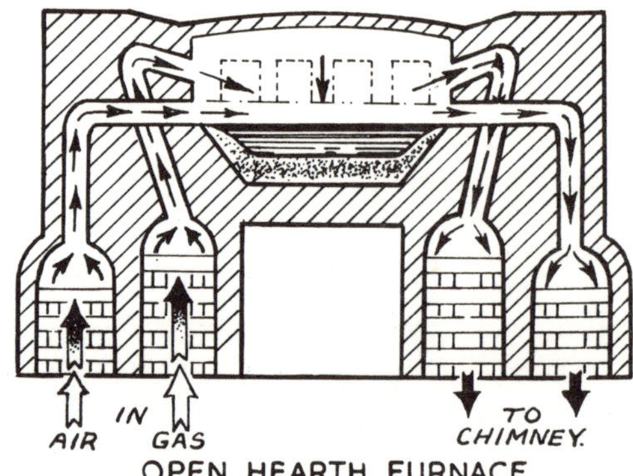

OPEN HEARTH FURNACE

Electric Furnaces are extremely important in modern steel making, especially in making special steels.

Electric Arc Furnaces are cylindrical with a saucer shaped hearth and a domed top through which pass three large vertical electrodes. They are smelting furnaces, i.e. the metal is melted and refined, and the charge, selected steel scrap, iron ore and pig iron is fed from the side, or above when the top is removable. The electrodes are positioned close to the charge so that it is melted by electricity passing down one electrode, arcing on to and passing through the charge and returning through the other two electrodes. Because electricity is clean and accurate control can be exercised high grade alloy steel, e.g. stainless steel, can be made in this furnace. The process takes several hours and for tapping the whole furnace is tilted.

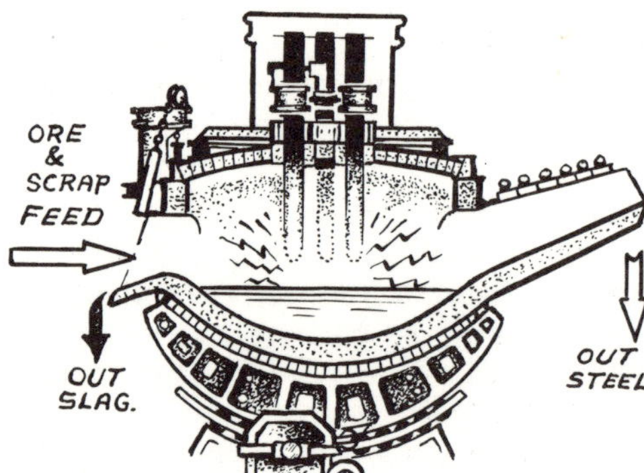

ELECTRIC ARC FURNACE

The High Frequency Induction Furnace is much smaller, seldom holding more than one tonne, and has superseded the crucible furnace. The charge is accurately weighed, and consists of special alloying metals and steel scrap. There is no slag and the metal is only melted. The induction furnace has a refractory lining surrounded by a water cooled copper coil.

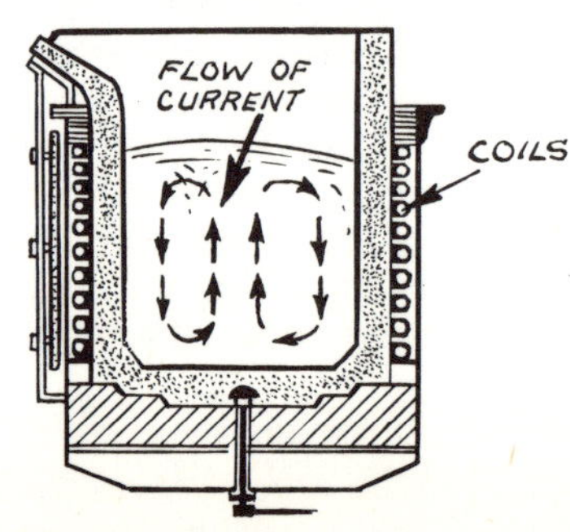

HIGH FREQUENCY INDUCTION FURNACE

A high frequency alternating current passes through the coil and sets up eddy currents which melt the charge and produce the finest alloy steels, e.g. high speed steel.

L.D. and Kaldo. It is significant that the latest developments in steel making are similar to the Bessemer process. The impurities in air, especially nitrogen, have been excluded by introducing first steam and now oxygen, which is blown into the molten charge from above and in two stages, before and after slagging. The new processes are L.D. and Kaldo.

The initials L.D. are derived from Linz and Donawitz, the two Austrian towns, where it was first developed, and Kaldo is a term representative of the name of Professor Kalling the inventor and of Domnarvets in Sweden, the steelworks at which he did his research. Speed and simplicity are the advantages of these new methods, a production of 200 tonnes an hour having already been achieved from one furnace. The original L.D. process is only for low phosphorus ores but it has been modified by injecting powdered lime with the oxygen and introducing a second slagging. This basic process was worked out in Arbed ironworks, in Luxembourg and CNRM, the research centre of the Benelux Iron and Steel Industry, hence the initials A.C. and the name **LD-AC** process. It takes a little longer but can use iron produced from English and Western European ore, which has 1%–2% phosphorus, to make low carbon steel, although the process is also used for medium and high carbon steels and certain alloy steels.

The Kaldo is also a basic process and both processes can use considerable quantities of scrap mixed with molten iron but the Kaldo Converter, which is a revolving furnace, has proved more flexible and is producing a wide range of steels from many grades of iron and scrap.

Mild Steel or low carbon steel is a soft steel and is produced in vast quantities for structural work and for motor cars, ships' plates, wire, nails, screws, rivets, buckets and tinplate.

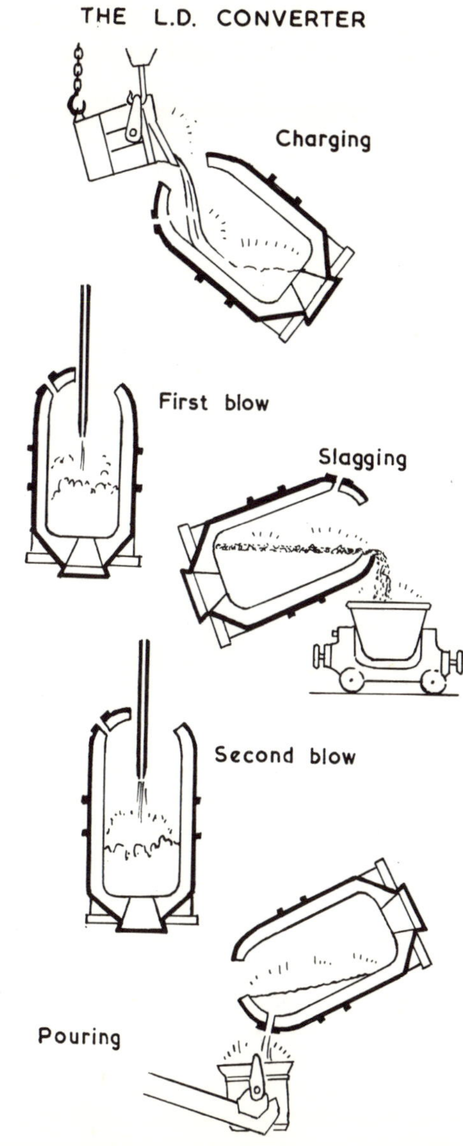

It files and forges well, can be pressed to shape, soldered, brazed and welded, and its fracture shows a light-grey crystalline structure. It contains up to 0.25% carbon and can be case hardened but not hardened and tempered. When mild steel is ground to shape the sparks are bright and yellow but not-star-like. **Bright Drawn Mild Steel** is cold drawn through dies, to give a bright, smooth accurate finish. **Black Mild Steel** is rolled hot and is less accurate, less strong and more difficult to machine.

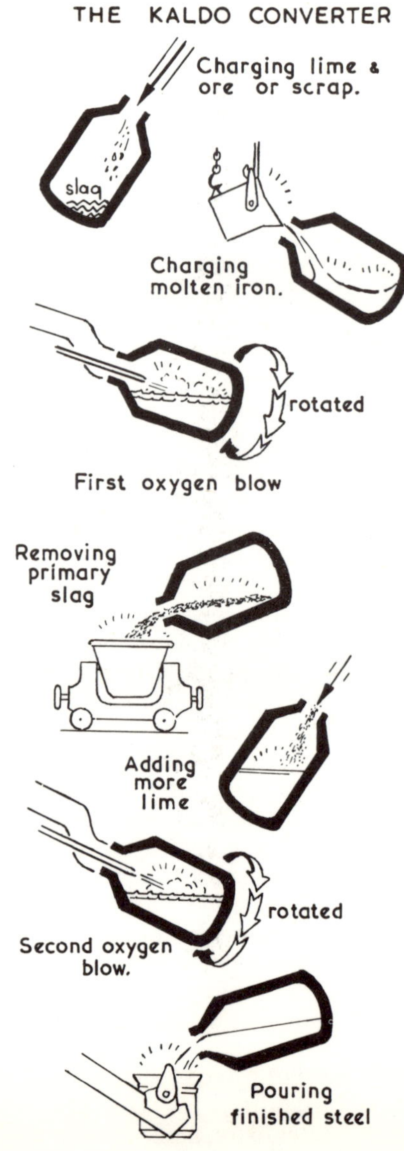

Medium Carbon Steel is similar to mild steel but is stronger and has 0.25–0.5% carbon. It is used for nuts and bolts, shafting and car and railway axles.

Cast Steel is high carbon steel with 0.7–1.4% carbon and is hardened by heating to redness and quenching after which it can be tempered. When the carbon content is above 0.9%, it is called **Tool Steel** and is used for razor blades, drills, taps and dies, shears, chisels, etc. It can be filed, turned and forged with care, gives a ringing sound with a high note when dropped, and is very smooth in appearance with a glittering black sheen. When broken, its fracture shows a pale-grey fine crystalline structure and, when applied to the grindstone, bushy streams of bright yellow bursting star sparks are given off.

High Speed Steel cuts at high speed retaining its hardness when hot and so saves time. A typical composition is 18% tungsten, 4% chromium, 1% vanadium, 0.7% carbon, 0.25% manganese and 0.15% silicon and the rest iron. It can be filed and turned, but is difficult to forge as it becomes brittle when red hot. It is hard but not so hard as cast steel and shows a fine blue grey silky fracture. It can be air-hardened.

Plate 25. **Stainless Steel Cutlery by David Mellor**

Campden cutlery designed for Walker & Hall and Old Hall Tableware. The first of the English stainless steel cutlery patterns, this received a silver medal at the Milan Triannale in 1958

"Provençal Style" made by David Mellor Cutlery, Sheffield. Stainless steel with rosewood handles and brass rivets

Plate 26. **Cutlery by Robert Welch**

Alveston cutlery manufactured by Harrison Fisher for Old Hall Tableware Ltd. This cutlery gained a Design Centre Award in 1965 and the Observer Award in 1969. It is available in stainless steel or sterling silver, was presented to the Heads of State in Russia and has been acquired by the Museum of Applied Art in Copenhagen and by the Stedelijk Museum in Amsterdam

Alloy Steels are special steels containing varying amounts of other elements as suggested below besides iron and carbon.

Aluminium induces a fine grain size, is used in heat-resisting steels and for special nitriding steels (case hardening in contact with ammonia).

Chromium increases the ability to harden, raises the tensile strength and gives unusual resistance to corrosion. Up to 30% may be used in heat resisting steels.

Cobalt is used for magnet steels and sometimes in high speed steel as it raises the tempering temperature and the hot hardness.

Manganese makes steel harder, so hard sometimes that it cannot be machined with steel tools, and increases the tensile strength. It is used to deoxidise steel before pouring, so is present in most steels.

Molybdenum gives greater strength and toughness and hardness without lessening machinability.

Nickel raises the impact resistance and the tensile strength and increases the resistance to corrosion.

Silicon is used for spring steels, for heat resisting, acid resisting and electrical resisting (transformer steels). There is at least a trace of silicon in all steels.

Titanium aids welding.

Tungsten strengthens steel at normal and high temperatures. It provides the quality of hardening in air, and, in high speed steel, the ability to cut when hot without becoming less hard.

Vanadium is used in small quantities up to 1% to increase hardenability.

Stainless Steel has 12–20% chromium but it can be austenitic, with a low carbon and high nickel and manganese content so that it can be pressed, hammered, or hammered to shape as for sinks and trays, or martensite, with a high carbon and low nickel and manganese content so that it can be hardened and tempered as for razor blades. The best known stainless steel is 18/8 i.e. 18% chromium and 8% nickel with a low carbon content.

Stainless steel cutlery presents interesting problems. Knife blades and handles are seldom made of the same material because the blades must be hardened and tempered to obtain and maintain a good cutting edge so martensite steel which can be hot forged and heat treated is essential e.g. 0.3% carbon, 0.4% silicon, 0.3% manganese, 13% chromium and 86% iron. Spoons and forks do not have cutting edges and like handles are made of austenitic stainless steel e.g. 0.03% carbon, 0.6% silicon, 1.0% manganese, 11.0% nickel, 18.5% chromium and the rest iron. Spoons and forks are rolled, stamped and pressed to shape and are worked cold so the steel must be softer and capable of intermediate annealing.

25

Non-ferrous Metals and Alloys

Aluminium, the most abundant metal, comprising 8% of the earth's crust, was not used in any quantity until the electrolic process of smelting was discovered in 1886. It is light in weight malleable and ductile, a good conductor of heat and, although it oxidises immediately on exposure to air, the thin film of oxide so formed prevents further corrosion. Aluminium is obtained from bauxite, named after Les Baux in France where it was first found, but it is now mined mostly in tropical areas, e.g. Surinam, and British Guiana in South America. Bauxite is treated with caustic soda to produce aluminium oxide, alumina, but, to separate the oxygen from the aluminium, alumina is dissolved in molten cryolite in an electric cell, a process which needs a heavy electric current. Britain lacks bauxite and sufficient electric power for such smelting, so very little of this metal is produced in this country although much ingot is imported for further fabrication. Uses for pure aluminium include electric cables, hollow-ware, and thin foil.

Pure aluminium lacks strength but this is overcome by alloying with many other metals producing many light metal alloys for many purposes. These are known by letters and numbers and have been classified by the British Standards Institution, e.g. LM. 4, the well known silicon (5%)—copper (2.5%) casting alloy. Some aluminium alloys, especially those containing copper and magnesium, can be further strengthened by heat treatment. Aluminium alloys are used on aircraft, road, rail and sea transport, architecture and engineering.

Copper is a soft reddish metal which conducts heat and electricity exceptionally well, is malleable and ductile, can be highly polished, soft soldered, silver soldered, brazed and welded. Occasionally it is found pure, but it is mostly mined from sulphur-bearing ore with 5% copper or less and found in Zambia, United States, Canada and Chile. It can be fairly easily smelted in a reverberatory furnace and pure copper is obtained by either fire or electrolytic refining. Half of the world's copper is used for electrical work, mainly as wire, and one quarter is used in making alloys of which brass is the best known.

Brass, of which 67% copper and 33% zinc is a typical composition, has excellent machining qualities and casts well. It is yellow, takes a good polish, is malleable, can be worked hot or cold and can be soft or hard soldered and brazed.

Gilding Metal as used in beaten metalwork and for cheap jewelry is mainly copper with 5–20% zinc.

Bronze originally contained tin and 90–95% copper but tin is now very expensive and plain bronze is seldom made.

Phosphor Bronze contains a little phosphorus 0.5% with 10% tin and 89.5% copper and is used for such diverse purposes as church bells and engineering.

Aluminium Bronze contains up to 10% aluminium mixed with copper and is a strong alloy used either cast or wrought in engineering.

Gunmetal is also strong and tough. It resists corrosion and is used for marine work and steam pipe fittings. The best, Admiralty gunmetal or U.S. Navy bronze, is 88 % copper, 10 % tin and 2 % zinc, but mostly it contains more zinc and less tin.

Nickel Silver is a copper-zinc alloy containing no silver and only a little nickel (10–20 %). Nickel silver is the best base for silver-plated ware.

Nickel, a strong tough metal with good corrosion resistance and a silvery white colour, is obtained from nickel-copper-iron sulphide ore (about 3 % nickel and 2 % copper), only after complicated processing which includes crushing, concentration by flotation, roasting, smelting and electrolysis. It is used in its pure state for plating, where it forms the vital corrosion-resistant layer under chromium, in chemical plant to resist alkaline and in thermionic valves for electrodes and lead wires. Nickel is most important in alloying, in steel for gears, shafts and other highly stressed constructional components, with chromium in stainless steel for domestic equipment, architecture and chemical plant, and with iron in controlled expansion alloys (Invar). Nickel chromium alloys are used for electrical resistance wires for heating elements and for heat and creep resistant alloys in gas turbines and for furnace components. The ore is mined mainly in Canada.

Cupro-Nickel is used for coinage and other nickel-copper alloys are used in chemical plant to resist attack by seawater, sulphuric acid and fluorine. One called by the trade name Monel alloy 400 is mined and smelted as an alloy.

Zinc occurs mainly as a sulphide ore, usually associated with lead and silver. Zinc sulphide is concentrated, roasted, and reduced to the metal by heating with anthracite or by solution in sulphuric acid followed by electrolysis. Brass was made by smelting zinc ores with copper or copper ores many years before zinc itself was known. Zinc is a blue-grey metal, almost as dense as steel and melting at only 419° C. About half the world's zinc production is used for galvanising steel. The other main uses are for die casting, as sheet and strip for roofing and batteries, in brass and zinc oxide.

Tin is a soft, white, shiny metal, malleable but weak, and, being resistant to corrosion, is used in great quantities for tinplate. It is smelted from tinstone (cassiterite) which is a tin oxide and is mined in Malaysia, Central Africa, Nigeria, Indonesia and Bolivia. Tin is now very expensive and is seldom used in its pure state except for tinplate. Tin alloys include soft solder, bronzes, britannia metal, white metal machine bearings and type metal. Antimony hardens the alloy and reduces shrinkage during solidification; hence its use in printing type (up to 30 %) which also contains up to 80 % lead and up to 25 % tin.

Pewter was originally an alloy of tin and lead, but there should not be any lead in modern pewter. A good grade of pewter is **Britannia Metal** which is 95 % tin, 4 % antimony and 1 % copper.

Lead is a heavy, weak, bluish grey metal. It has a low melting point and is widely used in soft solder, for cable sheathing, as sheet for building, as antimonial lead in battery manufacture, and for radiation shielding in the atomic energy field. Its ore is galena (lead sulphide) which comes from Australia, United States, Mexico, Canada and Peru. A little lead is now added to some steels and brasses to make them "free cutting".

The Properties of Metals 26

Properties of Metals can be classified as **Physical,** e.g. weight, colour, fusibility, etc., **Mechanical**—the effects of external forces, e.g. tenacity, and **Chemical**—resistance to corrosion and the effects of alloying.

Specific Gravity. Relative weights of metal compared to the weight of equal volume of water, e.g. gold 19.26, lead 11.36, iron 7.5, and aluminium 2.56.

Colour assists in identification and is important to architects and jewellers.

Lustre, the ability to reflect light, is associated with hard metal which can be highly polished and helps to resist corrosion.

Fusibility. The property of becoming liquid when heated, melted, as occurs in smelting, casting, soldering and welding.

Conductivity. Most metals conduct heat and electricity well. Silver, copper and aluminium, in that order, are the best conductors of heat and electricity.

Magnetism. Iron and steel are important magnetic metals but cobalt, nickel and manganese have some magnetic properties. Electro-magnets and their use in electric motors depend on magnetism.

Tension, compression and **shear** are the three simple mechanical stresses which determine the strength of a metal and are considered on pp. 137–139. In steel, **tenacity** is the most important strength and is the measure of stress which is often quoted and today is measured in newtons per square millimetre (N/mm^2). Tenacity used to be measured in tons per square inch varying between 20 and 100, which now becomes approximately 300 to 1500 N/mm^2. The conversion factor is 15.44.

Hardness implies resistance to scratching, marking, cutting and wear.

Elasticity is the ability of metal to return to its original shape and size after it has been deformed—stretched, compressed or bent—as in springs.

Malleability is the property of being bent, hammered or rolled without fracture.

Ductility is the quality of being drawn into fine wire.

Toughness is the ability to withstand bending, twisting or shock without breaking.

Impact Resistance is a form of toughness, resistance against shock.

Brittleness is the undesirable property of breaking without deformation or warning.

Fatigue is the puzzling property which has become so important recently in the study of fast-moving aircraft and rockets, that of causing metal to deteriorate in strength under repeated applications of loads previously borne with safety.

Creep is the gradual yielding of metals subjected to steady loads especially at extreme temperature, e.g. the slight deformation of an engine part which eventually causes the inexplicable failure of an efficient system.

Expansion and contraction. Most metals expand on heating and contract on cooling, antimony being the exception. This is why antimony is used in type metal, which produces clear, accurate letters for printing.

Plate 27. **Mace by Alex Styles**

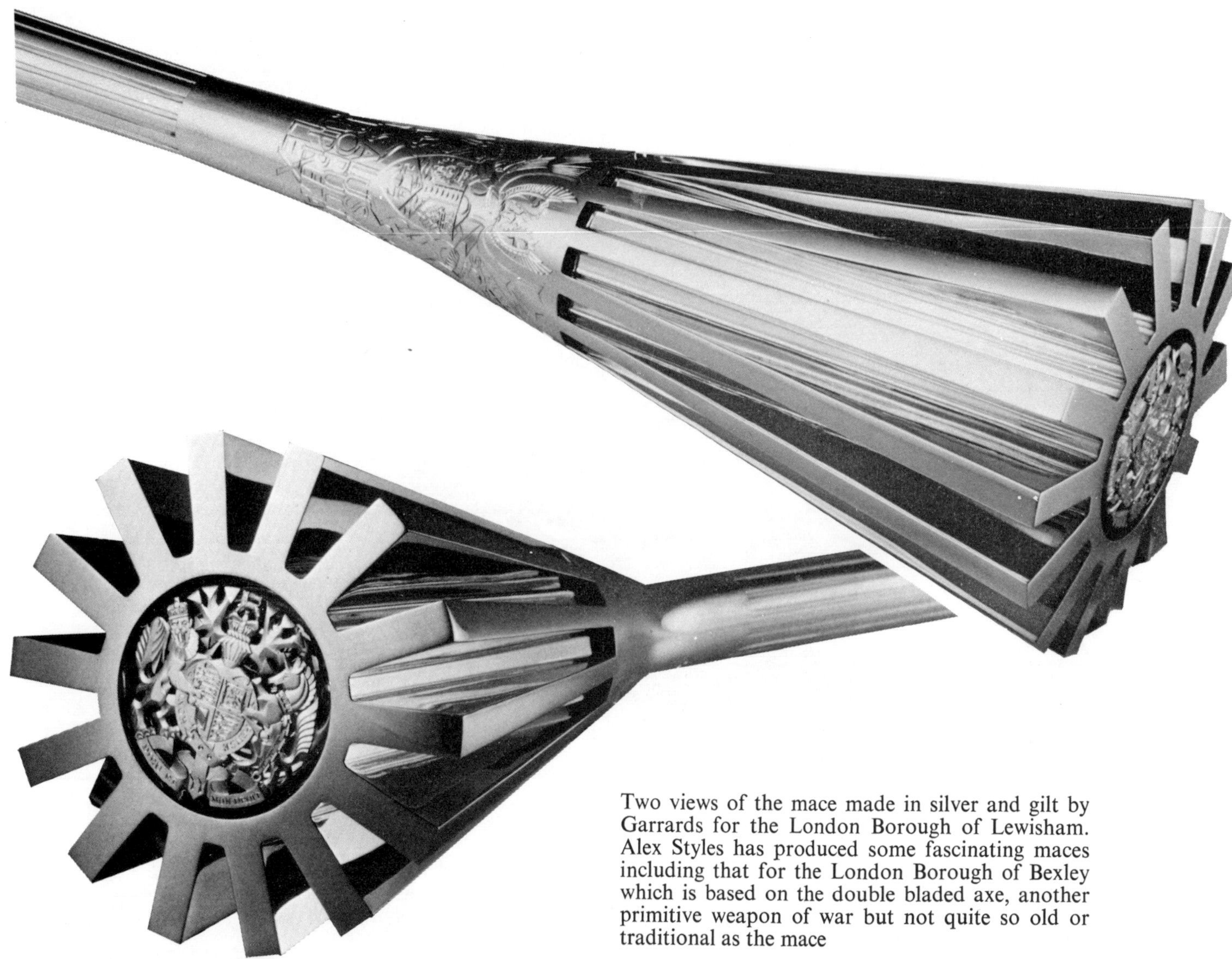

Two views of the mace made in silver and gilt by Garrards for the London Borough of Lewisham. Alex Styles has produced some fascinating maces including that for the London Borough of Bexley which is based on the double bladed axe, another primitive weapon of war but not quite so old or traditional as the mace

Plate 28. **Mace by Stuart Devlin**

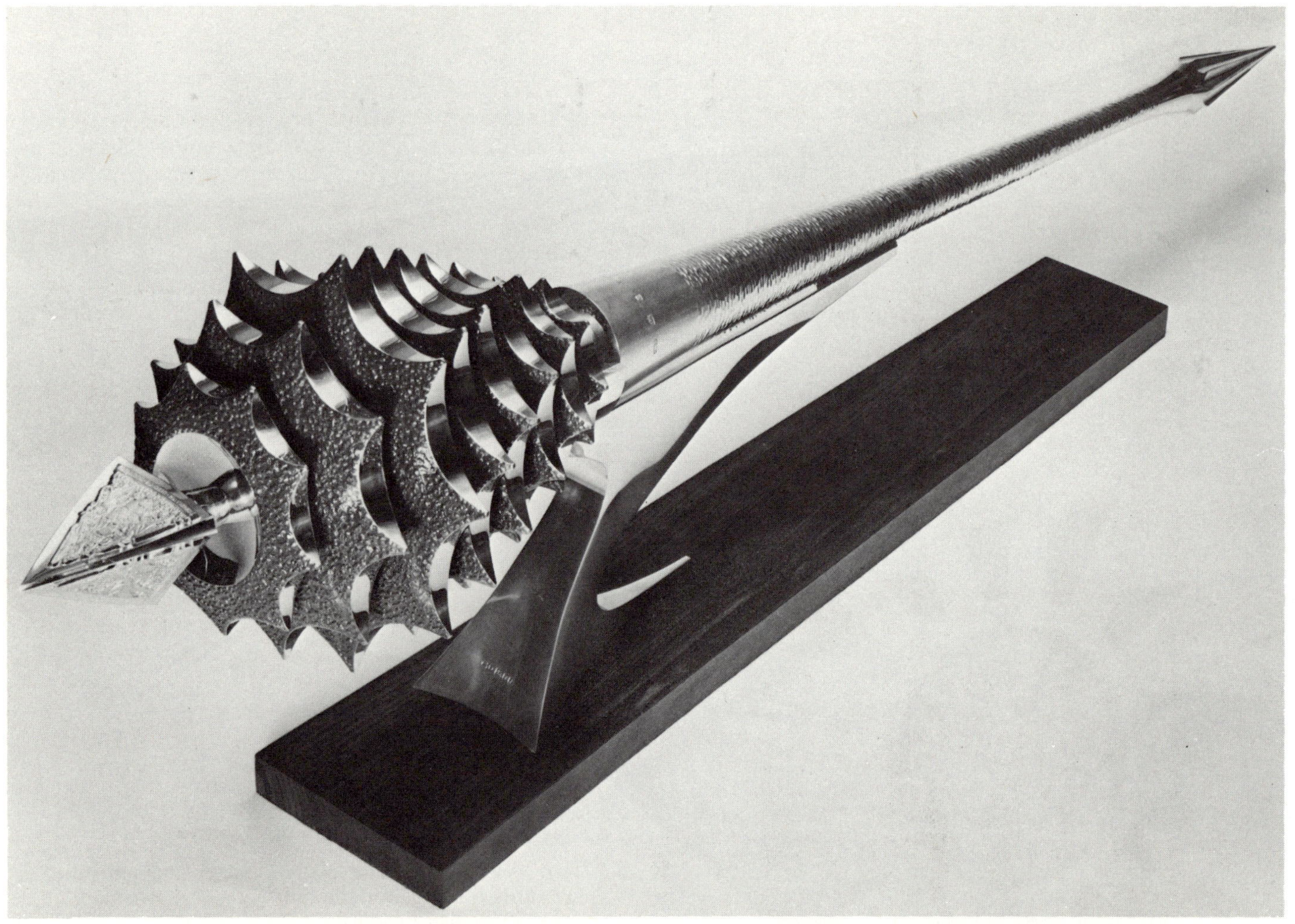

Made of silver with head part gilt and part black enamelled with end finial and badge gilt and mounted on a rosewood stand. Devlin made this for Bath University, formerly Bristol College of Science and Technology, and explained "The mace was originally a tribal weapon of war so a viciously spiked head is historically accurate"

27

The Story of Iron and Steel

The Earliest Iron

Nobody knows when iron was first discovered. It has been used continuously since the first century B.C., and although its value as a metal for tools and weapons was soon apparent it was not used extensively until the "Machine Age". The earliest iron may have come from meteorites, but it is more probable that it was accidentally smelted from iron ore used as stone for a rough fireplace, possibly a cooking pit, and the carbon from the fire helped to produce the iron. Unfortunately, iron rusts and disintegrates so it is likely that iron was discovered and forgotten several times in prehistoric times. The most ancient iron discovery is a blade which was protected from weather in an Egyptian Pyramid, and this may explain how Egyptian hieroglyphics were cut into hard stone.

Wrought Iron

Except for very small amounts occasionally contained in meteorites, iron is never found pure—yet it forms five per cent of the total substance of the earth. At first the ore, iron combined with stone, was heated in a charcoal fire until it melted and the iron ran out. This was smelting and the ore produced a white-hot, spongy mass of metal which was hammered promptly and vigorously to push out slag, waste stone and sand, which had not yet solidified, and to weld the pasty particles of iron into a coherent mass. This lump of incandescent iron was called a "bloom" and the primitive furnaces were called bloomeries. The earliest ones in England were built in the Forest of Dean and the Sussex Weald, among large forests. The metal produced was high-quality wrought-iron using haematite ore but the best iron was made from Swedish ore—Magnetite—a rich, 60–70% iron ore with magnetic qualities. Sweden had ample timber for charcoal so Swedish iron became famous.

Steel

Meanwhile, the blast furnace developed and, by the fourteenth century, large furnaces were producing pig-iron which it was found could be cast direct. The first iron cannon were cast in 1513. Steel was produced from the best ore by heating the blooms for a longer period of time with increased amounts of charcoal to enlarge the carbon content, but the first steel-furnaces were not introduced until the late-seventeenth century. The **Cementation Furnace** was like a square pottery furnace, about 6 metres square, with a tall chimney, up to 16 metres high, in which, just above a large fire, were placed Swedish iron bars packed in charcoal in large earthenware boxes which were sealed so as to exclude air and fumes. The boxes were kept at yellow heat for one week, and then allowed to cool slowly for a further week. The carbon caused the surface of the steel to be covered with ripples, and steel produced in this way was called "blister steel". Sometimes the bars were cut up, piled, reheated to welding-heat, and then hammered to produce "shear steel". Double shear steel, which some of the old Sheffield firms claim is unequalled for cutlery, was made by further heating and "cogging" (the hot rolling of large ingots). Early pictures of the city of Sheffield show these tall cementation-furnace chimneys prominently on the skyline. **Crucible-cast steel** was introduced by Huntsman, who, in 1740, seeking a better material for watch-springs realised

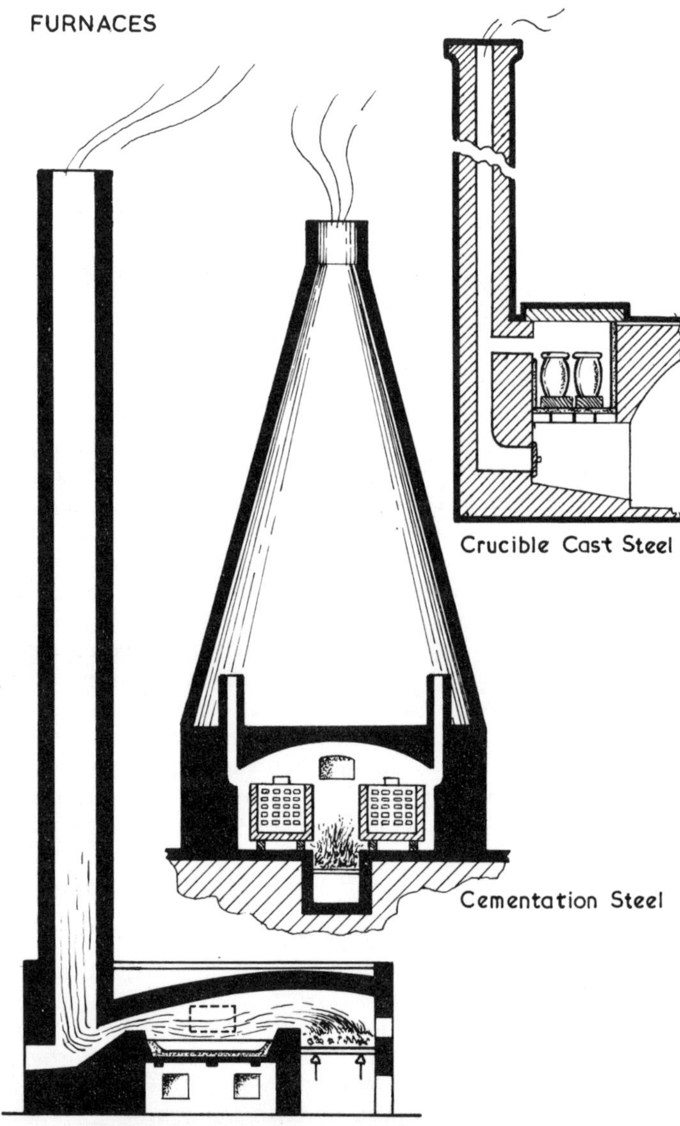

that a greater uniformity of structure could be obtained by fusing and melting selected blister steel in large crucibles. These crucibles each held 20–30 kilograms, and were lifted and poured by hand. This cast steel was of very high quality and later it was hammered and rolled to make "tool steel". By using iron of great purity with 0.75–2.0% carbon added, these methods produced good steel which could be hardened and tempered by heating and quenching; they were the only methods of steel-making until 1856 when Bessemer introduced mild steel.

The Industrial Revolution

Iron was not used extensively before the beginning of the Machine Age, in the eighteenth century, and much of that used had been imported from Sweden. The invention of the steam-engine, together with the introduction of locomotives, metal ships and the resultant increase in transport and industry, was responsible for a phenomenal increase in iron production and the introduction of new methods of steel-making—in order to have greater output for less cost. Cementation furnaces were slow and the process expensive. **The Bessemer Convertor,** the first furnace to produce steel quickly and cheaply, fulfilled a great need at a vital time. In Britain, however, both these furnaces were superseded by the **Siemens-Martin open-hearth regenerative** furnace which produced any kind of steel, and today the open hearth has given way to **electric arc-furnaces.** Crucible furnaces were used for making special steels until 1940, although high-frequency induction furnaces—a great improvement on the crucible furnace—came into production in 1925.

Metalworkers found in early times that iron has two invaluable properties: it can be hammered to shape and it can be welded. Wrought iron thus became the ideal material for the blacksmith.

The quality and amount of wrought-iron produced was improved and the costs reduced, in 1784, when Henry Cort designed the **"Puddling Furnace"**, a *reverberatory* furnace in which the heat of the fire or gas passed over the metal and then up a tall chimney. As the metal, about 250 kilograms of selected pig-iron, melted and boiled, it was "puddled" (i.e., stirred by men with long, heavy iron bars). As the iron became more pure its melting point rose, the iron became pasty on separating from the slag and, but for the stirring, would have stuck to the hearth. After half-an-hour's puddling, the puddler gathered the iron into balls, known as "muck balls" which weighed about 50 kilograms. Each was taken out, hammered and rolled to form muck bars and then cut up, piled together, reheated to welding heat and rolled again to form "merchant bars", the best wrought-iron. It was due to the Industrial Revolution and the growth of mechanical engineering that the demand for wrought-iron increased considerably during the eighteenth and nineteenth centuries, but it has now, been almost entirely superseded by steel and is a comparatively unimportant commodity. Bessemer was directly responsible for hastening the end of the "Iron Age" in 1856, and in 1877 Parliament allowed steel to be used for bridge-building.

Alloy Steels

Just as iron was important for armour, so steel became important in armaments. Alloy steels were made to resist bullets, and further alloy steels were used for shells to pierce the armour plate. In 1868, **Robert Mushet** found that steel containing tungsten could be air-hardened (i.e., hardened without quenching) and this led to the production of "high-speed steel"—steel for tools which would cut other steels at higher speeds. In 1883, **Robert Hadfield** discovered that manganese made steel harder and tougher and that it could be used for points and crossings on tram and railway lines and for bullet-proof steel. Later he introduced silicon steel. In 1889, it was found that the addition of nickel made steel more resistant, and a typical armour-plate steel was 0.5% carbon, 4% nickel, 2% chromium, 0.4% manganese, and 0.15% silicon—the remainder being iron. It was while experimenting to improve armour plate that **Harry Brearly**, almost by accident, discovered stainless steel, steel containing 10–20% chromium and up to 12% nickel, and 18/8 stainless steel became the popular steel which helped to solve the age long problem of rusting. Now after a hundred years, alloy steels are more important than ever.

The Forth Bridge

The railway bridge over the Firth of Forth was built by Sir Benjamin Baker and Sir John Fowler in 1889. It was the first important steel bridge and is still the most famous cantilever bridge in the world. It could not have been built, however, but for Thomas' discovery of the basic process for open-hearth steel. The bridge is 2½ kilometres long and has two main spans, each 510 metres wide, the cantilever construction showing how central supports can hold wide spans like men standing with their arms outstretched and holding hands. The bridge was able to be constructed in this way because steel is stronger in tension than iron; cast-iron has very little tensile strength, while the tensile strength of wrought-iron, which had been used for bridge-construction for the previous hundred years, is 340 N/mm^2. The tensile strength of the open-hearth mild steel used for the Forth Bridge was 510 N/mm^2.

The design of the bridge was such that every compression member was of steel-tube and every tension member was a lattice girder. It is interesting to compare the design with that of the Coalbrookdale Bridge of cast-iron, made nearly a hundred years earlier (*see* p. 158), and the reinforced-concrete bridge (*see* p. 137) built nearly a hundred years later, because both cast-iron and concrete are very strong in compression.

The Forth Bridge 1889

Plate 29. **Coffee Set by Gerald Benney**

Coffee set made for Marks & Spencers Ltd. who presented it to Bootle Corporation. Notice the interesting surface finish—a new style which has been perfected by Gerald Benney

Plate 30. **Presentation Silverware**

Centrepiece and candlesticks made by Gerald Benney for and given to the School of Pharmacy, London University by Sir Harry Jephcott

28

Men of Iron

Dud Dudley (1599–1684), first of the acknowledged ironmasters, was the natural son of Lord Dudley and was educated at Oxford University. He made iron at Worcester, using pit coal in preference to timber in order to avoid the rapid reduction of our forests. Dudley obtained a royal patent from James I, but was opposed by the charcoal-burners and other iron-makers from the outset, and eventually failed financially. His ideas did not spread. Dud Dudley, a staunch Royalist, was imprisoned by Cromwell during the Commonwealth—when the patent was granted elsewhere. Its recipient, like Dudley, failed in his enterprise to use coal in the making of iron. With the restoration of the monarchy Dudley regained favour under Charles II and persevered with his ideas until his death, but without real support. Iron-makers continued to use charcoal, and Britain continued to import most of her iron from Sweden. Nevertheless, Dud Dudley is remembered as a pioneer ironmaster, and the first man to smelt iron by coal.

Abraham Darby (1678–1717) was the founder of the famous family firm at Coalbrookdale, Shropshire. He began by casting iron cooking-pots in sand, but tried later to smelt his iron with coal (instead of charcoal). Finding this unsatisfactory, Darby next used coke, which is now used universally for smelting iron. The business prospered, and in 1779 Abraham Darby III cast the members for the world's first iron bridge. The bridge, now a national monument, spanned the Severn at Coalbrookdale and still survives, (*see* p. 158).

Benjamin Huntsman (1704–1776), a clock-maker from Doncaster, required a more homogeneous steel for his watch-springs. He managed to construct a large crucible capable of withstanding the heat necessary to melt and pour cementation steel. Huntsman's crucible-cast steel was found to be very hard, but was not accepted in England until the French had proved its excellence with their cutlery knives! It became acceptable as a good general-purpose, high-carbon steel, and was used extensively for tools and machinery.

John Wilkinson (1728–1808) was the most famous son of another "iron family". The Darby family, who were Quakers, had refused to produce armaments, but the Wilkinsons did not share these scruples and improved the process for making cannons, shells and grenades. John Wilkinson developed the *cupola* (a vertical, cylindrical furnace for melting pig iron), and his foundry was largely responsible for the popularity of cast iron; he cast a great variety of articles, from smoothing-irons to whole buildings. Wilkinson undertook commissions from the Adam brothers, especially for fireplaces, and he was responsible for the first, successful iron boat—a wrought-iron barge, 21 metres long and weighing over 8 tonnes. Working with Thomas Pritchard he designed the Coalbrookdale Bridge.

Henry Cort (1740–1800) introduced the "puddling" furnace, whereby the iron was heated on a hearth between the fire and a tall chimney which induced a powerful draught—a *reverberatory* furnace, as distinct from a blast furnace or a cupola, where the metal is heated with the fuel. The molten iron on the hollowed-out hearth of the puddling furnace is stirred by the "puddler". Cort developed and made great use of rolling mills—the "puddle bars" were put through iron rollers—but he did not invent them as is sometimes suggested.

James Neilson (1792–1865) conceived the idea of heating the air of the blast before forcing it into the blast furnace, in 1828. Eight years later methods were devised for utilising the waste gases from the blast furnace itself; today, the blast is heated by passing it through stoves previously heated by these waste gasses (*see* p. 142).

Sir Henry Bessemer (1813–1898) was an engineer with many inventive ideas, and it was while he was attempting to produce a more malleable iron in order to improve the manufacture of guns that he discovered that by blowing air rapidly through molten pig iron large quantities of what he described as "malleable steel" could be produced quickly. Previously, he had been unable to obtain sufficient heat to liquefy more than a few pounds of malleable iron. In the same year (1856), **Robert Mushet (1811–1891)** made this process practicable by advocating the addition of manganese in the form of "Spiegeleisen" which changed the iron into a low-carbon steel, called "mild" or "soft steel".

Sir William Siemens (1823–1883) was born in Germany and came to England to sell his brother's electro-plating process to Elkingtons. On deciding that England was the premier industrial nation, he returned to sell other inventions. Working with his brother, Frederic, Siemens built a furnace to heat wrought-iron billets (lengths of metal in semi-finished form, intermediate in size between ingots and bars, and usually between 75–150 millimetres-square and 1–2 metres long) using preheated gas; he achieved a seventy per cent saving in fuel requirements. Later the Siemens brothers met the brothers, Emile and Pierre Martin, who had made steel by melting pig iron with scrap. Between them, they devised the Siemens–Martin open-hearth regenerative furnace in 1868, which produced steel with a controlled carbon content. In 1878, Sir William Siemens patented an electric arc furnace.

Sidney Gilchrist Thomas (1805–1885) invented the basic steel-making process whereby the sulphur and phosphorous content of low-quality ore was separated from the iron. Bessemer steel, in spite of its early phenomenal success, failed abroad because Bessemer, without realising the effect of phosphorus, used high-quality ore containing small amounts of sulphur and phosphorous, whereas most continental ore had a high phosphorus content. Gilchrist Thomas introduced the dolomite lining and the 4-minute "after-blow" and, as a result, the Bessemer process was generally accepted; this acceptance, however, was more general in Belgium and Germany than in England. In 1879 the dolomite lining was adapted for the Siemens–Martin furnace and basic open hearth steel became a very important milestone in steel production in England.

29

A History of Mechanical Engineering

Mechanical engineering began with the use of a stone as a hammer, a stick as a lever and a sloping surface, the inclined plane, to reach heights: eventually the wheel opened the way for the design of machines. The Egyptian Pyramids, the Roman roads and bridges are all wonderful examples of feats of mechanical engineering. But rapid progress did not begin until the advent of the steam-engine. The earliest engines and machines were built by versatile and accurate craftsmen, skilled and thoughtful in the use of their tools. William Murdock (1754–1839), for example, who worked for James Watt, built a steam-carriage—forerunner of the locomotive—worked with compressed air, and experimented with the distillation of coal until he was able to introduce coal-gas lighting. Another ingenious mechanic of the period, Joseph Bramah (1748–1814), invented a hydraulic press, the water closet, a burglar-proof lock, a wood-planing machine with a rotary cutter, and worked on screw-propellers.

Thomas Newcomen (1663–1729) invented the first practical steam-engine in 1712. Newcomen worked with Thomas Savery who had patented a similar idea, but could not make it work. The first steam-engines were used to pump water from mines and Newcomen's engine lifted 10 gallons of water 150 feet (45 metres), each stroke taking 5 minutes. It was expensive, clumsy, slow, and not very efficient, but it was the first steam-pumping engine and over a hundred were installed.

John Smeaton (1724–1792) was a civil engineer from Leeds who improved upon Newcomen's piston engine and demonstrated that better fitting would increase its efficiency rather than larger cylinders which were favoured by his rivals. Smeaton conducted scientific studies on the design of windmills, which came to Europe in the fourteenth century after having been used for centuries in the East, and on the design of water-wheels, used by the Ancient Greeks and by the Romans who introduced gearing. Smeaton pioneered the iron water-wheel, worked on the construction of canals, especially the Firth and Clyde canals, and he improved the air-blast for blast furnaces by using a water-wheel to operate a blowing-engine. By bracing the stone rocks with iron girders, he rebuilt Eddystone Lighthouse, which stood from 1759 until 1882, when it was re-erected at Plymouth Hoe—where it stands still.

James Watt (1736–1819), the Scottish engineer, is known as the 'Father of the Steam-Engine'. After conducting scientific experiments on the properties of steam, he made the steam-engine quicker, more powerful and efficient—so making it successful technically and financially. In 1783, he introduced his double-acting engine which incorporated at least five of his inventions: (1) it had a condenser which condensed the steam without cooling the cylinder, so making better use of the steam supplied by the boiler and ensuring continuous action; (2) double-action was introduced by making the steam work on both sides of the piston, making each stroke a power stroke; (3) an ingenious parallel action connected the top of the piston-rod to the beam by a linkage which enabled the piston to push or pull the rod in a straight (usually vertical) direc-

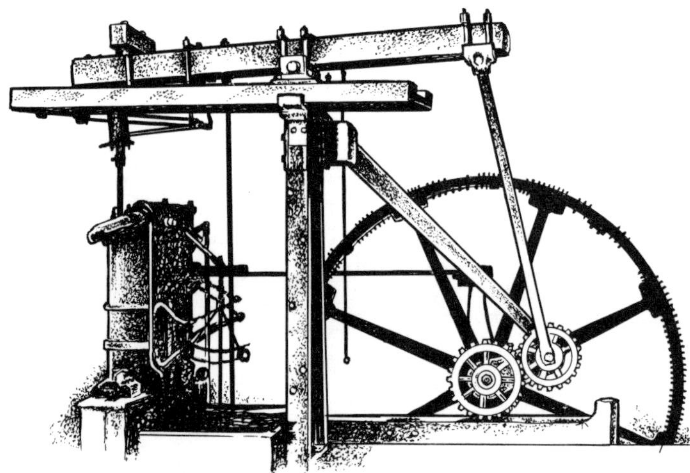

James Watt Double Acting Steam Engine 1783

tion; (4) centrifugal governors which automatically controlled the speed of rotative engines; and (5) sun-and-planet gear (an epicyclic gears system revolving within a larger, outer gear-wheel) which converted up-and-down action into rotary motion, thus enabling the steam-engine to turn wheels and work machines. Watt had to introduce a gearing system because he was prevented from using a crank which had already been patented by another engineer who had insufficient knowledge to make full use of it.

Watt was greatly indebted to **Matthew Boulton (1728–1809)** who had begun as a silversmith in his father's business and, while trying to improve and extend it, met James Watt whom he supported financially and encouraged technically. Matthew Boulton believed in steam to relieve the energy of his workers, and he started the famous Soho Works of Boulton and Watt in Birmingham. The success of Boulton–Watt engines began when they used John Wilkinson's (*see* p. 155) cannon-boring machines to bore accurate cylinders for their engines. As well as developing the making of engines and machines, Boulton improved the workmanship and artistic appeal of his silverware, introduced Sheffield Plate (*see* p. 186) to Birmingham, used his stamps and presses to improve the coinage, and was largely responsible (1773) for an Act of Parliament allowing Assay Offices to govern the hallmarking of gold and silver in Birmingham and Sheffield (*see* p. 185).

Richard Trevithick (1771–1833), the engineer and inventor, was a genius with boundless vitality who built the first passenger locomotive, but had little business sense and died penniless. Trevithick's great contribution to engineering was his development of the high-pressure steam-engine, of which Watt disapproved, but which, at the age of twenty, Trevithick used for locomotives which carried passengers along the roads. Two years later, he constructed a steam-assisted carriage for the streets of London.

The railway was born in the collieries of Northumberland. First pack-horses and then wagons were used to transport coal from the pit to navigable waters, but the roads did not stand up to the

Cast Iron Bridge at Coalbrookdale 1779

traffic and wooden tracks were laid for the wagons to negotiate. These quickly wore out and needed strengthening with iron. Later, metal strips were fastened on top, until, in 1767, Darby of Coalbrookdale (*see* p. 155) made cast-iron rails. Later still, these were made of wrought-iron and the first track for public transport was a tramway track in Surrey in 1803.

In 1804, Richard Trevithick built the famous tramroad locomotive which hauled 10 tonnes of ore and 70 men for 16 km—in Pen-y-daran, Wales. Trevithick used his high-pressure steam-engines successfully for rock-boring, rock breaking, and dredging and in 1812 he built a steam-threshing machine, arguing that the use of steam in agriculture would halve the cost of food and double the population—so making the country more prosperous (*see* pp. 166–171). In the same year he built the Cornish boiler—a horizontal cylindrical boiler with an internal fire-tube which was very efficient, and he advocated ideas for iron steamships. Trevithick began to make engines for high-altitude mines in South America, and in 1816 he went to Peru and later Costa Rica to superintend their working.

George Stephenson (1781–1848), father of Robert Stephenson, began work in the Northumberland collieries, and in 1815 introduced a miner's safety lamp, the 'Geordie lamp'. But he is known best as 'Father of the Railways', probably because of his association with the Stockton–Darlington Railway (1825), the first steam railway in the world with the first passenger carriages, and for which he built locomotives. Later, he was responsible for the Liverpool–Manchester Railway crossing the Chat Moss marshes, and in 1829 a £500-prize was offered for the most suitable engine for this railway. George and Robert won the competition with their *Rocket* which had a water-tube boiler, and eight of these engines were ordered. The following year they designed the *Planet*, their second locomotive, which set the pattern for all the best steam locomotives that followed. The Stephenson railway-systems included the Manchester–Leeds, the Leeds–Derby, the Derby–Birmingham, and the Birmingham–York railways.

The most involved project on which they worked together was the London–Birmingham Railway—part of the Grand Junction, linking London and Liverpool. George Stephenson enjoyed the glamour of the railways and was financially successful, but

George and Robert Stephenson. The Rocket 1829

he did not support or exploit the popular clamour for railways everywhere. He refused a knighthood, but because he was ineligible for the Institution of Civil Engineers, the Institution of Mechanical Engineers was founded with George Stephenson as its first President.

Meanwhile his son **Robert Stephenson (1803–1859)**, had turned to bridge-building, specialising in the tubular-girder construction, and was responsible for the Britannia Bridge over the Menai Strait, the high-level bridge at Newcastle upon Tyne, and bridges at Conway, Berwick-on-Tweed, and the Victoria (tubular) Bridge over the St. Lawrence River at Montreal, Canada. Robert Stephenson met Richard Trevithick in America and was his friend in England, but the two differed in technical opinions and they both disagreed with Brunel.

Isambard Kingdom Brunel (1806–1859), son of the great engineer, Sir Marc Brunel, was probably the greatest engineer in history. His work included the first transatlantic steamship, railways, tunnels, piers, docks, bridges, and guns. He built the Great Western Railway on a 7 foot broad gauge (2.132 m) as opposed to Stephenson's gauge of 4 feet 8½ inches (1.383 m) always used on colliery tramways. In 1841, passengers travelled from Paddington to Bristol at 60 miles per hour in comfort and safety. Five years later, broad-gauge railways were banned by Act of Parliament, but the Great Western Railway was so successful that Brunel extended the line from Bristol to New York by a steamship called the *Great Western*!

Long before steam locomotives ran regularly on rails, men had dreamed of building a ship which moved independently of wind and tide and man's power, but the steam boats of the eighteenth century were of wood and were paddle-driven—so they were not as fast as the clippers. Large, wooden ships could not withstand the uneven stresses and strains caused by large waves—a ship might be supported in the middle only, resting on one large wave, and then find itself immediately supported at the ends only, on two waves. Speed was increased by the screw-propeller, which acts like a short length of coarse screwthread boring its way through water as a screw does through wood. This knowledge and the success of the *Great Western* encouraged Brunel to build the *Great Britain*, the first large iron steamship and the first large ship to use the screw-propeller—and which, in 1886, after forty-one years' service, was wrecked on the Falkland Islands. Of a revolutionary design, the *Great Britain* was built three times larger than any previous ship and was 96 metres long, weighing 4 000 tonnes. She was the forerunner of all modern ships and her design dominated marine technology and showed the world the success of steam-driven iron boats. This famous boat has recently been salvaged and brought back to Bristol.

After the success of the *Great Britain* Brunel, in 1858, built, his third steamship, the gigantic *Great Eastern*, weighing 20 000 tonnes and 200 metres in length; she had two 90 tonne paddles which turned once every 6 seconds and a 36 tonne 4-bladed screw. The *Great Eastern* was intended to give 4 000 passengers luxurious travelling on five decks, non-stop from England to Australia. Unfortunately, this magnificent vessel was before its time, and although satisfactory technically it failed financially. Launching presented many problems and because of its great size the ship was launched sideways. The coal consumption of her 6 600 horse-power (5 000 kW) engines involved considerable bunkering-space, and basically there was not really sufficient demand at that time for such a large vessel. The *Great Eastern* was transferred to the Atlantic and after four voyages she was used to lay transatlantic and other cables until 1876 when she became a floating shop; she was broken up in 1888.

The early steam-engines were not really efficient because they used too much fuel, and wasted more than half—often three-quarters—of the power generated. Steamships had to carry so much wood or coal fuel that there was little room for cargo, and although the compound steam-engines allowed steam to be used again and again—passing through several cylinders in turn—it was not until 1894, when the turbine was introduced, that steamships really became successful.

Brunel built the first tunnel under the River Thames at Rotherhithe, where it still carries underground trains. He designed and built bridges over the Thames, Tamar and Wye in his final years, but his greatest memorial is probably the Clifton Suspension Bridge which was completed after his death.

The Hon. Charles Algernon Parsons (1854–1931) did not invent the turbine. An Ancient Greek, Hero, had the idea, Giovanni Branca worked on it, around 1630, and a Swedish contemporary, Gustav de Laval (1845–1913) worked on the steam-impulse system, but Parsons made it practical and successful and, after the steam-engine, the next great development in mechanical engineering. Using the principles of the windmill (air) and the Pelton wheel (water), the turbine is driven by jets of steam forced through nozzles at a high velocity on to vanes or blades mounted on wheels, several of which were mounted on a central shaft. This turbine shaft rotated fast enough to drive an electric generator which was the purpose of Parsons's design, but he also realised that the turbine would be more suitable than a reciprocating steam-engine for the propulsion of ships. He showed at Queen Victoria's Jubilee Naval Review that his ocean liner, the *Turbinia*, with her 35-knots speed could easily outdistance the Royal Navy destroyers' 27 knots.

The Great Eastern. Isambard Kingdom Brunel 1850

Machine Tools

Henry Maudslay (1771–1831) worked as a carpenter and blacksmith, became Joseph Bramah's foreman, and eventually established his own workshop where he became famous for his excellent craftsmanship. He standardised screwthreads and developed the first screwcutting lathe, which he patented in 1800. Maudslay, with the aid of Joseph Whitworth introduced back gear, self-acting traverse and automatic cross-feed.

Sir Joseph Whitworth, 1803–1887, a Manchester engineer who went to London to work for Maudslay, helped him to improve the lathe and became famous as a toolmaker—stressing that 'accuracy must go beyond the plus or minus one-sixteenth which was accepted in the eighteenth century'. Returning north, he introduced his standard system of gauges and, in 1841, the famous Whitworth 55° screwthread with standard taps and dies which served throughout the country for nearly a hundred and fifty years until the recent introduction of metric screwthreads. Whitworth was always anxious to replace hand work with machines, which he designed to work with great precision, and at the Great Exhibition (1851) he had the best display of machine tools.

James Nasmyth (1808–1890) also worked for Maudslay, improving machine tools, and he designed the shaping-machine. Later, he introduced the steam-hammer to forge a shaft for the steamship, *Great Britain*, and he used the idea to build a steam pile-driver. Nasmyth showed that steam tools could be used in any place—the tilt-hammer depended on water power—and he used small engines to power individual machines, as is common practice today with electric-motored tools.

The First Screw Cutting Lathe. Henry Maudslay 1800

Modern Times

Other nineteenth-century innovations were the gas-engine and the electric-engine—the South London Railway Line, opened in 1890, picked up its electric current from a third rail—and the petrol-engine (1885), was invented by two Germans, Gottlieb Daimler and Karl Benz, who made motor-cars and motor-cycles.

Henry Ford (1863–1947), the most famous name in mass production, was born on a farm, but soon realised he was a natural engineer. Finding the steam-driven farm machinery heavy and cumbersome, he sought lighter, simpler and less expensive mechanisms and became interested in the petrol-engine which had been introduced by Daimler and Benz. Henry Ford was anxious to introduce the motor-car to the masses, to create and satisfy a continuous demand which would lead to increased production, and which would lead to a reduction in costs and so further increase the demand. His method was scientific planning. Ford bought machines to make the parts quickly and to deliver them at the right time at the right place, so that the parts could be assembled without delay. This needed a continuous moving assembly line and in 1909 the Ford Motor Company decided to produce one car of one colour—black. Thus by mass production Henry Ford produced his Model T, the "Tin Lizzie", see below, a low priced car requiring the minimum of maintenance to suit the greatest

The Original Model T Ford 1909

number of people. Eventually the assembly line was putting together a car in 93 minutes, producing a new car every 15 seconds and by 1925 15 000 000 were produced, a record which was surpassed only in 1972 by the German Volkswagen Company. The car illustrated below is the saloon version of the Model T and it shows how Henry Ford set the style for years to come.

Mechanical engineering in modern times has been greatly influenced by electrical engineering and radio. Now we have rows of complicated machines programmed electronically, so that mass production has given way to automation. The programming of involved machinery from lathes to rockets which perform a series of operations, one after another in the right order, automatically, involves extremely difficult and accurate calculations and the need for computers which are capable of solving in seconds, problems which would take men years. Radio telecommunications and the radio telescope are increasing our knowledge of space.

In 1957, the largest radio-telescope in the world was completed at Jodrell Bank Observatory for the University of Manchester. It consists of a great metal dish, a parabolic bowl, 70 metres in diameter, which can be repeatedly revolved and tilted to point in any direction. It also has automatic control so that the telescope can follow the motion of any star or satellite. The telescope can receive radio signals through 100 million kilometres of space. In the same year, Russia launched the first satellite in space, *Sputnik I*, and since then men have travelled in space and we have been able to watch on television, men landing and walking on the moon.

Ford Saloon Car 1912

Radio Telescope at Jodrell Bank 1957

30

Agricultural Machinery

For the greatest part of the world's history agriculture has been by far the most important occupation and in this country it was the main industry at the time of the Industrial Revolution. We must wonder what those famous engineers we have just read about thought about agriculture. It was believed that a large population was essential for a prosperous country and Richard Trevithick supported the opinion that engineers should design machines to produce more food (*see* p. 159), but progress was very slow, possibly because farming was so many thousands of years older than mechanical engineering and the farmers distrusted the new ideas.

It is worth thinking about how engineers might have done more to help farmers, how those early machines might have been developed to dig and produce more food from the land more quickly and how more effort might have been used to persuade the farmers who were unwilling to use their profit to buy improved equipment.

A visit to a cowshed today shows how machinery produces milk more quickly than by hand. Some farms are now described as factories because animals are fed by a system which keeps them in pens and produces meat more economically than by grazing.

For agriculture, digging the ground and transporting the produce are essential operations and the wheel and the plough were the first mechanical aids; but even the simple wheel was not used in farming because of the soft nature of the soil. Wheels are most efficient where there is a suitable surface for them to run on and it was not until good roads were made that the full possibility of the wheel was realised. This was the main reason why the steam engine did so little for agriculture—it was too heavy to move around; the soil became packed under the wheels and the engines became hopelessly bogged down. It was not until 1850 that James Boydel invented a wheel which laid its own track as a "caterpillar" does today for military tanks. It was not until 1900 with the invention of the gas engine that the first successful land tractor was built.

The plough, at first operated entirely by man, must be almost as old as the wheel. There are many references to it in the Old Testament and drawings of ploughs are found on ancient Egyptian monuments. The first simple scratch ploughs used in Saxon times were shaped like a long point driven into the soil by the foot. Later, horse and oxen were harnessed to the wooden beam attached to the plough. The real advance came when a "mouldboard" and "coulter" were added. The coulter is a knife fixed upright in the beam of the plough which cuts through the weeds and stubble on the surface making a way for the "share". The share is the iron point on the tip of the plough which stirs the soil. The mouldboard is made of wood and is fixed to the plough, vertically, just behind the share and inclined slightly outwards. Its job is to scrape up the loose soil as it leaves the plough share and turn it over, leaving it in a long furrow behind the plough.

A leap forward was made when the wooden mouldboard plough became replaced by a similar but lighter type of plough made of iron. In 1710

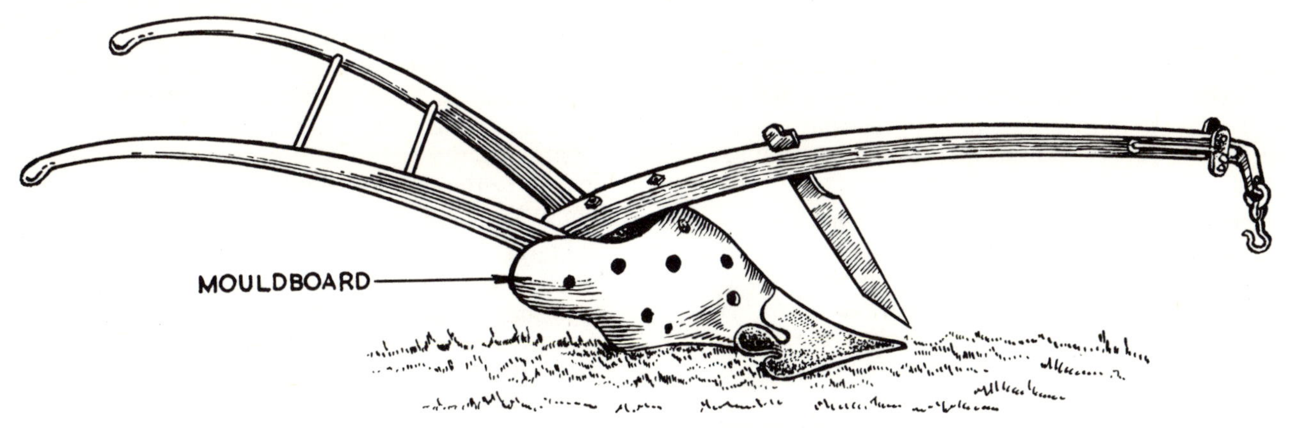

Above: The Rotherham Plough

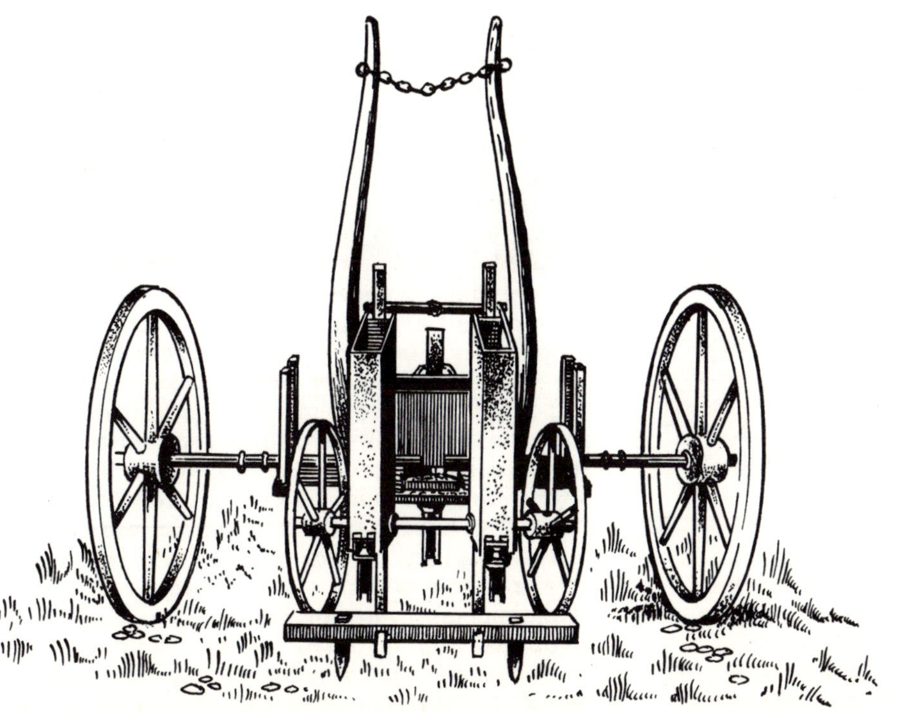

Left: Jethro Tull Seed Drill

a Scotsman named Lummis designed a new and vastly improved plough at his ironworks in Rotherham. In the same town James Small, another Scottish inventor, developed what was to become the Scotch Plough with a cast iron mouldboard.

Jethro Tull (1674–1741), famous for his agricultural inventions, introduced a seed drill, a horse-drawn machine which sowed seeds in regular drills or rows sufficiently wide apart to allow for tillage by the plough. He also studied the better use of manure and built a machine for pulverising it.

Andrew Meikle (1719–1811) invented the drum threshing machine in 1784. He is also famous for the work he did on windmills which were the first real power mechanisms used by farmers. He worked with John Smeaton and after improving the shafts by making them of cast iron, they invented a special gearing system to keep the sails automatically facing into the wind. Meikle improved the sails by constructing them in the form of venetian blinds adjusted by springs so that the high winds forced the strips to open, thus avoiding the excessive force of heavy winds which could cause enough frictional heat to set fire to the mill. Previously farmers prevented the sails from racing by reducing the exposed surface of the sails, a practice known as reefing. Meikle was the first to build a factory and to use Watt's engines for agricultural machinery. His son George worked on drainage and between them they invented and built a water raising machine.

Robert Ransome (1753–1830) was apprenticed to an ironmonger. From his early iron foundry he established the famous Ipswich firm and became the first agricultural engineer. In 1785 he introduced the tempering of cast iron plough shares by wetting the moulds with salt water and in 1803 he improved on this by casting the shares in special moulds, the lower half being made of iron and the upper half of sand. The metal chilled the molten iron and so hardened the lower part of the plough share and it was this under-surface which was exposed to the severest wear. This was an important innovation and is still practised.

James Allen Ransome (1806–1875), son of Robert, continued the work for his father and while conducting the family firm he took out patents to improve threshing machines, ploughs and scarifiers. It was in 1839 that Messrs. Ransome won the gold medal of the English Agricultural Society for an exhibition which included two new and interesting machines, a scarifier and a deep plough. The scarifier, a grubber with prongs, was invented by Arthur Biddell and, compared with the machines at that time, was an excellent mechanism. It had two rows of prongs fixed in an iron frame supported on wheels and preceded by a pair of smaller wheels. The depth of the scarifying, from 25 mm to 250 mm, was varied by two levers and chisel points were fixed to the tines which could be replaced by 100 mm hoes for partial hoeing or 225 mm hoes to cut the soil close. Its purpose was to improve tillage, to save time ploughing and to save horses. The Rackheath Plough was invented by Sir Edward Stracey and could break up the soil to a depth of 500 mm without disturbing the top soil and was especially recommended for the planting of trees. This deep plough had to be strong so it was made of wrought iron with a cast iron wheel but the beam and handles were of ash.

The majority of the engineers as well as the farmers thought that steam power was not an economic substitute for horses. The minority of engineers who favoured steam had to consider three options—(1) designing a steam tractor which would tow the conventional implements across

Scarifier

Rackheath Plough

the field (2) incorporating in the design of a steam engine some form of mechanical digger or cultivating machine and (3) designing a stationary engine to operate the existing machines.

John Fowler (1826–1864) is called the Father of Mechanised Agriculture and during the last fourteen years of his life he took out 32 patents concerned with reaping, sowing, ploughing, tractors and traction engines, brick and tile making and laying electric cables. He invented a steam plough which he used for drainage work on waste lands and in 1858 he won the Royal Agricultural Society £500 prize for mechanical cultivation using a stationary ploughing engine to move the plough up and down the field by means of ropes attached to a drum on the machine. Fowler was the only man who was successful in steam ploughing, making and selling more than a hundred ploughing sets and reducing the cost of cultivation by 30% but the machines were expensive. His greatest success was in supplying steam tackle for the reclamation of swamps all over the world which would have been quite impossible without his equipment.

The first recorded successful agricultural machine with its own inbuilt engine was a steam

Hart-Parr Gas Tractor 1900

digger designed by Thomas Darby but this was not until 1870 and this was after the death of Fowler whose method was then established.

It was not until the twentieth century, after the First World War, when the shortage of food was almost disastrous that agricultural machinery became generally mechanised. It was then that the petrol engine tractor was mass produced, and Fordson Tractors and Massey Ferguson Agricultural Machinery are now household words to all English farmers. Threshing and reaping machines have improved until one machine with one man will save the labour of seven or eight men and when a binder is added the saving is more than twice as much.

31

Art through Metalwork

Art has been expressed through metal for more than five thousand years. When the earliest craftsmen in stone discovered and first exploited metal, civilisation took a great step forward because, unlike stone, metal can be shaped by bending, beating, melting, and by pouring in a molten state into a mould. The first metal may well have been gold because when found pure it can be easily worked, it does not tarnish and is always attractive. But the first metal to be used in quantity was copper. Archaeologists, in their efforts to dig up the past, are still finding beautiful metalwork buried in the earth, sometimes in tombs.

Discoveries of the earliest metalwork of any importance were at the excavations of the **Royal Tombs of Ur in Mesopotamia**—Ur of the Chaldees which is thought to have been the home of Abraham—especially in the Royal Tombs which were built 3,500–3,000 B.C. Hundreds of examples of metalwork were found including fluted gold bowls with engraved patterns on the bases, finger rings and ear-rings, necklaces and much other jewelry of gold and silver, sculptures, daggers of gold and of copper with gold handles and silver sheaths and single and double axe-heads of electrum (an alloy of gold and silver). Perhaps the most remarkable example of metal craftsmanship was a ceremonial helmet of gold, hammered and chased into the form of a wig with holes around the edge for fixing a padded lining, found in an undisturbed, non-royal grave, that of Mes-Kalam-dug. Mes-Kalem-dug was not a king, since the grave is on its own and there are no subsidiary burials or evidence of human sacrifices, but he must have been a prince of the royal household or a famous warrior because apart from the helmet many of his personal possessions were found in his coffin—jewelry, a heavy gold bowl, a lamp, and two axes. He was wearing a broad belt of silver to which was fixed a gold dagger and a whetstone, used for sharpening the dagger, which was made of lapis lazuli—a mineral stone of beautiful ultramarine colouring—which had to be imported from Persia.

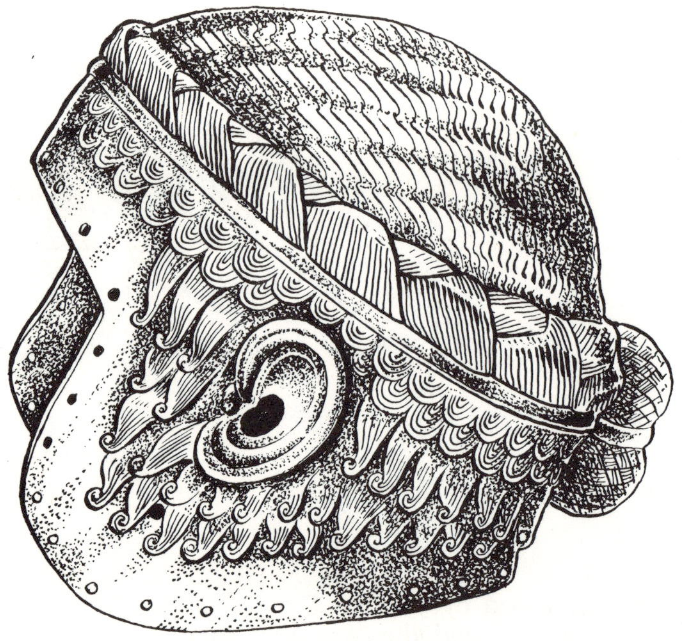

Golden Helmet—Royal Tomb of Ur. Sumerian 4th Centry B.C.

Gold Death Mask—Tutankhamun. Egyptian 2nd Century B.C.

Egypt

The history of Egypt can be traced over 5,000 years and many beautiful domestic vessels, weapons, and pieces of jewelry in gold, silver, copper, and bronze have been discovered. The best known examples of early-Egyptian art were those found in the tomb of Tutankhamun which contained furniture, shrines, statues, caskets, and mummies and which as far as we know is the only Ancient Egyptian Pharaoh's tomb which was not despoiled by tomb-robbers. The mummified body of the king was adorned with over one hundred gold objects and was encased in a coffin of 22-carat gold. The funeral-mask of burnished gold inlaid with obsidian, lapis lazuli and blue glass is of outstanding splendour, artistry and workmanship. The figures on the head-dress represent the head of the cobra and the vulture which with the false beard were emblems of royalty. Tutankhamen died in B.C. 1353, and his tomb was discovered in 1922.

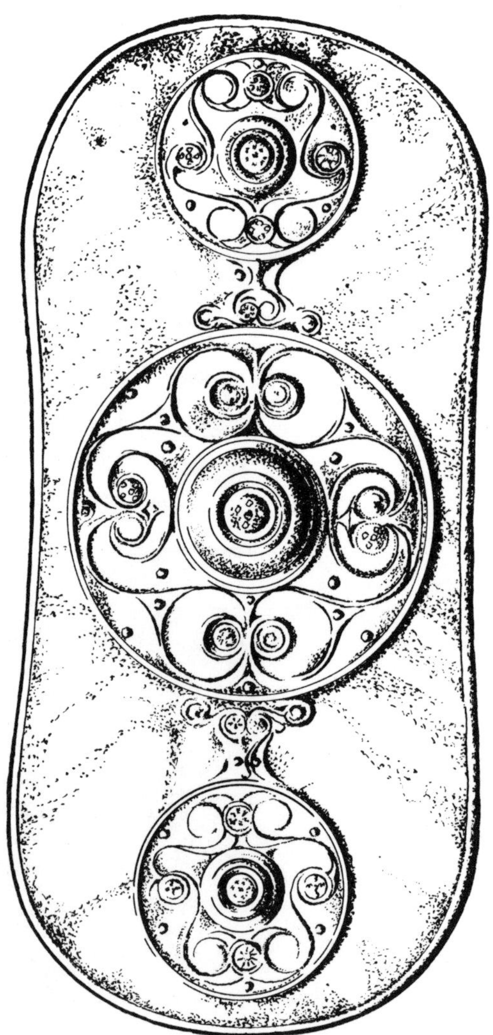

Bronze Shield—Celtic 1st Century B.C.

Roman Britain

The large British shield shown here was discovered in the River Thames; it has relief designs and was decorated with enamelled bosses. The Romans made and used lathes and valued the use of iron for currency, tools and agricultural implements—they were master metalworkers. The elaborate grilles, screens, rails, gates, etc., of later years may well have developed from their window bars. Lead was used for lining cisterns for baths and for the necessary pipes some of which are still in existence: they called lead *plumbum*, hence our word "plumber". However bronze was still the popular metal and much of it used for jewelry, vessels, spoons, lamps, razors and mirrors has been found in Britain.

Roman metalwork in Britain includes the Desborough Mirror and the Mildenhall Treasure, *see* p. 176. The mirror, kidney shaped with a graceful handle, has a finely engraved design on the back and is made of *Speculum*, a bronze with a high tin content which could be polished bright. While ploughing in 1946 at Mildenhall, Suffolk, a farmer turned up a bright piece of metal which he found to be a silver tray, over 600 millimetres in diameter, beautifully decorated with relief ornament of exquisite craftsmanship. This tray is known as the "Neptune Dish" and is only part of the Mildenhall Treasure, for on further digging, now more carefully with a trowel, thirty-three other pieces of silver tableware, including spoons, ladles, bowls, and platters, were uncovered. It is thought that this treasure was buried for safe keeping when the Romans left Britain in A.D. 410.

Anglo-Saxon Metalwork

The richest and most exciting event in the history of metalwork in Britain occurred in 1939 when archaeologists discovered the Sutton Hoo Treasure—an Anglo-Saxon burial-ship. A Viking ship, 24 metres long, had been hauled on to land near Ipswich and rested in a hollow to become a cenotaph or mausoleum for an Anglo-Saxon king or warrior who was probably killed in battle. It was not a grave because no body was found, but his personal possessions in iron, bronze, silver, and gold, including a famous, ornate gold buckle and a purse with gold coins, were placed in the centre of the ship inside a hut. The ship was buried under

Front of Purse—Sutton Hoo. Anglo Saxon 7th Century A.D.

Neptune Dish—Mildenhall Treasure. Roman 4th
Century A.D.

sand and earth and the mound eventually became a barrow. Three hundred years ago, some men, possibly grave-robbers, dug down to the ship, but missed the treasure by inches. An interesting aspect of this discovery is that the timbers of the burial-ship had completely rotted away, leaving only the nails and the stains of the wood on the sand, but from these detailed traces the size and the actual construction of the ship could be worked out. Patient work removing unstained sand left the outlines of the ship showing up the placing of its former ribs, planks and gunwales. The sea-going ship was rowed by thirty-eight oarsmen, and it was buried on land between A.D. 656–677.

The Blacksmith

"Smith" comes from an Anglo-Saxon word meaning "one who smooths metal"—meaning hammering, and including the goldsmith, silversmith and coppersmith; today it refers to the blacksmith who forges iron and steel. Early smiths were artist-craftsmen making tools for themselves and for other craftsmen, together with weapons for hunting and war. The smith worked for the Church and the home—generally assisting the woodworker by making hinges, handles, bolts, locks, and strengthening chests with iron hoops, straps etc., and we have some fine examples of Mediaeval and Gothic smithing. The illustration of the thirteenth-century door at Oxford University shows decorative hinges made by Thomas de Leighton who also, in 1295, made the grille over Queen Eleanor's tomb in Westminster Abbey to protect the cast bronze and gilt effigy. The hinge-work became more elaborate until eventually the ironwork was thought sufficient and wood was dispensed with—this resulted in beautiful iron gates which became famous in England's country houses. Exquisite grilles and screens were erected in many European churches. Railings, plain and decorative, were set

Wrought Iron Hinge-work Buttery Door, Merton College Oxford—English 13th Century

up instead of walls and hedges about the estates and buildings, and, later, to enclose parks and gardens.

The greatest blacksmith of all time was Jean Tijou who came from France in 1689 to work for William and Mary, first on Hampton Court Palace, which he embellished with large gates and screens. Part of one such screen is shown in the illustration and indicates Tijou's clever modelling, using a hammer, chisel and punches. Later he worked for Sir Christopher Wren, especially in St. Paul's Cathedral, to create some of the finest wrought iron screens in history. Wren had cast-iron railings erected outside the Cathedral, a new and very costly innovation.

Blacksmiths continued to work with architects, now making balconies, staircases, balustrades, and fanlights for the interiors of large houses to match the imposing gates and railings. All of them showed how well as artists in iron they understood their material. However, only the finest work is left today because so much ironwork was removed during the Second World War for use in armaments. The blacksmith's craft changed during the nineteenth century and in the present century when

Part of Wrought Iron Screen—Hampton Court Palace by Jean Tijou—English 17th Century

Wrought Iron Panel, polished and gilded, by Raymond Subes—French 20th Century

The Cellini Salt-cellar—Italian 15th Century

torch welding—oxy-acetylene and electric welding—and machine welding have superseded fire-welding, and the traditional long-flowing welds and rivet-and-collar joints have given way to short welds and spot welds, in which pieces of metal just touch each other and are securely welded (*see* p. 179). France has produced some highly creative and sensitively conceived ironwork in recent years as is illustrated by the radiator-grille in the illustration.

Benvenuto Cellini (1500–1571), the most famous craftsman in history, was an Italian metalworker and sculptor. He was a colourful figure—a man of genius and also a rogue. In spite of his boasting, swashbuckling extravagant ways and bad temper he was commissioned by kings and popes because of his wonderful craftsmanship. King Francis I of France wrote "I will choke you with gold" in an attempt to obtain Cellini's services, and it was while in France that Cellini made his celebrated salt-cellar of solid gold which is now in the Vienna Museum. The female figure symbolises the earth, and the male, holding a trident, the sea. He is particularly famous for his *cire perdue*, or waste-wax, method of casting which is described on

p. 126, and which he used for his greatest work, the statue of Perseus, now in the Loggia del Lanzi, Florence. The story of how when casting this statue his bronze would not run, and he used all his household pewter, about two hundred dishes, is told vividly in Cellini's autobiography.

Pewter

The introduction of pewter vessels for ecclesiastical and domestic uses began in the tenth century and was an important innovation. This well-known alloy (largely tin with lead, and sometimes copper, added) gradually replaced stone, wood and horn, and became very popular for plates, dishes and tankards. The illustration on this page shows a pewter communion-set which was used at Midhurst Church, England, for many years; the flagon and cup were made *c.*1670, but the communion plate bears pewter marks—a crowned rose with "Made in London"—and is eighteenth-century work. As well as in England, pewter was used extensively in Scotland and on the continent of Europe until the end of the nineteenth century when it was replaced by the manufacture of britannia metal, a superior alloy containing 95% tin, 4% antimony, and 1% copper which is used in modern pewterwork and eliminates the risk of lead poisoning.

Mediaeval Metalwork

The **Royal Gold Cup,** now in the British Museum, was made in the fourteenth century in Paris and is an excellent example of late Mediaeval metalwork. It is brilliantly colour-enamelled on solid gold showing the story of St. Agnes and it belonged to the Kings of France; it was part of the English Royal Treasure from Henry VI, until the reign of James I when, in 1604, it was presented to the King of Spain on the occasion of the peace-treaty between the two countries. The Cup as it is now is shown overleaf and opposite, page 183, is shown the drawing of the

Pewter Communion Set—English 17th and 18th Century

The Royal Gold Cup—French Mediaeval. British Museum

The Royal Gold Cup—French 14th Century.
Copy from original drawing

Cup as it was made. It is now taller because the stem was twice lengthened—firstly in England during the reign of Henry VIII by a gold ring on which are riveted Tudor roses, and secondly in Spain, in 1610, when the Latin inscription in black enamel was added. The cover has since lost its cresting of pearls together with its knob. But the Cup is the sole-surviving example of gold Mediaeval secular plate (while in Spain, however, it was consecrated for use in religious services). As a sumptuous and technically excellent piece of metalwork it is unique.

Armour

Men have always lavished much care and money on their accoutrements of war, and armour has been responsible for some of the finest metalwork ever produced. Spain, because of its natural mineral wealth and national ambitions has probably produced more armour than any other country. In the East, heavy armour and unwieldy weapons were most uncomfortable and lighter and more highly tempered swords were made in Damascus. These swords were often decorated by *damascening*—which consisted of cutting intricate patterns in the surface of the steel and of beating gold and silver wire into the engraved hollows. When the Moslems conquered Spain, they took their craft with them and the blades of Toledo and Seville became famous throughout Europe. In the fifteenth and sixteenth centuries, Spain, Germany and Italy attained a degree of perfection in the craft of the armourer that has never been excelled in any metalwork.

Armourers combined with artists and goldsmiths to produce exceptionally fine decorative work, using chasing, damascening, chisel-work, and fluting. Most of the best work was parade-armour, encouraged by wealthy patrons, each anxious to be more magnificently arrayed than his rivals. Charles V of Spain and Maximilian I of Bavaria were liberal patrons of the most famous armourers, including the Negroli brothers of Milan and the Colmans of Augsburg. When Henry VIII became King of England he was most annoyed to find that all English armour had to be imported. In 1511, he employed European metalworkers at Southwark, London, and seven years later at Greenwich; the

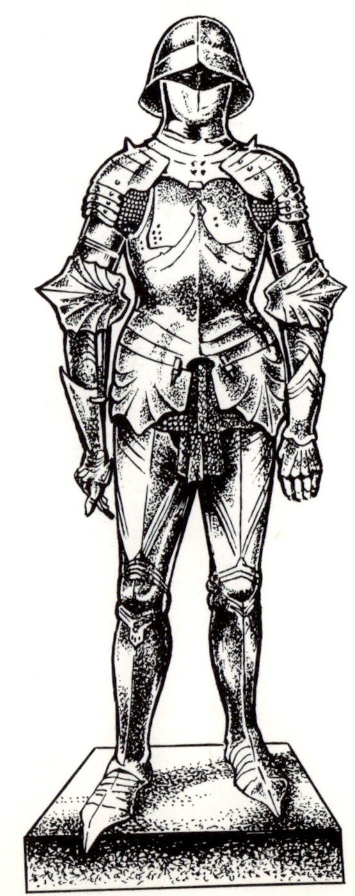

Cap-à-pie Armour—German 16th Century

craft continued in London until 1637. The best examples of their work is in the Tower of London, where one suit has a steel skirt for use on horseback which has a decorated border of *H*'s and *K*'s (Henry and Katherine), a touching reminder of the young king's love-life. His armour was always carefully fitted and the magnificent collection today shows how the King's girth increased with the years. The illustration is of a suit of early sixteenth-century *cap-à-pie* (head to foot) German armour, showing the mail-shirt worn underneath.

The Silversmith

England has always excelled in the production of good silversmithing and for many years she was supreme in this art. It was the practice for ambassadors and other representatives of foreign countries to be presented with rich gifts made from silver which were the work of our native craftsmen, and ambassadorial plate was often worth thousands of pounds. Silverware was often referred to as "plate" in England and, like the Roman Mildenhall Treasure, it was made both to be used and as a sign of affluence. At the end of the seventeenth century and in the eighteenth and nineteenth centuries plate was almost the equivalent of a private bank account. Much of the gold plate referred to in early inventories was silver-gilt, and for many years it was thought that the Royal Gold Cup was made of silver and afterward gilded. Silver is a precious metal, both attractive and durable, but it has a low melting-point, and during these times, although it was the accepted practice to display the silver, it was not thought unusual to melt it down either for money or to make something more fashionable. Samuel Pepys tells us of this in his famous *Diary*.

In 1335, an Act of Parliament made it compulsory for all silversmiths to mark their work with registered punch-marks, and in 1477 the London Goldsmiths' Company decreed that pieces of silver of the accepted standard should be stamped with the leopard's-head mark, while in the following year the date-stamp was inaugurated. Thus, since 1478, English silver had been hallmarked, so that we are able now to date with certainty many historical items, and often ascertain the actual maker of the piece.

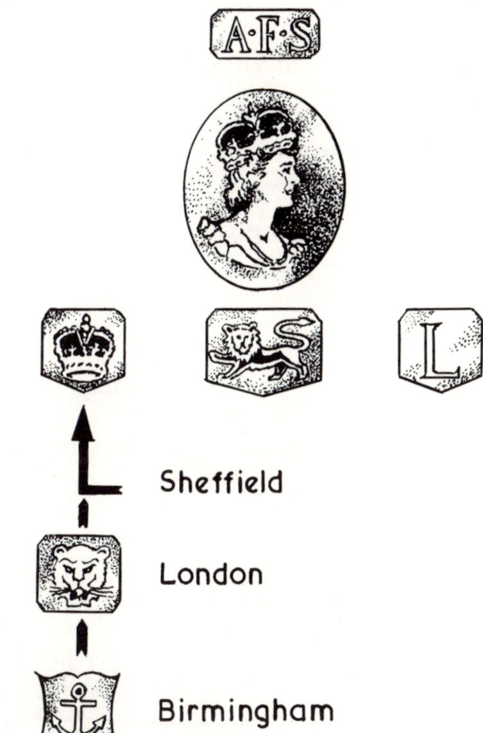

The Author's Hall Mark. The initials of the maker A.F.S. The Crown to show that the work was marked in Sheffield Assay Office. The Lion to indicate silver. The date letter L—1953 and because it was the time of the Coronation, the Sovereign's Head, Queen Elizabeth II, was added. The Leopard's Head is the Assay Office Hall Mark for London and the Anchor for Birmingham

Some excellent silversmithing was carried out in Tudor times but there is little of it left. A better collection than ours is in the Kremlin, Moscow. Henry VIII was a patron of the arts but much of the silverware confiscated from the monasteries was melted down, and James I, when he came to London from Scotland gave much away; and again, the Roundheads destroyed many of the treasures belonging to the Crown and its supporters. Standing salts, tall salt cellars, of which the Gibbon Salt (1576) is an excellent example were regarded with veneration in Elizabeth's reign and were fashionable for two centuries. Their position on the table was significant often indicating the position of the host or special guests. Our best Tudor pieces include Elizabethan dishes—six richly engraved with Biblical scenes (1573) and the Queen's coronation cup, the Bowes Cup dated 1554.

Knives and spoons have been used since earliest times—daggers made of stone being the first knives, together with spoons made of clay and bone—but forks did not come into use until the sixteenth century. At this time, however, ewers and salvers made of silver were very important—rose-scented water was poured from the ewer, a large jug, into the salver, a dish for guests to rinse their fingers after eating. Meanwhile, silver alms-dishes, chalices, paten covers, steeple cups, and flagons were made for the Church.

After the Restoration (1660), silver-work became ostentatious and extravagant and punch-bowls, silver candlesticks and chandeliers were popular as well as drinking mugs, wine cups, tankards with

Sheffield Plate—English 18th Century

lids and toilet sets. Coffee, tea and chocolate were all introduced about 1660, and silversmiths were called on to make coffee pots, chocolate pots, teapots, jugs for cream, and basins for sugar. It was during the eighteenth century that many refugee French silversmiths—the Huguenots—came to England and their technical skill and refinement of design reached very high standards. Paul Lamerie (1688–1751) was one of the most famous craftsmen of the period and he worked with William Hogarth, the great painter and pictorial satirist, who was first an engraver. As in ironwork, the influence of the Adam brothers was important, and in silverwork we find teapots, jugs and tureens shaped like classical urns and decorated with pierced, trellised galleries which were cut with the new piercing-saw; festoons and palm leaves were engraved, hammered in low relief, or applied.

Sheffield Plate

The desire for this beautiful, but expensive, domestic finery led to a most interesting development in metalwork—the introduction of Sheffield Plate by Thomas Bolsover, in 1742. The illustration shows three early pieces, when the work was at its best. Sheffield Plate was a sheet of copper faced with a thin sheet of silver, the two being fused together. The proportions of the two thicknesses was maintained however thinly the Sheffield Plate was rolled. Articles were made up in the usual way, but parts subject to heavy wear were often of solid silver, as were mouldings and handles which could not be made of sheet, although white metal-alloys and silver-foil stampings filled with lead were used in the later work. Joints were riveted or soft-soldered, because the heat necessary for silver-soldering the copper tended to melt the plate's thin silver surface. Sheffield Plate was immensely popular, it had the appearance of solid silver and was cheaper, and it was only in its latest stages that it became more ornate and the designs deteriorated. It lasted a hundred years, however, until superseded by electroplating, which enabled the articles to be made entirely of base metal and then very thinly coated. Unfortunately, some silversmiths tried to compete with Sheffield Plate, making toilet sets, candlesticks, etc., which were little more than thin, silver sheaths over a core of resin or lead. Later, this cheaper work was encouraged by mass production and at the end of the nineteenth century silverware had profoundly deteriorated. The Victorians were especially fond of silver-plated britannia metal for tableware.

Fabergé (1846–1920)

About this time there was in Russia a famous goldsmith and jeweller working for the Russian Imperial Court, **Peter Carl Fabergé** who has been described as a modern Cellini. He was renowned for his Easter Eggs, of which he made more than fifty, most being presented to the royalty of other countries. The egg illustrated was made in 1897 for Nicholas II and is in translucent lime-green enamel trellised with gold with double-headed eagles in black enamel and rose diamonds. A large diamond is shown at the crown of the egg and there is another at the point. A working model of the coronation coach in gold and red enamel, 125 mm long, was inside the egg.

Royal Easter Egg by Fabergé—Russian 19th Century

Twentieth-century Metalwork

Little art was expressed through metalwork at the beginning of the twentieth century in Great Britain, when with the continuation of the Machine Age, mass production was developing strongly. There was a great desire to produce more articles at less cost, and the emphasis was on ease of production rather than good design. The hand-craftsman, especially in metal, was completely out of favour and the work of a certain group, Ernest Gimson and the Barnsley brothers, who, blaming the machine for a deterioration in craft standards, had followed William Morris into the English Cotswold Country, was considered old-fashioned. "Fitness for Purpose" was now the popular phrase. Design emphasised the "Functionalism" of things that *worked*—locomotives, rifles, ships, and machines.

Georg Jensen 1866–1935. Meanwhile craftsmen were progressing in Scandinavia and nowhere was this more evident than in silversmithing.

Fire-dogs by Ernest Gimson c 1900. Sheet brass, hammered, pierced, chiselled and filed

Copenhagen was already famous for its porcelain when, in 1904, **Georg Jensen** began working as an artist-craftsman practising silversmithing and jewelry. His early work showed a liking for sculptured forms and ornamental details which reflected his interest in early works of art and his studies of natural forms. He understood and resurrected the nature of silver which he maintained the Machine Age had lost. As his fame and his business spread over Europe and America he found collaborators and they, with his successors, produced work which combined an animated style with a tranquil simplicity of form as illustrated. Intricate details gave way to elegant new shapes in jewelry and tableware which were enhanced by attractive surface treatment so making Danish jewelry and tableware distinctive and modern (*see* pp. 20 and 22).

Silver Pitcher by Jensen. Designed by Henning Koppel—Danish 20th Century

English Craftsmen

By the middle of the century the Scandinavian influence on craft design in other parts of Europe was obvious. Industrial design, now referred to as "styling", remained important, obviously so with cars and aeroplanes, but also in architecture, street furniture, transport, and domestic equipment. English craftsmen accepted this challenge and began to regain their importance, many emerging as successful designers. This is particularly true of a number of young men e.g. **Gerald Benney, David Mellor, Alex Styles, Robert Welch** and the Australian **Stuart Devlin** who designed his country's new decimal coinage, who were trained as silversmiths and have been supported by the Goldsmith's Company and assisted by the new universities and new towns desiring to build collections of plate. These men have shown their understanding of new materials, of the changed working conditions and the widened interests of the people.

Two new materials have made an impressive impact on domestic metalwork during this century, namely, aluminium and stainless steel; the former can be cast, spun, or pressed to shape and anodised, so that we now have brightly coloured metal articles which are light in weight, while the latter can be pressed, spun, or hammered and polished brightly, or given the new and attractive "satin" finish.

Index

Acknowledgements

Plates 1, 23b, 25a and *b*, David Mellor Esq., Dennis Hooker Photographers.
Plate 2, Anne Maria Shelton, The Design Centre.
Plate 3, Above: George Wolstenholm and Son Ltd. Design Council.
Below: Needham, Veall and Tyzack Ltd. Design Council.
Plate 4. Above, Below and *Right:* Dryad Metal Works Ltd.
Plate 5, Peter Hayte Esq., Design Council.
Plate 6, Rupert Oliver Designs, Design Council.
Plate 7, Frank Wardle and Vono Ltd., Dave Draper—Artist.
Plate 8, Above: Arkana Limited, Studio Warne, Bristol.
Below: William Plunkett Ltd., David Lavender, photographer.
Plate 9, Left: New Dimension, Barbara Prime Associates.
Right: The Modern Lighting Company, Martin Coombs of Creative Photography.
Plates 10, Left, 15 and *27:* Alex Styles of Garrard and Company, The Worshipful Company of Goldsmiths.
Plate 10, Right: Davis and Elson Ltd., Peter Parkinson, photographer.
Plates 11, Left and *28:* Stuart Devlin.
Plates 11, Right, 12, Left and *20, Right:* Robert Welch.
Plates 12, Right, 21, 24 and *26:* Robert Welch and Old Hall Tableware Limited, Dennis Hooker, photographer.
Plate 13, Right, Left and *Middle:* Yvonne Poulton.
Plate 14, Above: L. Connell, M.Sc., Ph.D., Principal, City of Leeds and Carnegie College and Paul Bridge.
Plates 14, Below and *22:* L. Connell M.Sc., Ph.D., Principal City of Leeds and Carnegie College and Robert Rignall.
Plate 16, Louis Osman, Worshipful Company of Goldsmiths.
Plates 17 and *18, Right* and *Left:* Oslo Kommunes Kunstantsamlinger Vigeland-Museet.
Plate 19, Left: Sir Basil Spence, Henk Snoek, photographer.
Right: Provost and Chapter of Coventry Cathedral, Thompson Limited Coventry, photographers.
Plate 20, Left: The Dean of Llandaff Cathedral, Stanley Travers, Cardiff, photographer.
Plate 23, Left: David Mellor, Design Council.
Plates 23, Right; 25, Left and *25, Right:* David Mellor, Dennis Hooker.
Plates 29 and *30:* Gerald Benney.
Illustration on page 163: Ford Motor Co.
Illustration on page 182: British Museum.
Illustrations on pages 18, 20 and 190: Georg Jensen, Design Council.